T0418165

Amish Women and the Great Depression

YOUNG CENTER BOOKS IN ANABAPTIST AND PIETIST STUDIES
Steven M. Nolt, *Series Editor*

Amish Women
and the
Great Depression

KATHERINE JELLISON *and*
STEVEN D. RESCHLY

Johns Hopkins University Press
Baltimore

Johns Hopkins University Press
2715 North Charles Street
Baltimore, Maryland 21218
www.press.jhu.edu

Library of Congress Cataloging-in-Publication Data

Names: Jellison, Katherine, 1960– author. | Reschly, Steven D., author.
Title: Amish women and the Great Depression / Katherine Jellison and
Steven D. Reschly.
Description: Baltimore : Johns Hopkins University Press, 2023. |
Series: Young Center books in Anabaptist and Pietist studies |
Includes bibliographical references and index.
Identifiers: LCCN 2023003589 | ISBN 9781421447971 (hardcover) |
ISBN 9781421447988 (ebook)
Subjects: LCSH: Amish women—Pennsylvania—Lancaster County—Social life and
customs—20th century. | Amish—Pennsylvania—Lancaster County—Social life
and customs—20th century. | Depressions—1929—Pennsylvania—Lancaster
County. | Lancaster County (Pa.)—Social life and customs—20th century. |
Sex role—Pennsylvania—Lancaster County—History—20th century.
Classification: LCC F157.L2 J45 2023 | DDC 974.8/15042—dc23/eng/20230126
LC record available at https://lccn.loc.gov/2023003589

A catalog record for this book is available from the British Library.

*Special discounts are available for bulk purchases of this book. For more information,
please contact Special Sales at specialsales@jh.edu.*

To Sandra and Randy Jellison-Knock and
in memory of Keenan Jellison-Knock (1994–2013)
—Katherine

For my Amish and Mennonite ancestors
—Steven

CONTENTS

We wish to extend our gratitude to the Gerald R. Ford Foundation, the Pennsylvania Humanities and Museum Commission, the Young Center for Anabaptist and Pietist Studies at Elizabethtown College, and our respective Departments of History for their financial support of the research for this book. Many student assistants at Truman State University worked on various parts of this project, and we thank them for their diligent efforts. We are grateful to the staff at the Gerald R. Ford Presidential Library, Ann Arbor, Michigan, and to Gertrude Enders Huntington, Diane LaBarbera, and John Taylor for providing advice and assistance in our use of the Study of Consumer Purchases data. For assistance in accessing additional research materials, we thank Tom Conrad at Ohio State University and the staffs of the Pennsylvania State Archives, Harrisburg; the National Archives II, College Park, Maryland; the archives of the Mennonite Church, Goshen, Indiana; the Lancaster Mennonite Historical Library, Pennsylvania; and the Pequea Bruderschaft Library, Gordonville, Pennsylvania.

Cory Anderson, Linda K. Kerber, Donald B. Kraybill, Paul C. Milazzo, Steven M. Miner, Steven M. Nolt, Nancy Grey Osterud, Malcolm J. Rohrbough, Shelton Stromquist, Melissa Walker, and Jacqueline H. Wolf read earlier portions or full drafts of the manuscript and offered valuable suggestions. Conference session commentators, article reviewers, and book manuscript evaluators added useful comments and different perspectives. Many Amish persons, who prefer to remain anonymous, became oral history narrators who generously shared their stories of the Great Depression with us.

Our family members patiently supported our many years of work on this project, and we are grateful to them: Katherine's spouse, David Winkelmann, and her sister, brother-in-law, and late nephew—Sandra, Randy, and Keenan

Jellison-Knock—to whom this book is also dedicated; and Steven's children—Leah Cech, Jessica Frazer, and Joel Reschly—and his siblings, Daniel Reschly and Janice Miller. Amish history often merged with family history, and they were precious companions on the journey.

Out of respect for Old Order Amish prohibitions against prideful behavior, the authors have agreed not to use the real names of oral history narrators who were Old Order Amish at the time of their interviews. Religious proscriptions prevented the use of recording devices for these interviews, and the notes for all Amish interviews are in the authors' possession. The real names of non-Amish narrators are used with their permission, and the recordings and transcripts of their oral histories are in the authors' possession.

In note citations for diaries from Tom Conrad's private collection, the diarists are identified by initials as requested by Mr. Conrad. The authors have created pseudonyms for the diarists when mentioned in the main text.

Where necessary, the capitalization in quoted material has been adjusted to conform with modern conventions.

Amish Women and the Great Depression

Introduction

On July 14, 1936, Agent Rigdon, representing the Bureau of Home Economics in the US Department of Agriculture (USDA), conducted an interview with a farm wife in Salisbury Township, Lancaster County, Pennsylvania. On that day, Rigdon—who never recorded her own first name—asked several hundred questions and filled out four of the five separate survey forms created for documenting farm and household expenses for the woman's family during fiscal year April 1, 1935, to March 31, 1936. The 50-year-old woman reported that she and her 47-year-old husband farmed 78 acres with their six children, ranging in age from 9 to 19, and made a profit of $2,098.60 ($43,293.06 in 2022).[1] During the year, they had sold wheat, potatoes, milk, eggs, chickens, 27 steers, and a horse and had received an Agricultural Adjustment Act benefit of $192 for taking tobacco land out of production. Their only farm labor expense was the 18 meals the wife served to helpful neighbors during threshing season. The family raised and ate most of their own food, which had an estimated value of $337. In addition to data about the family's farming operation, Rigdon also recorded personal information, such as the wife having purchased 12 pairs of light cotton hose at 20 cents apiece. Rigdon left one section of the survey entirely blank—the portion dealing with automobile expenses—and with the exception of 10 cents for a dog license, she recorded no recreation expenses for the family. By way of explanation, Rigdon noted in the margin, "This is an Amish family who's [sic] religion does not permit paid for recreation."[2]

Agent Rigdon and her Old Order Amish host were only a small part of a large research project, the Study of Consumer Purchases (SCP), conducted during 1935/36. It was organized by the Bureau of Labor Statistics of the Department of Labor and the Bureau of Home Economics of the Department of Agriculture and conducted by the Works Progress Administration (WPA). The survey that Rigdon and the Amish woman completed that summer day is one of approximately 400 similar files from Lancaster County selected for this examination of Amish women's lives during the Great Depression.[3]

The organizers of the SCP chose Lancaster County to represent general agriculture. Some officials at the USDA had developed an interest in the Old Order Amish as a potential model for viable rural communities. The Amish appeared to have a history of agricultural innovation that still preserved a small-scale, semi-independent, and economical way of life. These officials sometimes competed with other USDA leaders who advocated a large-scale, mechanized, monocultural, capital-intensive model of agriculture—as promoted by the Farm Bureau—and scientific agriculture characterized by advocacy of herbicides, pesticides, artificial fertilizer, and ever-larger farm machinery. Both models of agriculture still visibly exist in rural areas of North America, with the Old Order Amish continuing to represent small-scale, diverse agriculture. As a result, outsiders often view the Amish as idealized Jeffersonian yeoman farmers. The following study attempts to break through romanticized images of the Amish to provide a more authentic re-creation of their lives during the years of Franklin D. Roosevelt's presidency, a period in which the federal government exhibited a keen interest in their way of life and compiled a mountain of evidence about their experiences.

Several possible reasons existed for the Roosevelt administration's fascination with the Amish. In the segregated United States of the 1930s and 1940s, the Amish and other northern white farm families were safer subjects for New Deal celebrations of the nation's "common man" than were members of the more racially diverse urban working class. The seemingly firm Amish division of labor between male farmers and female homemakers appealed to New Dealers eager to reinforce traditional gender roles at a time of high male unemployment. In particular, the Old Order Amish, with their theologically based commitment to nonconformity and agricultural self-sufficiency, neatly reflected the national creation myth. Noting the Amish community's resemblance to Jefferson's fabled nation of farmers, members of the Roosevelt administration hoped these thrifty, hard-working Christian agrarians would be admirable role models for Depression-weary Americans of the 1930s and war-wary Americans of the early 1940s. The physical circumstances of the Old Order Amish even seemed to resemble those of the nation's rural forebears because of their rejection of highline electricity and automobiles, use of horse-drawn transportation and farm equipment, and tradition of plain, unfashionable dress. The extensive data that Roosevelt administration investigations engendered, however, ultimately revealed a greater complexity to the Amish beneath their image as counterparts to America's agrarian founders.[4]

Members of the Roosevelt administration most frequently turned to the nation's best-known Amish community, the Old Order Amish of Lancaster County, as a subject of study. The data that WPA workers gathered among the Lancaster County Amish for the SCP constitute the principal source for the discussion in this book. Translating numbers and statistics into narrative is a challenge with quantitative history, but fortunately, significant qualitative sources exist to help elaborate on and interpret the SCP data. In 1993 we published an article in *Agricultural History* that presented a quantitative skeleton constructed from SCP statistics. After many years of subsequent research and consideration, we are now putting qualitative flesh on those bones by adding the voices of Amish women, their family members, and their neighbors. Their voices emerge through Old Order Amish women's diaries and memoirs; accounts by and about Lancaster County Amish women in *The Budget*, a weekly newspaper published in Ohio; federal and state government reports about the Lancaster County Amish and correspondence regarding the research and writing of those reports; oral histories with elderly Old Order Amish women and men about their experiences in the 1930s; an extensive oral history we conducted with Walter M. Kollmorgen, author of a 1942 Bureau of Agricultural Economics (BAE) study of Old Order Amish community stability; and photographs of Old Order Amish farms, farm families, and their neighbors taken by federally employed photographers working for the BAE, the WPA, the Farm Security Administration (FSA), and the Office of War Information (OWI). Together with our original quantitative data, this qualitative evidence helps present a much fuller picture of Amish life, especially of Amish farm women's experience, than our frequently cited 1993 article provides.[5]

Numerous books have been published about the Amish, but relatively few by academic historians. The scholarly studies that do exist are largely the work of social scientists who focus principally on Amish men and contemporary communities. Exceptions to this trend include the scholarship of anthropologist Karen Johnson-Weiner and the work that feminist sociologist Julia Ericksen has coauthored with rural sociologists and anthropologists. While these scholars have indeed examined the unique experiences of Amish women, their attention has been on the contemporary period. Historians such as Marlene Epp and Royden Loewen, who have delved into the past experiences of Anabaptist women and their family labor systems, have concerned themselves primarily with the much larger Mennonite population rather than the Amish. Nevertheless, their insights into the historic centrality of Anabaptist women's labor to the efficient functioning of family farming indeed laid important groundwork for the present study.[6]

What distinguishes our book in part from previous scholarship is its temporal focus. A thoroughly researched study of Amish women in the 1930s makes it a unique contribution to Anabaptist studies as both a work of history and a study of gender. Its interweaving of extensive statistical data with the narrative voices of Amish women is unprecedented. This approach also offers views that challenge standard assumptions about the Great Depression. Historians of that period and of American women's history have not traditionally viewed Amish women as having agency and therefore neglected their role in the story of the 1930s. Amish women disrupt preconceived notions of significance, and they contradict the archetypal rural women of the period—the desperate and displaced—such as the woman in photographer Dorothea Lange's *Migrant Mother* or Ma Joad in novelist John Steinbeck's *The Grapes of Wrath*. Indeed, Amish women represent successful rural women who remained on the land, fed their families, and kept family farming alive. They, and farm women in general, contributed greatly to keeping American agriculture viable between the two world wars. The experiences of Amish women in Lancaster County demonstrate in sharp relief the characteristics and practices that enabled successful family farming during the Great Depression. It is because of such history that their stories deserve to be heard and studied.[7]

The Amish owed their farming success to what Americans today would refer to as "sustainability." This was what the social scientists of the BAE were investigating in their community studies during the early 1940s—that is, how Amish customs and practices allowed them to sustain family farms from one generation to another. In the study here, we employ two categories of comparison to assess the sustainability of Amish farming. First, the SCP data provide insight into the greater productivity of Old Order Amish farms in comparison to non-Amish farms in 1930s Lancaster County. Second, the BAE data establish the greater sustainability of Amish farming in comparison to other types of farming communities around the United States. In the first instance, Amish farms were, in some cases, only slightly more productive than their non-Amish neighbors while significantly more so than others. In the second instance, the BAE evidence indicates the Lancaster County Amish were much more likely to maintain their farms to pass on to the next generation than were the other communities the BAE investigated. We argue that in both categories of comparison, the productive and reproductive labor of Amish women proved necessary to farming success.[8]

As acknowledged throughout the book, farm communities in many regions of the United States experienced a substantial increase in women's gardening, dairying, poultry-raising, and field activities in the 1930s as compared to the 1920s. In the 1980s and 1990s, rural sociologists, anthropologists, and historians—including Deborah Fink, Katherine Jellison, Mary Neth, Grey Osterud, Carolyn Sachs, Sonya Salamon, and others—demonstrated the significance of women's work to sustainable family farming in the late nineteenth-century and twentieth-century Mid-Atlantic and Midwest. In the twenty-first century, a new generation of scholars, most significantly historian Jenny Barker Devine, has continued the conversation on women's significance to family farming. As these scholars have noted, a key to sustainable family farming was the mutuality of men's and women's labor. Despite the seemingly rigid gender roles that Amish men and women appeared to project to the outside world and reinforce in their highly patriarchal rhetoric, mutuality of labor was central to farm-family life. In fact, the extent to which the Amish crossed gender-role boundaries to ensure farm sustainability surpassed that of many other successful farming communities in the Roosevelt era.[9]

By the 1930s, most of the nation's mainstream farm households were in a period of transition, moving away from the general family farming practices of the nineteenth century and toward greater crop specialization, mechanization, and reliance on consumer goods that farm journals, agricultural college farm services, home extension services, and most Department of Agriculture agencies were urging upon them. In contrast, the productive activities of Old Order Amish women were a continuation and expansion of their usual chores rather than a resumption or selective extension of earlier practices amid the economic disruption of the Depression. As Walter M. Kollmorgen noted in his BAE-sponsored study of their community, the Old Order Amish belief that the Lord had commanded them to lead a labor-intensive life on the land lay behind their strong and sustained commitment to productive activities that involved all members of the farm family. Hard work continued to distract family members from worldly influences outside the Amish community, and home production ensured that members of the Old Order Amish faith—with their history of religious persecution—could remain relatively self-reliant and independent of potentially dangerous outsiders. For Old Order Amish women and girls, a central role in home and farm production thus represented a permanent way of life rather than a temporary survival strategy or the final stage of reliance on the practices of an earlier era before continuing down the road toward capital-intensive mechanized farming when the economy recovered. As this book shows, Old Order Amish women's long-established and wide-ranging production efforts, and their limited involvement in consumer activities, served their households well during the crisis years of the Great Depression and helped them weather related conditions more successfully than most other farm families. The individual chapters of this book tease out features of Amish success during the Great Depression, utilizing the data collected by the SCP and BAE and supplemented by additional qualitative sources.

Chapter 1 reveals how cooperation between the sexes was one of the most significant keys to the Old Order Amish accomplishing the work necessary to successfully maintain their farms during the Great Depression. The men did not own gasoline tractors or other large power farm implements that might amplify their manhood, and Amish women did not own mechanical household appliances to symbolize their feminine role as housekeepers. In rejecting the notion of mechanized, capital-intensive agriculture in favor of traditional, labor-intensive family farming, the Old Order Amish of Lancaster County practiced a system of labor that necessarily required the crossing of strict gender-role boundaries. Although men primarily identified as farmers and women as homemakers, agricultural success among the Amish necessitated a significant degree of cooperation and mutual labor.

Chapter 2 focuses on sewing, an activity that occupied a sizeable portion of Amish women's time. During the Depression, Amish women continued their long-standing custom of making most of the textile products that their family used. Nearly all Old Order Amish households owned treadle-powered sewing machines, which women used to make women's and children's clothing and to mend or alter the clothing their husbands purchased from local seamstresses specializing in Amish menswear. Amish women's sewing activities significantly outdistanced those of other Lancaster County women, allowing their families to keep bedding, linen, and especially clothing costs to a minimum.

Chapter 3 analyzes how Amish women's long-established baking, canning, poultry dressing, and dairy production activities helped feed their families and earn necessary cash during the Great Depression. In the mid-1930s, the average

Old Order Amish woman canned 357 quarts of fruits and vegetables a year and was responsible for raising and processing $466 worth of her family's total annual food supply—more than twice the amount she spent on purchased groceries. Women also often sold food items at farmers' markets throughout Lancaster County, such as pies, for 25 cents apiece, and cup cheese or "schmierkase" (in standard German, *Schmierkäse*), for 10 cents a carton. In total, women's food production accounted for nearly a third of all agricultural products exchanged or consumed by the typical Old Order Amish farm family in the 1930s.

Chapter 4 examines women's outdoor work. In the mid-1930s, when the average Lancaster County family netted $1,271 a year from cash crops and livestock, women's work helped Old Order Amish families realize $1,710 in net farm profit. Most women regularly took a turn in the grain, tobacco, potato, or hay field during busy seasons. They also reproduced the farm-family labor force at a higher rate than their neighbors, making their farms less reliant on paid field laborers.

Chapter 5 considers women's recreational lives. As members of a religious community that prohibited radio ownership, movie attendance, and even the reading of novels, Old Order Amish women and girls rejected pastimes popular among most of America's female population in the 1930s. They participated instead in recreational activities that reinforced the Amish work ethic, religious beliefs, and community solidarity. Girls organized neighborhood teams for playing ball games with other Amish youths; young women met their beaux at local hymn singings; women gathered at neighborhood "frolics" to construct quilts and straw hats; and everyone participated in frequent visits to the homes of friends and relatives. These noncommercial entertainments continued long-time Old Order Amish traditions and incidentally spared scarce cash resources.

Chapter 6 looks at women's religious practice. Old Order Amish women not only organized their lives around the agricultural calendar, but also around a regular series of religious events and rituals. Because the Old Order Amish held worship services in their homes rather than church buildings, the wife and daughters of a family spent hours cleaning and rearranging furniture before and after their turn to serve as hosts to the rest of the community. Women performed similar tasks and also cooked large meals on the occasion of a family funeral or a wedding, the latter typically occurring in November, after the harvest. Again, traditional, home-based and -produced rituals saved the Old Order Amish limited cash resources that many other farm families would have paid to commercial institutions.

Chapter 7 discusses women's role in times of medical crisis. Frequent farm accidents, illnesses, buggy collisions with automobiles, and at-home births took their toll on Old Order Amish families. They sometimes relied on the assistance of medical professionals, but they frequently turned to Amish women to tend the sick and injured and console grieving and worried friends and neighbors. In a community that eschewed ownership of telephones and automobiles, women's letters to friends and relatives and their submissions to Amish-read newspapers were often the most efficient means of disseminating health-related information throughout the Old Order community. As with other long-held traditions, women's healing practices saved community members money that otherwise might have been spent on medical bills.

Chapter 8 focuses on Walter M. Kollmorgen's classic 1942 analysis of the Amish agricultural success story. In an extensive report for the BAE, Kollmorgen, a cultural geographer, argued that the Old Order Amish of Lancaster County had so masterfully weathered the Great Depression that they were undoubtedly the most stable and successful rural community in the nation. Kollmorgen, the organizers of the SCP, and other government investigators recognized and acknowledged the patriarchal system under which Old Order Amish farmers and homemakers functioned, but their statistical data and impressions of Amish gender role prescriptions often obscured an important reality: Women's labor, sometimes conducted under male supervision and sometimes performed autonomously, played a significant role in Amish agricultural success. This book, as an addition of Amish women's voices to the government study, reveals the vital nature of their work.

CHAPTER ONE

Working Together
Women and Men on the Amish Family Farm

Work among the men folks is stripping tobacco while the women
are sewing, and some help to strip tobacco.
                                                —*Katie Y. Beiler, 1936*

Providing agricultural advice in *Georgica curiosa aucta* (1682), Wolf Helmhard
von Hohberg set forth the ideal working relationship for wives and husbands
heading rural households in German-speaking early modern Europe. "A household without a woman," Hohberg wrote, "is like a day without sunlight, a garden without flowers, a lake without fish. Without her assistance an economy can
never be undertaken and carried on in proper order. . . . [T]he household will
malfunction if the marriage partners do not help one another harmoniously."[1]

Hohberg, a member of a noble Protestant family, had fled Catholic Austria
to establish new landholdings among other Protestant exiles in Bavaria's Upper
Palatinate. He wrote his guidebook for people like himself—well-educated aris-
tocrats. All socioeconomic levels of the agrarian hierarchy, however, from manor
lords to peasants, would have recognized and appreciated the interdependence
of male and female labor during this period of agricultural innovation in western Central Europe. Yet in the late seventeenth century, a time when literacy
and the ability to publish accounts of rural life remained the preserve of the
upper class, men like Hohberg provided the only extant appraisals of the era's
new agriculture—featuring crop diversification and crop rotation—and of that
system's gender relations. Further insight into the central role that women's
work and cooperation between the sexes played in the new agriculture's success

may be gleaned from the experiences of the Old Order Amish of southeastern Pennsylvania—the descendants of early modern agriculturalists who began immigrating to North America just 50 years after the publication of Hohberg's treatise. Over the years, the Pennsylvania Amish would selectively adopt a number of new customs while also retaining the most salient features of early modern agrarian life.[2]

Characteristics of early modern new agriculture included subsistence farming with some market participation, maintenance of soil fertility through the planting of legumes and the application of manure, crop diversification, and keeping large numbers of animals. Implementation of the new method rested on the concept of patriarchal authority over the household labor force.[3] In Alsace, Baden, the Palatinate, and other areas where the new agriculture emerged, the agricultural household was both hierarchical and team based. The male head of household held ultimate authority, but he and his wife, along with their children and servants, recognized that the household's survival relied on interdependent male and female labor. Like the crop diversity and crop rotation system that nurtured the soil of the new agriculture, its household labor arrangements relied on the concept of balance. Men and boys labored in the fields with horses and oxen, while women and girls worked in the house, the garden, the poultry yard, and the dairy. The other major task for adult women was to produce the household labor force through frequent childbirth. When the agricultural cycle demanded it, however, female members of the household worked alongside men and boys during planting, harvest, and haying seasons.[4]

Within this system of complementary male and female labor, the male head of household supervised the work of other men and boys while his female counterpart managed that of the women and girls. From the sixteenth through the eighteenth century, common nomenclature in German-speaking Europe reflected the economic interdependence of male and female heads of household, with the man designated as *Hausvater* (father of the household) and the woman as *Hausmutter* (mother of the household).[5]

Evidence that the Amish, who began relocating to Pennsylvania in the early 1700s, retained the customs of rural Central Europe remained obvious more than two centuries later. In the state's largest Amish settlement, in Lancaster County, Amish husbands and wives continued to speak a German dialect, referred to as Pennsylvania Dutch, and address and refer to one another as "father" and "mother." They maintained the tradition of general, diversified farming to provide for the agricultural market and at the same time feed their own families. To do so, they embraced the cooperation between the sexes necessary to maintain the farm. Although men primarily identified as farmers and women as homemakers, agricultural success among the Amish necessitated a significant degree of mutual labor. As one twentieth-century Amish woman noted when reporting that she and her husband made equal contributions to the farm economy, "We're in it together. We're partners."[6]

The reasons the Amish relocated to Pennsylvania lay in the religious upheavals that shook Central Europe in the early modern period. Like the Mennonites and other European Anabaptists, or "re-baptizers," who emerged from the Reformation, the Amish faced persecution from Catholics as well as mainstream Protestants, who disapproved of the Anabaptists' resolute pacifism and embrace of adult baptism and other unconventional practices. Their status as religious dissidents often precluded Amish ownership of land, but pursuing an occupation unrelated to agriculture was not an option in the era's agriculturally based economy, nor were Anabaptist dissenters typically allowed to practice crafts regulated by the guild system. In addition, Amish interpretation of the Bible dictated that they, like Adam in Eden, tend the garden and the beasts. The Amish thus often became leaseholders, managing the estates of absentee landowners who traded toleration for lease-holding loyalty. As tenants, they relied on the labor of their own family members and invested in animal stock and other movable property, but also experimented with such techniques as crop rotation and manure application to make their marginal farmlands thrive. In other words, the Amish stood in the vanguard of the new agriculture that by trial and error eventually spread throughout Central and Western Europe.[7]

Continuing to face religious discrimination and fearing that Central Europe's growing armies would take their young men into military service, many Amish ultimately assimilated into other Protestant faiths or left Europe altogether, most of the latter heading to North America, where they initially settled in the British colony of Pennsylvania. There, in a colony founded by another religious pacifist, the Quaker William Penn, they found a hospitable location to practice their faith and a climate and terrain similar to what they had known in Europe. In colonial Pennsylvania, the Amish could continue the agricultural practices and gender role arrangements of Europe's new agriculture.[8]

Family farming was the norm in colonial Pennsylvania by the time the Amish began arriving, but the newcomers' almost exclusive dependence on family labor set them apart from some of their neighbors. Amish families sometimes hired one another's youngsters to perform farm work on a temporary basis, and some might also purchase the labor of German-speaking redemptioners—Pennsylvania Mennonites, religious cousins to the Amish, certainly did so—but it seems the Amish history of relying primarily on family workers and their theology of humility and simplicity kept them from purchasing enslaved Blacks; slave owning in southeastern Pennsylvania was regarded as a mark of ostentation or conspicuous consumption rather than a necessity.[9]

British observers often praised Pennsylvania German speakers' agricultural know-how—celebrating the large vegetable gardens the women tended and praising the field labor they performed alongside husbands and sons at harvest time—but such observers did not differentiate among confessional groups or single out the Amish.[10] Indeed, the Amish population in colonial Pennsylvania was relatively small—likely only about 500 immigrants of all ages in total—and it paled in comparison to the number of colonial-era Lutheran or Reformed who were also German speakers. Amish households initially clustered in what would become Berks County, though some Amish settled in what would become Chester, Lancaster, and Lebanon Counties. By the early 1800s, however, the dispersed Amish population had consolidated in eastern and northeastern Lancaster County.[11]

Without reading later expressions of Amish distinctiveness back in time, it is difficult to know in exactly what ways the early nineteenth-century Amish were distinctive in their appearance, household goods, or architecture. The 1798 federal direct tax records suggest that all but a few Amish households were living in log homes, even as many of their better-established neighbors had farmhouses of stone.[12] Other differences are harder to pin down, but Lancaster Amish bishop David Beiler (1786–1871) provides some hints. Beiler spent his later years critiquing the material refinement and market-oriented changes that had engulfed the United States and had begun transforming the household economics of his neighbors. In his youth, there had been "no talk of fine shoes and boots nor did one know anything of light pleasure vehicles." Wagons were unpainted, and "there were not such splendid houses and barns." Instead, he recalled, "It was customary to hear the spinning wheel hum or sing in almost every farmhouse." Later, the household production system began giving way to "the large amount of imported goods with which our country is flooded, and also the domestic cotton goods which are to be had at such [a] low price [that they] have almost displaced the home-made materials so that the daughters who now grow up no longer learn to spin."[13]

These developments did not go unanswered in the Lancaster Amish community and in fact contributed to a dramatic schism in the 1870s. On one side were tradition-minded folks like Beiler, soon called Old Order Amish, who upheld integrated household economies, and on the other side stood the change-oriented Amish who would later be nicknamed "Church Amish" because, in 1882, they constructed meetinghouses in which to hold Sunday services while the Old Order continued their time-worn practice of gathering for worship in members' homes.[14] The split between the Old Order Amish, or House Amish, and the Church Amish was complex and involved disagreements over church practice and theology. Although the schism cannot be reduced simply to economics, the commitment to household production that Beiler championed continued to mark the Old Order Amish into the twentieth century and was evident in the 1930s.

The Old Order were never entirely isolated or cut off from the broader rural neighborhoods in which they lived, but they were highly committed to what they called nonconformity to the world, and that included rejection of most of the new agricultural, household, communication, and transportation technologies that late nineteenth- and early twentieth-century industry produced. By the turn of the twentieth century, they had adopted some new equipment, such as treadle sewing machines and gasoline-powered lamps for the poultry house, but they assiduously avoided other technologies that most of their neighbors, including the Church Amish, were adopting, such as gasoline-powered tractors and automobiles.[15] Complicating this scene, after 1910 a third group emerged, splitting from the Old Order and positioning itself between the Old Order Amish and the Church Amish. It would eventually be known colloquially as Beachy Amish and, after 1927, its members would also drive cars.[16]

Old Order agriculture was not only traditionalist in its rejection of tractor farming. It also continued firmly to resist the separate spheres model of family farming that agricultural experts in the United States and back in Germany were now prescribing. With the industrialization of agriculture, these advisors increasingly championed the notion that farm households should become more like bourgeois urban households, with men thinking of themselves as businessmen farmers, who specialized in the production of cash-making field crops and livestock, and women envisioning themselves as full-time homemakers. These prescriptions greatly influenced the most prosperous agriculturalists, and in nineteenth-century Germany, the term *Landwirt* (farmer or agricultural proprietor) began to replace *Hausvater,* and *Hausfrau* (housewife) replaced *Hausmutter.*[17] As numerous scholars have noted, however, the economic realities of most nineteenth- and early twentieth-century farm operators meant that "work flexibility, shared responsibilities, and mutual interests" continued to characterize the labor of farm men and women.[18]

In addition to maintaining the mutuality model of family labor for practical economic reasons, the Old Order Amish also clung adamantly to this system on theological grounds. The concept of farming as a business was entirely alien to them, a people who believed it to be a divinely ordained way of life. To the Amish, tending farmland was a Christian responsibility that all family members should assume and pass on as a sacred way of life to subsequent generations.[19]

As a result of the developments described above, by 1930, after living in Pennsylvania for two centuries, the Old Order Amish of Lancaster County emerged as a distinctive group who remained committed to many aspects of the life their ancestors had known. They rejected ownership of telephones, radios, automobiles, electrical appliances, and birth control devices. At a time when a high school education was becoming a near universal experience throughout the rest of the northern United States, they gained national notoriety for refusing to send their children to consolidated elementary or secondary schools. Members of the faith continued to speak Pennsylvania Dutch and dress in a decidedly plain and unfashionable manner, with the men sporting beards and flat black hats and the women wearing modest head coverings and aprons. Most significantly, in an increasingly urban, industrial United States, the Amish remained committed to an agricultural way of life. They farmed in Lancaster County (and other areas of Amish settlement) without the benefit of tractors—relying instead on the power of horses and mules—and at a time when other farmers were increasingly specializing in production of a few major cash crops, the Old Order Amish remained committed to small-scale, mixed crop agriculture. Old Order men and women believed that the Bible sanctioned their devotion to an agrarian way of life, as it did their other distinctive practices. As a Lancaster County Amish man told cultural geographer Walter M. Kollmorgen in 1940, "The Lord told Adam to replenish the earth and to rule over the animals and the land—you can't do that in cities."[20]

The distinctive practices that the Old Order Amish continued to maintain in the 1930s made them attractive research subjects for Kollmorgen and other social scientists affiliated with President Franklin Roosevelt's New Deal. Kollmorgen's employer, the US Department of Agriculture's Bureau of Agricultural Economics, was only one of several federal organizations that sent investigators to Lancaster County in the 1930s and early 1940s to determine, in part, how effective Old Order Amish reliance on labor-intensive agriculture and rejection of modern consumer culture had been in helping them weather the Great Depression. Across the board, these studies found that eighteenth-century practices served the Amish well during the economic crisis of the 1930s. In Kollmorgen's report published in 1942, he in fact determined that the Old Order Amish of Lancaster County were the most stable rural community of the Depression era.[21]

One of the most extensive New Deal investigations took place as part of the 1935/36 Study of Consumer Purchases. Under the auspices of USDA's Bureau of Home Economics and the US Department of Labor's Bureau of Labor Statistics, the SCP organizers selected families in large and small cities, villages, and farming communities throughout the country for exhaustive analysis using detailed questionnaires. Lancaster County was among the 66 farm counties included in the study, with survey workers collecting questionnaires from more than 1,200 farm families in the county, including 74 Old Order Amish families. Survey investigators approached the women in participating families to gain information about their households' spending habits as well as data about farm crops and income, farm and household equipment, family size, home production, recreational practices, and dietary habits. The SCP data gathered in the 1930s provided the first systematic measure of the interdependent nature of male and female labor among the Old Order Amish and the economic value of women's work among agriculturalists whose labor arrangements approximated those of early modern farm families.[22]

The SCP data indicate that Amish adherence to farming practices of the early modern era yielded positive results. In the mid-1930s, when the average Lancaster County family netted $1,271 ($26,220 in 2022) a year from cash crops and livestock on a 60.5-acre farm, Old Order Amish families realized $1,710 ($35,276) in net farm profit on 67.6 acres.[23] The flexibility of Amish labor roles was one key to the success of these families. In an amendment of gender roles practiced in early modern Europe and colonial Pennsylvania, women no longer predominated in dairy work. As the scale of Amish dairying grew in the twentieth century, it engaged both sexes roughly equally. Women and girls nevertheless remained the predominant labor force in the home, garden, and poultry house, while men and older boys continued to be in charge of large livestock and cash crops. At harvest time, male and female family members, with the exception of the youngest boys and girls, all labored in the fields.

The lines between women's and men's work, household and farm labor, and house and farm equipment are difficult to draw on any family farm. When historian Sarah Elbert visited a modern farm household in the late twentieth century and asked the farm wife to estimate the number of hours she devoted to work for the farm versus work for the home, the frustrated woman flung open the lid of her automatic washing machine to reveal a load of laundry that included grimy farm coveralls, children's play clothes, and furniture slipcovers. The jumble of work clothing and household laundry in the woman's washing machine graphically revealed the difficulty of trying to divide labor for the marketplace and labor for the family when workplace and home place, as well as workforce and family, are one and the same.[24]

The situation on Old Order Amish farms was no different in the 1930s. For example, when SCP agent J. I. Byler asked an Amish family to determine whether their horses were primarily a family expense for buggy driving or a farm expense for powering field equipment, they were thoroughly stymied, leaving her to report, "No extra cost for driving horses. Uses farm horses only. Cannot give any amount for family." Like horse labor, human labor was often difficult to categorize as primarily serving the family or the farm. SCP agent Rigdon recorded a typical catchall response when she reported the farm and household labor arrangements of a middle-aged Amish couple with four teenage children: "All work done within family both in house and farm."[25]

In farming communities around the United States, men and women's access to particular types of equipment and the sources to power them theoretically differentiated their labor. According to the dominant patriarchal model, the male farm operator and his older sons chiefly operated expensive farm equipment. Elsewhere in the northern United States, this increasingly meant that older males claimed primary or exclusive use of the gasoline-powered tractor. In Amish country, however, men's chief claim remained the use of farm horses and the plows, wagons, and other equipment the animals powered. In contrast, wives, younger sons, and daughters primarily performed their work by hand. When they did employ implements in their farm labor, these were likely to be less expensive tools that all family members used regardless of age or sex. In some instances, this equipment might even be difficult to categorize as either principally a farm or household tool.[26]

A common symbol of the mutuality of men's and women's work in Amish farm families was the decidedly low-tech floor broom, a tool that received heavy use in households lacking vacuum cleaners. SCP agent Margaret F. Fratantono recorded three dozen new brooms in an Amish household comprised of a middle-aged couple, their 20-year-old daughter, three teenage children, a 21-year-old hired man, and an elderly female boarder. The farm family raised their own broomcorn and then paid a broom maker to make enough for the eight-person household at 25 cents per broom. At a total cost of $9, the investment in three dozen new brooms was a wise one, even in cash-scarce times. The women of the family would immediately press some of the new brooms into daily service, sweeping the large farmhouse and its porches and yard. They would put the implements to more rigorous use when they thoroughly cleaned the house for hosting Sunday worship services, visiting guests, or perhaps a wedding or funeral. The investment in new brooms to tidy the house also generated dividends on farm work. As Agent Rigdon described the scenario on multiple Amish survey schedules, "Brooms purchased for household, used first in house then taken to barn." With the arrival of clean new brooms, veteran implements lived out the remainder of their service in the barn. While women and girls were the primary users of new brooms, men and boys more frequently handled used models to sweep the barn and outbuildings; female family members, particularly younger girls, might also take a turn sweeping farm buildings with a retired household broom. The difficulty the Amish women and the SCP agents encountered in defining a broom as a household or farm investment, as house or barn equipment, or as a female or male tool demonstrated the interwoven nature of Amish family life and farm work and the mutuality of female and male labor.[27]

Despite the reality of the situation on Amish farms, in a rhetorical practice common on family farms throughout the United States, the families downplayed the extent to which male and female members shared labor and equipment. Instead, they insisted, like one Lancaster County Amish woman, "The women keep the house and the men work the farms."[28] When the Amish did acknowledge the labor women performed in the barn and field, they did not characterize it as farm work but as "helping" male family members with the men's work. Although the Amish employed a rhetorical strategy that reflected the patriarchal structure of their households—privileging male labor—and seemingly rendered women's farm work "invisible," SCP data demonstrate a different reality: regardless of the rhetoric, the Old Order Amish acknowledged and valued women's work wherever it took place.[29]

The market value of the labor Amish family members contributed to their own households and farms may be determined by the wages they earned when they took that labor to their neighbors' homes and fields. In a practice familiar to their ancestors in Reformation-era Europe, an Amish family with enough children to spare might send a son or daughter to labor at a neighboring farm where the children were either too young to work or were old enough to begin marrying and leaving home. Working at a neighbor's place was an important coming-of-age experience for many Amish youngsters, providing them with a sense of personal responsibility and a chance to practice the work skills they had learned at home and that would soon be taking them into adulthood. Work on a neighboring farm also provided young people with a wage to take back to their families or to invest in establishing their own farm households one day.[30]

Prevailing wage rates designated male hired labor—which centered on cash crop production in the spring, summer, and fall—as worth more than household-centered female labor, which might be done year-around. Over the course of a year, however, girls' more frequent work resulted in total wages that were roughly equal to those of their brothers. During the 1935/36 survey year, for instance, one 16-year-old Amish girl earned $156 for performing "household work on farm" for a neighboring family at a rate of $3 a week for 52 weeks, while her 18-year-old brother received $160 for doing "unskilled labor on farm" at $20 a month for eight months. As such evidence indicates, both male and female labor had significant economic value for Lancaster County farm households, and Old Order Amish families, who had the county's highest birth rate, benefited from this system whether their children exerted all their efforts at home or earned cash resources by sometimes taking their labor elsewhere.[31]

Theology as well as the need for family labor encouraged the Amish community's high birth rate. Taking seriously the biblical injunction to "be fruitful and multiply," Amish women did not view childbirth as potentially threatening but as status enhancing, and they and their husbands considered babies gifts from God rather than extensions of their parents. In the 1930s, Amish farm families rejoiced in the birth of each baby regardless of gender. Birth announcements in *The Budget*—an Ohio-based newspaper to which many Amish, both Old Order and change-minded, submitted content in the form of community news—emphasized a child's status as a future worker and designated whether a new baby would eventually perform indoor female labor or outdoor male labor. In autumn 1934, for example, Katie F. Lapp reported from the Lancaster County community of Gordonville that a "little dish washer" named Sarah had "arrived at the home of Samuel Blank," while Mary Ann Byler spread the news from Crawford County that folks at the Jake A. Byler household were "all smiles since the little woodchopper came to stay with them. He answers to the name of Andrew." In addition to reifying gendered labor roles, such announcements also clearly reinforced the patriarchal structure of Amish family life. A woman gained greater personal status with the birth of each child, but that did not mean her name would make it into the newspaper. The household she lived in and whose workforce she enlarged continued to be known by her husband's name.[32]

Although the Amish themselves as well as federal investigators categorized girls' and women's work as primarily household labor, female family members necessarily performed periodic outdoor labor, particularly during busy harvest seasons, as noted above. In most instances, this was unpaid labor on their own family farms. Occasionally, however, Amish girls performed outdoor work on neighboring farms, and the wages they earned in these instances indicate the market value of their labor. For example, in autumn 1935, a 17-year-old Amish girl earned $1 a day picking apples in a neighbor's orchard. The $5 she earned in total for working Monday through Friday matched the wages of the 18-year-old male laborer previously discussed when his $20 monthly earnings are broken down by the week. In other words, as gauged by local wage rates, Amish families valued male and female farm labor equally, at least during peak seasons, when a crop had to be harvested or else lost.[33]

The experiences of a 19-year-old "hired girl" and the household she labored in offer insight into both the value of female labor and the imprecision of the term "household work on farm." In 1935/36, this young woman worked on a 55-acre general farm rented by a 30-year-old wife and 29-year-old husband who had a 5-year-old son and 3-year-old daughter. The farm wife reported to SCP agent Viola J. Hambright that playing and sleeping were the main activities of her son and daughter. With children too young to labor on the farm, the Amish couple hired both farm (male) and household (female) labor. Due to skepticism of outsiders—including the belief that they lacked the training, strength, and perseverance to work successfully on Amish farms—the youngsters the couple hired were likely Amish. The couple reported paying just $25 for farm labor, which suggests that they only hired male help during the busiest weeks in the farm calendar, such as during the wheat harvest and at haying time. In contrast, the young woman Hambright classified as the couple's "hired girl" apparently worked throughout the spring, summer, and fall, earning the going rate of $3 a week. She received $105 as well as room and board for the 35 weeks she worked on the farm.[34]

Although Hambright listed the 19-year-old's daily labor as "housework," the extent to which her work was tied to the household's farming tasks is demonstrated by her employers not requiring the young woman's services during the winter months. While the household's wife and mother worked in the garden, poultry house, dairy barn, and farm field, the hired girl washed dishes, dusted, swept, and kept an eye on the children. When her female employer processed fruits, meats, and vegetables for market sale or home consumption, the hired girl assisted her. In the winter months, however, with the woman's gardening, canning, and fieldwork completed, her small household did not require the services of a hired female laborer.[35]

The SCP data that Hambright compiled demonstrate the impressive results of the work that the hired girl and her female employer performed. During Hambright's visit in late November 1936, the household consumed an extensive list of vegetables and fruits that the farm woman had raised and canned with the hired girl's assistance, including fresh cabbage and apples and canned green beans, tomatoes, carrots, beets, pickles, and applesauce. That the hired girl still resided with her employers during the last full week of November indicates that she continued to provide assistance while the wife and husband did the late autumn hog butchering and processing that provided the household with hams, sausages, and pudding pork, the head and organ meat to be ground and pressed together for later slicing and frying as scrapple. Also while the hired girl did the housework and minded the children, the farm wife devoted time to the family's poultry and dairy operations, which provided food for both the household and the market and earned the household a gross income of $195 in chicken, chicken egg, and duck sales and $1,325 in milk sales.[36]

The hired girl and farm wife also played an important role in field crop production. Her employer likely would not have allowed the hired girl to work with farm horses or the equipment they powered in the grain and hay fields. The meals that she and the wife prepared for male field hands, however, were vital to the laborers' success during the harvest and haying seasons, and while the hired girl worked indoors, the young farm wife undoubtedly worked alongside her husband and hired male laborers doing the handwork of shocking grains, gathering hay, and harvesting a potato crop that grossed $100.[37]

The wife and mother, if emblematic of other Amish women in the county, also labored in the farm's tobacco fields, helping her household earn $170 in gross tobacco income. Tobacco profits accounted for nearly 10 percent of her family's total income, which was typical for Lancaster County farms. Tobacco was the county's major cash field crop, although dairy, poultry, and livestock each produced more of the county's total farm income. Lancaster County produced more than 90 percent of Pennsylvania's total tobacco crop.[38]

Amish farm families contributed significantly to the county's high rate of tobacco production. While during 1935/36 the average Lancaster County farm raised a tobacco crop worth $398, the typical Old Order Amish household raised a crop valued at $461. Tobacco was the quintessential Amish crop.[39] The Columbian exchange of crops between the Americas and Europe meant that their ancestors may have had the opportunity to cultivate this "New World" plant in the Palatinate long before the Amish left that region for their new life in Pennsylvania even though Amish church disciplines forbade them from smoking tobacco or using snuff because such activities were considered worldly luxuries that transgressed Anabaptist commitments to plain living.[40] Tobacco cultivation came to Lancaster County in the mid-nineteenth century and took hold in the 1860s and 1870s in the areas where the Amish lived.[41] Tobacco appealed to Amish families as a labor-intensive crop. Stripping, sorting, and baling the crop took place during the winter months, a period devoid of major field tasks; the Amish thus prized tobacco as a crop that kept "boys from being idle in the winter."[42] Tobacco also kept Amish mothers and daughters busy weeding with hoes in summer and harvesting the crop with hand shears in late August and September. Women, in fact, were so associated with this type of agricultural work that when the weekly news and opinion magazine the *Independent* published an essay on Amish women's labor in June 1903, the article featured a photo of two Amish women working in a Lancaster County tobacco field.[43] Later, tobacco farming gained the added attraction of not being dependent upon the purchase and use of gasoline-powered farm equipment.[44]

All told, the 30-year-old wife—with her labor in the farm's tobacco and potato fields and its poultry and dairy operations—contributed to cash earnings of $1,790, or 63 percent of the household's gross farm sales income for the year.[45] The joint efforts of this Amish woman and the hired girl she supervised were impressive and made a significant economic impact on their household. This reality becomes more apparent when comparing this Amish household to the non–Old Order Amish household it most closely resembles in the SCP's Lancaster County survey records (table A2.1).

Like the Old Order Amish household described above, with its teenage hired girl and two young children, its non-Amish counterpart included three youngsters—a 12-year-old and 8-year-old sons and a 5-year-old daughter. The couple heading the family was relatively young, the husband age 37, the wife 36, both a few years older than their Amish counterparts. Having moved up the agricultural hierarchy, they owned rather than rented their farm, which at 60 acres was 5 acres larger than the one the Amish couple rented. Like the Amish farm, nearly

10 percent of this farm's income came from tobacco, but a smaller percentage of its income derived from its poultry operation (defined as women's work) and a much smaller percentage from its dairy enterprise (which engaged both men's and women's labor). In contrast, a larger proportion of this farm's income derived from wheat farming (predominantly men's work) and a much larger proportion from its large livestock operation (defined as men's work).[46]

Since the non–Old Order Amish farm relied on cattle, hog, and wheat farming for 71 percent of its income, it depended more significantly on hired male labor than did the Old Order Amish household. During a mid-August 1936 visit to the household, SCP agent Hambright characterized the family's 12-year-old son as engaged in "odd jobs" or "farm chores," but he was still too young to drive the farm truck the family listed in its equipment inventory. At five feet, five inches tall and 106 pounds, the boy was not yet developed enough to do the physical labor of a full-grown man. The family thus hired a man to assist the husband and father with grain and livestock farming. During the survey year, the hired man earned $2 a day and three meals a day for the 260 days he worked on the farm, but he did not reside with the family.[47]

In contrast to the hired farm laborer, a household worker employed by the family worked only fifteen days during the survey year. She earned $1 a day and, like the farm laborer, ate three meals a day with her employers but did not stay overnight with them. The short duration of her employment suggests that the house worker assisted the family's wife and mother, whose reported activities were "housekeeping" and "gardening," only during busy harvest seasons. Although her garden produced food for home consumption, and she provided a total of 780 meals to the farm's field hand over the course of a year, the woman's direct role in production for the market was more limited than that of her Old Order Amish counterpart. The family's poultry operation and small dairy enterprise undoubtedly took up a portion of her time, and she likely did some work in the tobacco fields. Although the family did not grow potatoes as a cash crop, they did grow asparagus and rhubarb for the market, and the wife and mother likely provided labor in producing these vegetables. In contrast to the wife and mother in the Old Order Amish family, however, the market-oriented labor of the non-Amish woman was minimal. Her efforts in the tobacco and market vegetable fields, the dairy barn, and poultry house accounted for only 28 percent of the family's farm income. With less involvement in outdoor activities, this woman could devote more time to household chores and simply did not require the services of a hired live-in girl.[48]

The general differences between this household and its Amish counterpart illustrate broader trends throughout Lancaster County. As SCP data indicate, Old Order Amish husbands and wives were on average a few years younger than most couples who headed farm households in the county, and Amish farms were less dependent on hired farm labor. Most significantly, Amish women played a larger role in production for market.[49]

Most farms in 1930s Lancaster County, including those operated by members of other Anabaptist groups, were transitioning from the diversified, labor-intensive agriculture of an earlier era to the specialized, mechanized farming that most agricultural experts of the day advised. The Old Order Amish, however, clung to the older model of family farming. The non–Old Order Amish household described above was a farm family in transition. With their gasoline-powered truck, highline electricity, and livestock operation that generated 64 percent of their income, this family was moving toward the type of capital-intensive, male-oriented farming that the agricultural experts prescribed. Although the wife and mother provided garden produce for home consumption, her market-oriented activities accounted for much less of the household's income than her husband's work in the livestock pens. As a result, although the household engaged in numerous other agricultural activities, the SCP characterized their farm as an "animal specialty" enterprise. In contrast, the SCP described the comparable Old Order Amish farm as primarily a poultry and dairy operation. In other words, it was a farm whose profits derived significantly from women's labor.[50]

The non-Amish farm household made a substantial investment in mechanized equipment and the acquisition and care of hogs and cattle. Its reliance on hired male labor throughout most of the survey year illustrates the male-oriented character of this type of farming. The Old Order Amish farm household made no investment in modern farming equipment and focused expenditures primarily on its poultry and dairy operations. Its reliance on hired female labor throughout most of the survey year illustrates the extent to which women's labor contributed to this type of farming. During the Depression years, when cattle and hog prices were low, and cash to invest in mechanized equipment was scarce, "animal specialty" farming could be risky. Nevertheless, during the SCP survey year, the non–Old Order Amish farm made a profit of $1,584. The Amish farm, which incorporated both male and female labor in its dairy operation and primarily women's work in its poultry venture, turned an even higher profit of $1,823.[51]

Amish families were not unique in the 1930s, even in the face of prescriptions to adopt the role of homemaker. Out of economic necessity, millions of farm women throughout the United States stepped up their production activities and decreased their reliance on purchased goods. Farm communities in many regions witnessed a substantial increase in women's gardening and poultry-raising activities in the 1930s as compared to the 1920s. By the 1930s, however, most of these women's families were in a period of transition between the family farming practices of an earlier era and the crop specialization, farm mechanization, and consumer culture participation that farm journals, equipment manufacturers, agricultural colleges, and many within the USDA prescribed. Once the economy recovered, most farm women and their families would continue on the path toward greater capital investment, mechanization, specialization, and consumerism. Over time, this path led to prosperity for some and failure for others.[52]

For the Old Order Amish, their productive activities in the 1930s represented a continuation rather than a resumption or extension of earlier practices. The belief that the Lord had commanded the Old Order Amish to lead a labor-intensive life on the land lay behind their strong, sustained, and highly successful commitment to production activities involving all members of the farm family. Hard work distracted family members from worldly influences outside the Amish community, and home production and consumption of their own farm products ensured that members of the faith—with their history of religious persecution—could remain relatively self-reliant and independent of potentially dangerous outsiders. For Old Order Amish women, their extensive role in farm production was not a temporary survival strategy in hard economic times but a permanent way of life. As the SCP data indicate, women's long-established and wide-ranging production efforts—and their limited involvement in consumer activities—helped Amish families weather Depression conditions more successfully than the majority of other farm families and allowed them to maintain a stable life on the land for decades to come.

Rejecting the separate spheres prescriptions of nineteenth- and twentieth-century experts on both sides of the Atlantic, the Amish instead maintained the practice that Wolf Helmhard von Hohberg had described in the seventeenth century as helping "one another harmoniously." While their rhetoric upheld the notion of a rigidly patriarchal labor system in which men alone performed cash-making outdoor work, Amish families' real-life labor and cash-earning experiences represented a different reality and demonstrated the interwoven nature of women's work and men's work—and family life and farm labor—on the Amish farm. The SCP data also demonstrate the extent to which the Old Order Amish continued the agricultural practices and gender-role arrangements that their ancestors had brought from western Central Europe to Mid-Atlantic North America in the early eighteenth century. The gender roles of the early modern Palatinate translated well to 1930s Pennsylvania.

CHAPTER TWO

Quilts and Clothing

Sewing for the Amish Family

Work among the women folks is sewing.

—*Leah F. Glick, 1936*

Like other farm women of the Depression era, Old Order Amish women were skilled at "making do" with the resources at hand. At a time when making and mending clothing and reusing old fabric for new purposes were common activities throughout rural America, the breadth and diversity of Amish women's sewing work nevertheless remained remarkable. Perhaps more so than any other category of labor, Amish women's extensive work with needle and thread set them apart from their peers in other farming communities. Their sewing activities significantly outdistanced those of other Lancaster County women, allowing their large families to keep bedding, linen, and especially clothing costs to a minimum.[1]

During the Depression, Amish women continued their long-standing custom of making most of the textile products that their family used. Study of Consumer Purchases surveys reveal that the Old Order Amish outpaced most other Lancaster County groups in their ownership of treadle-powered sewing machines. SCP data show that 72 of 74, or 97 percent, of Old Order Amish households in Lancaster County owned pedal sewing machines in the mid-1930s, with the remaining two households owning neither a pedal nor electric machine. In comparison, among the county's population not affiliated with the Amish or other Plain Anabaptists—whom the Amish referred to collectively as the "English"—76 of 86 households owned pedal sewing machines, 3 owned electric machines, and 7 owned neither. In short, 92 percent of English households in the county possessed some type of sewing machine. While English sewing machine ownership lagged only somewhat behind that of the Old Order Amish, additional SCP evidence indicates that Amish women used their machines more extensively than the county's English women and most other Anabaptist women.[2] Amish women's nearly universal ownership of the treadle sewing machine allowed them to make most women's and children's clothing, construct a portion of men's clothing items, and mend or alter the clothing their husbands purchased from local seamstresses specializing in Amish menswear. One Old Order Amish woman remembered making "twenty or more pairs of pants every winter" during the Depression, and another frequently noted in her 1933 diary entries that she "was patching all day" (figure 2.1).[3]

Sewing headed the list of indoor activities that occupied Amish women. When winter came and outdoor farming responsibilities lessened, women were particularly keen to pick up the needle and thread or work the pedals of their sewing machines. Throughout January and February, women's reports to *The Budget* newspaper stressed the indoor nature of family labor in Lancaster County, noting, "Work among the men folks is stripping tobacco while the women are sewing." In an examination of Amish women's diaries of the 1920s and 1930s, Patricia T. Herr, a scholar of Lancaster County quilts, found that some women spent up to half of February engaged in sewing activities. Fannie Esch, an Amish woman, estimated that she could work on as many as twelve or thirteen dresses in lengthy sewing sessions, during which her young daughters performed all the remaining household tasks. Like other local women, Fannie also made pillowcases, bed sheets, and tablecloths out of discarded chickenfeed bags during the Depression.[4]

Old Order Amish women's sewing activities ensured that they spent less money per person clothing women and children than their non-Amish counterparts did in Lancaster County. The larger size of Amish families and their need to purchase specialized hats, suits, and bonnets in conformity with the Amish *Ordnung*—unwritten guidelines that promote obedience, humility, and conformity—meant that Amish households averaged higher total clothing costs, $123.20 ($2,541.55 in 2022), than English households, $107.42.[5] Nevertheless, on a per-person basis, while the mean cost of clothing an Amish man was $2.78 higher than for an English farmer, the cost of clothing an individual Amish woman or child was less than for their English counterparts. While English farm women averaged $27.45 for clothing expenditures in 1935/36, Old Order

2.*1* A treadle sewing machine. At the time of the Study of Consumer Purchases survey in 1935/36, foot-powered sewing machines were ubiquitous in Old Order Amish households. Photograph by Marjory Collins, Lancaster County, 1942. (Courtesy of Farm Security Administration / Office of War Information Collection, Library of Congress, Washington, DC)

Amish women spent $24.18. Amish families also spent an average of $13.91 more than English farm families on clothing their children in total because there were more children in the family unit. When it came to clothing each child, however, Amish expenses were lower than those for English families. The difference lay in the portion of the wardrobe budget devoted to sewing supplies versus ready-made clothing purchases. The average English household spent only $5.61 on sewing materials in the mid-1930s, while the Amish spent an average of $37.78 on them. The greater investment by the Amish in fabric and thread benefited their families significantly when clothing each woman and child.[6]

SCP agents who visited Lancaster County Amish families felt it necessary to explain the households' minimal per woman and per child clothing expenses in marginal comments on their survey forms. Agent Rigdon's comments on the survey schedule for a seven-person family she visited in May 1936 were typical: "Amish family who make all their own clothing & repairs possible." Total annual clothing costs for the 45-year-old father were the highest, at $60.50, owing primarily to his purchase the previous fall of a light wool suit for $25. The other $35.50 spent on the man's clothing included the purchase of a $4 felt hat in the fall, a 50-cent straw hat in the summer, 15 pairs of socks, 2 pairs of work shoes, 1 pair of street shoes, 1 pair of overshoes, 2 union suits (meaning long underwear, or long johns), a $2.50 winter sweater, and $10.75 in sewing costs, including $4.50 for 30 yards of cotton fabric and $5.25 for "Other materials and findings." The man's wife and perhaps his 21-year-old and 17-year-old daughters used the cotton fabric to make the man's shirts and everyday trousers and probably used a portion of the other "materials and findings," including feed sacks, to make his light spring and summer underwear. Thus, even when clothing a member whose wardrobe included a significant number of purchased premade items, the family spent a noticeable amount—18 percent of the father's total clothing costs—on homemade attire.[7]

Total clothing costs decreased as one descended the family's age and gender hierarchy. Clothing for the family's 19-year-old son, categorized as a "man" on the survey schedule, cost a few dollars less than his father's wardrobe, at $57, and included a $25 heavy-wool winter suit as well as a variety of purchased items appropriate for a young man performing male outdoor labor. These latter purchases included a $3.75 jacket in the fall, a $2 wool cap in the winter, and a $3.50 pair of rubber boots in the spring. Other expenses resembled those for his father, including $4 for a broad-brimmed felt hat in the fall, 50 cents for a straw hat in the summer, and the purchase of three pairs of shoes and a year's supply of socks. In contrast to purchases for the father, however, the family bought the son only one union suit and spent less money on the construction of his everyday shirts, pants, and light underwear. While the young man's mother and others used 30 yards of cotton to construct his father's wardrobe, they required only 25 yards to clothe him. The difference perhaps resulted from the younger man's smaller size.[8]

As the SCP agents moved from consideration of men's clothing expenses to those of women and children, they witnessed a striking increase in the proportion of homemade clothing and a dramatic decrease in total clothing costs. In contrast to the findings for the household's father and oldest son, Agent Rigdon's records indicate that home-constructed garments constituted a substantial portion of other family members' wardrobes. Homemade clothing constituted 48 percent of the $36.35 clothing budget for the 45-year-old mother, 51 percent of the $46.20 clothing expenses for the 21-year-old daughter, and 39 percent of the $33.75 wardrobe bill for the 17-year-old daughter. As these data suggest, home-produced clothing was so central to an Amish woman's wardrobe that a larger proportion of homemade garments correlated to higher total clothing costs per woman. At prime courting age, the 21-year-old daughter probably required a larger wardrobe than her mother and teenage sister to attend the many singings, taffy pulls, and other social events that attracted young Amish couples. That the young woman bought two pairs of dress shoes during the fiscal year and went outside the family labor force to spend $5 for the services of a seamstress perhaps indicate that she was already preparing her bridal trousseau.[9]

Clothing expenses for the household's two youngest members further illustrate differences between providing garments for male and female family members. Total clothing costs for the family's 13-year-old son were nearly twice as much as those for his 5-year-old sister. Even with the outside purchase of his fall felt hat, summer straw hat, socks, two union suits, a pair of overshoes, and the four pairs of shoes necessary to keep a growing boy's feet appropriately shod over the course of a year, the homemade portion of the boy's wardrobe was still significant, accounting for 29 percent of the $40.60 total spent on his clothing that year. Expenses for his little sister's clothing totaled $20.95, with the purchase of two pairs of shoes, a pair of boots, a pair of overshoes, a pair of wool gloves for the winter, a sweater, and a year's supply of socks. The remainder of the child's wardrobe for the year was homemade and accounted for 27 percent of her total clothing costs. The similar proportion of homemade clothing expenses for each child indicates that although male clothing always included more purchased items, and thus generally outpaced the cost of female attire, the gender gap in the proportion of homemade clothing constituting the total wardrobe budget decreased as one descended the age ladder.[10]

The differences in clothing costs according to gender and age that Rigdon found for the seven-member family in May 1936 followed the same patterns as other Amish households in the mid-1930s. While the proportion of homemade clothing in an adult male's wardrobe might vary from household to household, the need to purchase distinctive Amish headgear, a plain suit, and protective garments for outdoor farm work in inclement weather habitually necessitated a greater investment in purchased items, and thus higher total costs, for grown men's attire. Even in the household that Agent Shoemaker characterized as an "Amish family [who] make all clothing including men's overalls & suits," the proportion of the 35-year-old father's wardrobe expenses for purchased items, at 67 percent, far exceeded the percentage of purchases for his wife as well as for each of their six young children.[11]

Another Amish family who completed the clothing survey in October 1936 followed the typical pattern, with outlays for ready-made clothing going primarily for the purchase of distinctive Amish headwear and men's and boys' suits. The household's major clothing expenditures included $3.50 on a hat and $28 on a suit for the 51-year-old father, identical purchases for the 19-year-old son, and a $2 hat and $8.50 suit for the 11-year-old son. For the women in the family, bonnets were the major ready-made clothing purchases, costing $3.50 for the 49-year-old mother and $3 each for the 15- and 13-year-old daughters. The $34 the household spent that year on sewing materials primarily translated into several new dresses for the teenagers and their mother.[12]

While the SCP agents took pains to remark that the "Amish make all their own clothes including men's shirts & some underwear," women's sewing activities in reality made a larger contribution to their own wardrobes and those of their children, particularly daughters, than to Amish menswear. Rigdon, Shoemaker, and other agents made a point of commenting on the home-construction of Amish men's clothing because this practice set the Amish and members of some other Plain religious groups apart from the nation's other households. Throughout Depression-era rural America, women made clothing for themselves and their children out of feed sacks and other materials, so the Amish were not unique in this regard. Even by the standards of rural America in general, however, and certainly in comparison to other Lancaster County groups, Amish women and children relied heavily on the garments that women constructed. This situation resulted from the proscription against elaborate and fashionable clothing. By religious necessity, an Amish woman annually purchased dozens of yards of what Agent Rigdon characterized as "special Amish dress mat[erial]" and used this solid-colored fabric—without any checks, polka dots, or other decorative patterns—to make dresses for herself and her daughters according to the principles of their Plain religion. In addition, she and her daughters refrained from buying the stylish berets, fur coats, negligees, and dozens of other fashion accoutrements that made the printed survey form for female family members twice as long as the one for males. In place of these fashionable items, agents handwrote seldom-heard terms such as "bonnet" or "heavy shawl" along with the explanation that in an "Amish family, shawl takes place of coat." The $3 cost of a bonnet or $11 for a shawl was a noticeable cash outlay for an Amish family, but considerably less than the purchase of more worldly attire would have been. Thus, Amish women, in adhering to the rules of their faith, combined both their limited purchase of clothing items and their extensive sewing activities to clothe individual female household members at a less expensive rate than those of other Lancaster County groups.[13]

While the larger size of Amish families inevitably meant that the total average cost of clothing an Old Order Amish household exceeded that of other Lancaster County groups, men's clothing was the primary driver of this higher expense. The need to purchase several elements of the distinctive wardrobe prescribed for Old Order Amish men, particularly their suits and headgear, took a toll on family clothing budgets. Amish women's diligent work at their sewing machines, however, diminished the cost of clothing other members of their large households while also keeping the cost of some adult male clothing items—light underwear, shirts, and pants—relatively low. The need to construct Plain garments unavailable elsewhere certainly contributed to women's extensive sewing activities. After all, one could not order an Amish-style dress from the Sears catalogue nor purchase one at a local department store. The importance of thrift in the Amish value system, magnified even further under depression conditions, also played a role in promoting women's extensive sewing activities.

Amish, Mennonite, and other Plain Lancaster County residents frequently quoted the Bible when explaining their satisfaction with simple, home-produced food and clothing: "Having food and raiment, therewith be content" (I Timothy 6:8). Amish women's traditional food and clothing production activities proved especially valuable in keeping their families well fed and clothed during the hard times of the Great Depression. Women also marketed surplus food and textile items to earn needed cash resources and typically used the fabric scraps left over from their construction of clothing and linens to make colorful yet practical quilts and rugs. Once their own homes were sufficiently stocked with these items, they might then sell others to non-Amish customers at local stores or farmers' markets.[14]

Construction of rugs and quilts, unlike the making of Amish clothing, also allowed women a modicum of culturally sanctioned creative expression. Whereas clothing had to conform to the strict guidelines of a Plain wardrobe, leftover fabric from a variety of monochromatic dresses and shirts could become a swirl of colors as a braided rug or when pieced and quilted atop a backing made of

2.2 The female members of a Moravian congregation quilting together. Old Order Amish women also gathered to quilt. Old Order Amish proscriptions forbade posing for photographs, which was considered contrary to biblical injunctions against pride and graven images. Photograph by Marjory Collins, Lancaster County, November 1942. (Courtesy of the Farm Security Administration / Office of War Information Collection, Library of Congress, Washington, DC)

bleached feed sacks or other reused or newly purchased fabric. Construction of these items was also often a social occasion, as frequent mention of rugging and quilting bees in *The Budget* suggests (figure 2.2).[15]

The Depression-era experiences of Amish-raised author Louise Stoltzfus's grandmother are instructive. With the death of Stoltzfus's maternal grandfather, whom she described as a mediocre farmer, his wife Mary was left an impoverished 51-year-old widow with thirteen children. To secure her family's survival, Mary turned to her homemaking skills. Like other Lancaster County Amish women, she was an expert at using fabric scraps to create rugs and quilts for household use; the sale of such items could also "provide much needed income." In addition to the financial benefits of her quilt and rug making, Mary's work provided her an acceptable creative outlet that also rendered psychological advantages. Amid the severity of her hardship, Mary was "an artist" who spent

2.3 A Plain Mennonite bedroom with the type of quilt typically found in Anabaptist farm homes. The original caption noted that the frilly window curtains "would not be permitted" in an Old Order Amish home. Photograph by Irving Rusinow, Lancaster County, March 1941. (Courtesy of the Bureau of Agricultural Economics Collection, National Archives II, College Park, MD)

long hours in her "sewing room retreat . . . stitching quilts and braiding rag rugs which became masterpieces of color, reflecting an inner life quite unlike the reality of her everyday existence." Stoltzfus notes that while collectors later considered Mary's quilts and rugs works of "artistic genius" and hung them on the walls of museums, members of her grandmother's Old Order Amish community simply considered them practical items whose creation kept a grieving widow busy and with a few dollars in her pocket (figure 2.3).[16]

Creating decorative family birth records was another way in which Plain women simultaneously used their needle skills to serve the family and express their artistic talents. Old Order Amish women as well as their Church Amish and Mennonite neighbors frequently embroidered the names and birthdates of family members and then displayed the resulting pieces in their parlors. Other women took a more creative approach. For example, Hannah Beiler Smoker, a

2.4 Hannah Beiler Smoker's cabinet full of useful wares in her farmhouse parlor. The original caption to the photograph drew attention to "the beautiful illuminated record listing the birthdates of the members of the family." Photograph by Irving Rusinow, Lancaster County, March 1941. (Courtesy of the Bureau of Agricultural Economics Collection, National Archives II, College Park, MD)

Church Amish member, created an illuminated family record on paper with colorful ink and a series of fine pin holes. Constructing the elaborate record allowed Smoker a creative outlet that fell within the parameters of her Plain culture. Smoker displayed it in her parlor alongside other decorative, but utilitarian household items, such as patterned dishware and embroidered sofa pillows (figure 2.4).[17]

Like the other labor women performed on the family farm, sewing tasks were also viewed as part of their commitment to their Plain way of life. Looking back on the Depression years, one Old Order Amish woman, Fannie Esch, remem-

2.5 A Mennonite farm woman constructing Plain clothing on her treadle sewing machine. Old Order Amish women also did such work. Photograph by Marjory Collins, Lancaster County, 1942. (Courtesy of the Farm Security Administration / Office of War Information Collection, Library of Congress, Washington, DC)

bered it as a time when she and her husband, Davie, labored on both sides of the farmhouse threshold to maintain their farm and family. They worked together in the wheat field at harvest time and in the dairy barn every morning. While she weeded the garden, he took a turn at childcare. The cooperative relationship the couple established when they wed in 1929 continued into their old age, when Fannie invited Davie to join her in what in their culture was a quintessentially female activity: "When we retired, we made quilts together. Davie cut all the patches and sewed them together. I quilted them. We made one for each grandchild. Oh, we had so much fun!" The pleasure and sense of accomplishment that Fannie Esch achieved in creating an object that was both practical and beautiful was something she could now share in retirement with the man who had been her partner on the family farm for sixty years.[18]

As Fannie Esch's comments suggest, although Amish women of the Depression period functioned within a highly structured, patriarchal religious culture, their economic and social contributions provided them a sense of purpose and self-worth. These women, whose contentment was inextricably bound to the welfare of family, farm, and religious community, took satisfaction from contributing to the stability of these institutions. Examination of Amish women's experiences in the 1930s indicates that much of the labor they performed not only benefited their families and farms, but also provided the women themselves with culturally acceptable means of self-expression and creativity in an environment that emphasized community cohesion over individual achievement. The image of a devout woman creating a colorful quilt or a practical garment on her treadle sewing machine is thus one of the most appropriate depictions of Amish womanhood in Depression-era Lancaster County (figure 2.5).

CHAPTER THREE

Kitchen and Market

Producing Food for Family and Income

We baked 100 pies at a time.

—Naomi Fisher, remembering the 1930s

Amish women's long-established baking, canning, poultry dressing, and dairy production activities helped feed their families and earn necessary cash during the Great Depression. In the mid-1930s, the average Old Order Amish woman canned 357 quarts of fruits and vegetables a year and was responsible for raising and processing $466 ($9,613 in 2022) worth of her family's total annual food supply—more than twice the amount she spent on purchased groceries. In comparison, "English" households averaged 303 quarts and $332 in food raised and consumed. Even when adjusted for the larger size of their households, Old Order Amish women's self-provisioning—especially their garden production—significantly outpaced that of other Lancaster County groups.[1] Amish and other farm women also often sold their food items door-to-door or at farmers' markets throughout Lancaster County. One Old Order Amish woman reported annual sales of $130 on her homemade potato chips alone. Another made $150 selling "home baked products." In total, women's food production accounted for nearly a third of all agricultural products exchanged or consumed by the typical Old Order Amish farm family in the 1930s.[2]

Evidence about home-produced food for family consumption appears in several sections of the Study of Consumer Purchases (SCP) surveys. SCP agents recorded this information on the Family Schedule under the heading "Value of

Products Furnished by Farm for Family's Own Use during the Schedule Year." Similar information appears on the survey's Expenditure Schedule in several categories: "Usual Expense for Food at Home during Each Season of Schedule Year," "Money Value of Food Raised at Home or Received as Gift or Pay during Schedule Year," and "Food Canned at Home during Schedule Year." It was also recorded under the section of the survey headed "Food Consumed during Last 7 Days" and on the very detailed Food Record, which only a minority of families completed. Those who completed the Food Record provided specific information about a day's worth of family meals and thorough data on the home-produced and purchased foods on hand in the kitchen pantry.

The comparison in chapter 1 of an Old Order Amish household and a non–Old Order Amish household, likely Lancaster Conference Mennonite or Reformed Mennonite, demonstrates the value of Amish women's food production to the family economy. The women in both households served three meals a day, seven days a week to five people. At the Amish dining table were the husband and wife, their 5-year-old son and 3-year-old daughter, and a 19-year-old hired girl. Those dining in the non-Amish home consisted of the husband and wife and their 12- and 8-year-old sons and 5-year old daughter.[3]

In describing a typical day's meals to SCP agent Viola J. Hambright in late November 1936, the Amish wife cited bread, crackers, cornmeal, Postum, and potatoes as the only purchased items she served. The household reported raising potatoes, but primarily as a cash crop. All the other vegetables they consumed at mealtime were home-produced, including fresh cabbage, canned green beans, and pickled beets. According to the Food Record, all of the meat and dairy products that the household consumed on the third day of the sample week had been home-produced. Where the Amish wife acquired the filling for that day's raisin pie remains a mystery because she did not list the dried fruit on her inventory of either purchased products or home-produced items. She certainly did not need to purchase lard for the pie crust because she reported the household had plenty on hand from its recent butchering activities.[4]

In contrast, while the wife in the non–Old Order Amish household reported that her family members ate a number of home-produced foods during their specified meal day, they nevertheless consumed a greater number of purchased products than their Old Order Amish counterparts. The meals the woman described to Agent Hambright were also more elaborate than those the Amish wife served. Like the Amish meals, there was bakery bread, but unlike them the non-Amish also ate store-bought corn flakes and desserts made with purchased chocolate and lemons. During the survey week, the non–Old Order Amish wife additionally used several other purchased items not found in the Amish home, such as cantaloupe, peanut butter, and Jell-O, and she reported a greater variety of purchased breakfast cereals than her Amish counterpart. This household, particularly in its greater use of national brand name products, such as Jell-O and popular breakfast cereals, demonstrated a larger engagement with national commercial culture than was typical for the Old Order Amish.[5]

The most noticeable difference between the food supplies of the two house-holds was the extent to which they relied on home-canned fruits, vegetables, and meat. SCP data showed that both women owned pressure cookers but that the Amish wife put hers to greater use during the survey year. The Amish woman reported producing 355 quarts of canned goods, while the other woman re-ported preserving only 221 quarts of fruits, vegetables, and meats. In both instances, the women reported that the majority of the products they canned were raised on their own farms rather than purchased at produce stands or markets. The Amish woman's greater canning output was consistent with gen-eral patterns in the county. In total, SCP data showed that Old Order Amish women averaged 357 quarts of food canned per year, while the overall average for Lancaster County farm women was 315.[6]

Nevertheless, the non–Old Order Amish wife estimated that the total value of home-produced food that her family consumed in a year's time was $407, which was $24 higher than the estimated total for the Amish household. That difference likely resulted from two factors. First, with the hired girl absent from the Amish home during the winter, the household contained only two adults and two small children for a quarter of the year and thus did not need to con-sume as many farm products as a five-person household whose members all resided and ate their meals at home for a full 52 weeks. Second, at a time when potatoes had become such a staple of the rural Lancaster County diet that one woman recalled eating fried potatoes up to three times a day in the 1930s, the non–Old Order Amish family consuming its own potato crop further raised the total value of its home-produced food consumption. While the Amish house-hold raised potatoes primarily as a cash crop, the other family raised them strictly for their own use. The Amish household earned $100 in potato sales during the survey year but themselves consumed only $12 worth. As a result, the house-hold was experiencing a potato shortage by the time of Agent Hambright's November visit and had to purchase the potatoes the Amish woman fried for breakfast on the day of the sample meal. In contrast, the other family consumed $20 in home-grown potatoes over the course of the year, and they indeed ate potatoes at all three meals of their sample menu day. The farm wife served fried potatoes for breakfast, buttered potatoes at noon, and creamed potatoes for supper.[7]

While the shortage of home-grown potatoes in the daily diet of the Amish household was unusual, in all other ways the family was typical of others in Lancaster County. Significant reliance on home-produced foods was the norm for Old Order Amish families. As SCP data indicate, Old Order Amish home food production outpaced that of every other ethno-religious group in the county. In 1935/36, the monetary value of home-produced food for all farm households averaged $372, while the average for Old Order Amish families totaled $466.[8]

Of course, some Amish households far exceeded this average, while others fell short. In one of them, the 39-year-old mother of six children, who ranged in age from 1 to 9, reported to SCP agent Rigdon that the value of the food she and her husband produced for home consumption during 1935/36 came to $590. She alone had canned 650 quarts of fruits, vegetables, and meats and had baked all the family's bread. On the other hand, when Agent M. C. Miller visited another Old Order Amish family during the August 1936 threshing season, the wife apparently worried that Miller would perceive her and her husband as poor household providers. To feed her household, which included five children ages 9 to 18, the 48-year-old woman had canned 404 quarts of food during the survey year, and her family had butchered pork worth $140 and beef worth $98 for their own use. Nevertheless, when she had to feed two extra meals a day to the five adult men who did two days of threshing on her farm, the woman resorted to purchasing a 10-pound chuck roast for $1.90. One imagines the Amish woman apologized profusely for the purchase because Miller took great pains to explain the unusual situation, writing at one point on the survey schedule, "Do not as a rule buy meat but did this week for threshing men. As home cured meats were all used & it was necessary to buy this meat." Commenting later in the document about the threshing crew's temporary presence in the household, Miller drove the point home by referring to them as "five extra thresher men for to eat extra meat bought."[9]

As Miller's comments suggest, Lancaster County Amish families purchased foods at butcher shops, bakeries, and grocery stores only sparingly. After marrying in 1934, Lydia Stoltzfus, an Old Order Amish woman, and her husband "bought with care" at the grocery store, purchasing only items they could not produce on their own farm, such as "three boxes of corn flakes for 25 cents." Prepared cereals frequently headed the list of items Old Order Amish families purchased in the 1930s. Looking back from the vantage point of the late 1990s, Daniel Zook, his wife, Rebecca, and his half-brother Amos all agreed that corn flakes and puffed wheat—along with sugar, salt, and coffee—were their chief grocery purchases in the 1930s. Lydia Stoltzfus summarized the situation, stating, "We raised everything we needed on our own farm. In the garden. We made our own butter. We bought only staples at [the grocery store], and occasionally some candy. That's just how things were."[10]

Along with data on purchased and home-produced foods that household members ate, SCP agents also recorded information about products that family members made to sell to others. That information appeared on the survey's Family Schedule, under the heading "Money Earnings of Family from Employment Other Than Operation of Farm during Schedule Year" and in marginal comments that agents provided to explain unusual consumption patterns. For instance, on May 15, 1936, when Agent R. Groome visited an 84-acre rented farm in Salisbury Township, she reported that the small Amish household had "consumed" 10 pounds of sugar and 10 pounds of white flour during the previous week. Perhaps realizing how unusual it appeared for the 30-year-old husband, 27-year-old wife, 2-year-old son, and a hired man to have consumed 20 pounds of sugar and flour in only seven days, Groome explained at the bottom of the page "made pies and candy takes lot of sugar and flour." Very likely, the young farm wife made the large volume of sweets to take to market, and based on the household's use of two dozen bananas during the previous week, a portion of those baked goods were banana cream pies.[11]

Making and selling baked goods was labor-intensive but could result in a tidy profit. A Mennonite woman in her 60s reported to Agent Shoemaker in May 1936 that she had spent 156 days baking pastries during the past year and had earned a $500 profit on their sale. That was nearly half of the $1,075 annual income for a farm household that included only herself and her husband. Naomi Fisher, an Old Order Amish woman, said that she and her mother and sister "baked 100 pies at a time" during the Depression. She recalled, "We got up early and started. The range baked four pies at a time. When it was hot, we just done it. There was no such thing as it being too hot. We just went and did it." According to Fisher, the profits were significant. Minimal investment in ingredients yielded pies that sold for 25 cents apiece. As Fisher noted, "Mother figured that if she made 100 pies she had $25. We paid 19 cents for a 12-pound bag of flour and three cents for one pound of lard." Not every farm family made even small investments in their baking enterprise. One Old Order Amish household reported that it purchased only half the 20 pounds of flour they used in a week and milled their own wheat for the other half. Along with providing their own flour, many Lancaster County farm families also baked with lard preserved from their own butchering activities.[12]

Pie fillings were also inexpensive, with the exception of banana cream pies or some other kind that required the purchase of imported fruits. Families used fresh or canned produce from their own gardens and fruit trees to make rhubarb, peach, apple, and other assorted pies. If they did not grow their own fillings, Amish women might employ other methods to acquire them with little to no cash outlay. Fisher recalled that her family picked up "drops"—apples that had fallen to the ground at a nearby commercial orchard—"for nothing." They used the free apples, along with those they had purchased, to make both pies and "40 gallons of apple butter at a time." Making apple butter and pear butter were in fact ubiquitous autumn activities for Lancaster County Amish women. As the New Holland correspondent noted in her late October 1936 report to *The Budget*, while the local men were "busy husking corn," the women were "canning pears and boiling pear butter." Once they had made enough for their own families' use, women could then market these products to others. In 1936, one Old Order Amish woman reported to SCP agent Ella Veit that she had canned 481 quarts of fruit, vegetables, and meat to feed herself, her husband, her three children, the "extra farm help," and occasionally her elderly parents or in-laws. She had enough surplus pear butter, however, to sell it for a total of $7. She reported to Veit that she was adding cash to the family income in other ways as well. She had invested $200 to increase her poultry flock at a time when eggs were selling for 18 cents a dozen and dressed chickens for 80 cents apiece; she ended up grossing $700 in egg sales and $500 in chicken sales for the year. At a time when every penny counted, she also earned an additional $2 selling soap that she made from butchering lard.[13]

Lard itself was another product that Lancaster County women marketed. Elizabeth Benner, a Mennonite, remembered that after butchering, her family would have enough lard to fill 50 one-pound cans. They would keep enough for a year's worth of cooking and soapmaking and then sell the rest to a grocery store for cash or exchange it directly for grocery items they could not produce on the farm, such as sugar, cocoa, and shredded wheat cereal. Like many other Depression-era farmers, her family also sometimes exchanged eggs for their groceries.[14]

Families marketed their pies, eggs, and other home-produced foods in a variety of ways. Since as Lydia Stoltzfus recalled, the Amish farm families' "non-Amish neighbors also grew all their own things in their gardens," most of the customers for Amish vegetables, fruit, poultry products, and baked goods were town and city dwellers. After families had sold their cash-crop potatoes or milk to the commercial broker or dairy and had provided for their own food supply, they often took their surplus foodstuffs to town. Daniel and Amos Zook estimated that approximately half the county's Old Order Amish families marketed products directly to urban customers in the 1930s, and the brothers themselves peddled potatoes door-to-door in the city of Lancaster, with a population of approximately 60,000 persons in 1930. Other farm families in the county also frequently sold their products door-to-door. Grace Summy, a Mennonite, remembered that her widowed mother made cupcakes and potato chips that Grace and her three siblings sold door-to-door in Lititz, a town of about 4,300 people in 1930. Hazel Bergey's Mennonite farm family lived 26 miles south of the city of Lancaster but traveled there to sell their surplus produce at the "curb market," where they rented space along the street curb and sold lima beans, chickens, and eggs to customers who traveled by train from as far away as Philadelphia to purchase fresh foods. Amish and Mennonite farm families frequently sold their products on the street because renting a stall at one of the big indoor markets, such as the Southern Market or Central Market in Lancaster, was too expensive. Eventually, however, the city outlawed curbside sales, and if families wanted to sell their products to city customers, they had to pay for space in an indoor marketplace.[15]

The variety of products that families sold was impressive. Mennonite teenager Edith Thomas spent every Friday and her older sister spent every Saturday with their father at the Southern Market, where they sold her mother's homemade angel food cakes, bread, and sponge cakes. The girls also sold the butter and cheese they helped their mother process and the asparagus and radishes they assisted her with in the garden. The children in Rebecca Zook's Old Order Amish family also took turns in the marketplace alongside their father, but the products they sold were primarily the result of their mother's labor, including dressed chickens, homemade potato chips, red beans, and carrots. The children and their father also marketed berries at a time when large strawberries sold for 25 cents a quart, small strawberries for 10 cents a quart, and raspberries for 16 cents a quart. Among the products that Anna Yoder's Old Order Amish family marketed in the 1930s were apple butter, dressed chickens, eggs, and fresh flowers. After Lydia Stoltzfus's oldest sister became a widow in 1932, Lydia helped her make sticky buns, bread, cakes, and pies that they sold at the Southern Market (figure 3.1).[16]

Whether it was fathers and children who marketed products, as in Rebecca

3.1 The floor of Lancaster's Southern Market. Photograph by Irving Rusinow, Lancaster County, March 1941. (Courtesy of the Bureau of Agricultural Economics Collection, National Archives II, College Park, MD)

Zook's family, or the women themselves who stood in the market stall, as Lydia Stoltzfus's sister did, the labor that produced the market products was primarily female. Naomi Fisher's hard-working mother exemplified the diversity of tasks an Old Order Amish woman performed so her family could market its products to city dwellers. According to her mother's 1933 diary, the Fisher family "went to market" every Tuesday, Friday, and Saturday. That meant that every Monday, the mother, 21-year-old Naomi, and Naomi's 14-year-old sister did the family laundry and "got things ready for market," such as baking pies or dressing chickens from their poultry flock. In the summer, it meant readying fresh vegetables for sale and in the fall entailed making apple butter and retrieving endive, cabbage, carrots, and red beets from the cellar and arranging them in bunches for sale. In the winter, it involved organizing the cheese, butter, eggs, and sweet potatoes they had stored in barrels in the attic. They might also use the raw milk from the three or four cows in their dairy herd to make the Pennsylvania Dutch version of cream cheese, called "schmierkase" (in standard German, *Schmierkäse*), or cup cheese, which they dolloped into small cardboard containers to sell for 10 cents apiece. According to Naomi, on the three days a week they marketed their goods, family members "stood on the Southern Market in Lancaster and peddled from door to door." Apparently, everyone but her two youngest brothers, who were still in school, took their turn at marketing. On Wednesdays and Thursdays, when they did not go to the market, Naomi's father chopped and loaded firewood, her mother and sister "did various things around the house," her 16-year-old brother made horseshoe pads from discarded rubber tires to sell to local blacksmiths, and Naomi did housework for Amish neighbors for 50 cents a day. On Sunday, of course, the family worshipped and rested.[17]

In the final analysis, all the hard work that women put into making their products was wasted effort if they did not display their goods in an attractive way that enticed their city customers. In a July 1941 *National Geographic* article describing life in Lancaster County, writer Elmer C. Stauffer paid tribute to women's careful presentation of their market produce: "Look at those apples shining as though individually and painstakingly polished; crisp, cool lettuce having a handled-with-white gloves freshness about it; big tomatoes, red and firm, glistening like clever wax copies; gourds and pumpkins, fresh and full, glowing like plump children just out of the tub." As such testimony indicates, Amish women dedicated concerted effort in displaying as well as producing their market products.[18]

The same year that Stauffer published his article, photographer Irving Rusinow traveled throughout Lancaster County taking pictures of Amish and Mennonite activities to illustrate an upcoming study of agricultural stability by the Bureau of Agricultural Economics. Among the photographs Rusinow took were some of women selling their products at the Southern Market, where they arranged their dressed chickens and baskets of eggs in orderly, eye-catching rows (figure 3.2). The following year, Office of War Information photographer Marjory Collins captured Lancaster County women selling their goods at the Lititz farmers' market. Among her pictures was one of a woman neatly arranging her pies and dinner rolls on a table covered with a clean white cloth and backed by a mirror that reflected and seemingly doubled the abundance of her baked goods (figure 3.3). In another Lititz market photo, Collins captured a woman whose large bunches of celery, radishes, and other vegetables nearly spilled over the front of her market table, inviting customers to sample her garden's bounty

3.2 Amish and Mennonite farm women waiting for customers at Lancaster's Southern Market. Photograph by Irving Rusinow, Lancaster County, March 1941. (Courtesy of the Bureau of Agricultural Economics Collection, National Archives II, College Park, MD)

(figure 3.4). In documenting Anabaptist women, Rusinow and Collins highlight their savvy retailing skills through the artful presentation of their products. The photos also reveal that Plain women used their market stalls as culturally appropriate spaces for aesthetic expression.[19]

Women's careful arrangement of their market stands also indicated a sense of accomplishment in their labors. Their religion frowned on displays of personal pride but prized diligent labor, commitment to family and community, and a self-sufficiency that enabled separation from worldly influences. In raising, processing, and sometimes marketing their own food, Amish women demonstrated commitment to the tenets of their culture and religion. In their marketplace displays, they literally exhibited the fruits—and vegetables, poultry products, and baked goods—of their labor. They thus provided tangible evidence of their

3.3 A Mennonite woman standing by the carefully arranged baked goods she brought to sell at the Lititz farmers' market. Photograph by Marjory Collins, Lancaster County, November 1942. (Courtesy of the Farm Security Administration / Office of War Information Collection, Library of Congress, Washington, DC)

adherence to Old Order Amish norms and conformity to their culture's vision of female competency. More than 60 years after the fact, Naomi Fisher's detailed recitation of the many tasks she performed alongside her mother illustrates the satisfaction women achieved in a job well done. In contrast, Agent Miller's explanation for another Amish woman's threshing-season meat shortage demonstrates the loss of self-esteem a woman might have experienced if she felt she had fallen short of the prescribed ideal.

Old Order Amish women achieved many goals in their extensive production

3.4 A Mennonite woman displaying her garden produce at an overflowing stall at the Lititz market. Photograph by Marjory Collins, Lancaster County, 1942. (Courtesy of the Farm Security Administration / Office of War Information Collection, Library of Congress, Washington, DC)

of food products. Work in their large vegetable gardens, in the dairy barn and poultry house, and at their kitchen stoves kept family grocery expenses lower than they otherwise would have been. When they marketed their home-produced goods, Amish women earned money they could then spend on coffee, sugar, bananas, and other foods they could not produce at home. Money saved or earned through home production could also be reinvested in the family farm. Home food production could result in extra cash for increasing the poultry flock, repairing farm equipment, or maybe even purchasing farmland. Along with feeding the family and fulfilling their prescribed roles as industrious wives and mothers, Amish women through their food production enabled their households to meet the most important goal of the Old Order Amish in the 1930s: continuing to live their lives as pious tillers of the soil.

CHAPTER FOUR

Field and Barn

Raising Crops and Livestock

I shocked wheat. But I never helped with the hay.
—*Fannie Esch, remembering the 1930s*

In the mid-1930s, when the average Lancaster County family netted $1,271 ($26,220 in 2022) a year from cash crops and livestock, women's work helped Old Order Amish families realize $1,710 ($35,276) in net farm profit. A woman with a fondness for animals might sometimes work with large livestock, but almost all women regularly took a turn in the grain, tobacco, potato, or hay fields during busy seasons. One Old Order Amish woman remembered, "I threw bales until I was 50." Girls from predominantly female families might frequently work in the farm fields alongside their fathers, risking the same debilitating accidents as their male counterparts. When Israel Zook's daughter Susie "had the misfortune of hurting her foot . . . while working in the fields" in spring 1935, her injury merited mention in *The Budget*. Acknowledging the accident's negative impact on the Zook family economy, correspondent Katie F. Lapp lamented that the injured foot had rendered Susie Zook "[un]able to do much work" for several weeks.[1]

The Amish farm benefited not only from women's productive labor, but also from their reproductive efforts. Old Order Amish women gave birth to the farm-family labor force at a higher rate than their neighbors, making its operation less reliant on paid field laborers than non-Amish farms. While the average county farm woman who responded to the Study of Consumer Purchases had

2.53 children living at home in 1935/36, the typical Old Order Amish respondent had 3.43 children in her household. The size of Old Order Amish families also outdistanced that of all the other Anabaptist groups in Lancaster County.[2]

Recalling the 1930s at the end of the twentieth century, Lancaster County farm woman Lydia Stoltzfus remarked, "I do not remember of my father having hired hands, because there were plenty of us children." As the youngest of 10 children born between 1897 and 1914 to an Old Order Amish family near the community of Bird-in-Hand, Lydia milked cows and worked in her family's corn and tobacco fields until 1934, when she married and performed similar work on the farm she rented with her husband. Her experiences were typical, and her memories provide a general outline of Amish gender relations and farm labor: The family patriarch supervised farm work and determined whether the farm required the services of "hired hands" (paid male labor) or could rely strictly on family labor, both male and female. As the result of family size, birth order, and her father's say-so, Lydia performed men's work on the family farm.[3]

Like Lydia Stoltzfus, Ada Lapp believed that birth order played a role in determining that she routinely performed farm work. Rather than the youngest in a long line of family workers, however, Ada was the oldest of eight children in an Old Order Amish family. She reasoned that since she was the oldest, her father had no choice but to put her in the field once she could do the work. She also continued to harvest potatoes and do any other necessary farm labor even after she had brothers old enough to do it. She recalled working in the fields as much as her brothers, a pattern that continued after the family left Lancaster County in the mid-1930s for a farm in nearby Chester County.[4]

Birth order sometimes trumped gender in household labor arrangements too. In those instances, the family's wife and mother made the decisions. As the oldest of nine children in a Lancaster County Mennonite family, Mahlon Hess found himself in an unexpected role when the family's hired girl suddenly "took off" one summer in the 1930s. Mahlon's mother, recognizing that her husband had adequate assistance with the farm, drafted her oldest son for household service. She told her husband, "Now Father, you still have a hired man, but I have no help. This summer, Mahlon will work in the house!" In the end, Mahlon appreciated the benefits he derived from learning how to perform household tasks, noting, "When I went to college, I could sew on buttons!"[5]

The necessary flexibility of gender work roles sometimes allowed space for personal preference to play a part in whether a woman or girl performed outdoor farm work. Elizabeth Benner was the fourth of eight children in her Lancaster County farm family, and she thought of herself as her father's "hired man" because she did every type of outdoor work except hauling manure and plowing. In her words, she would rather do farm work than "wash dishes, thank you." Her penchant for outdoor work was highly useful when she married and began farming with her husband in 1928. Throughout the next several years, she worked alongside her husband in the farm fields, driving horses for harrowing and discing and loading hay, until her sons were old enough to take on the responsibility. In contrast to Elizabeth's experiences, however, some Lancaster County women performed outdoor work in spite of their lack of interest in it. For instance, Edith Thomas, recalling her 1930s Mennonite girlhood, bemoaned the arbitrary nature of her father's work assignments: "I always said I didn't know why my dad made me work outside in the fields. I should have worked in the house. My older sister worked in the house, and she'd just as soon worked out in the fields."[6]

Working as a household helper was the more common way for Amish and Mennonite girls and young women to earn money away from home, but they sometimes might also earn a little cash doing short-term agricultural labor on a neighbor's farm. Harvesting fruit, whether in a neighbor's orchard or berry field, was a common type of paid farm labor for them, as well as for young boys in Lancaster County. Paul Weaver, the son of a Mennonite truck farmer, remembered that in the early years of the Depression, Amish youngsters constituted the bulk of his father's labor force during strawberry and raspberry season. One local farm household reported to SCP agent Shillot that the $40 paid to "children [who] picked strawberrys [*sic*]" had been their only farm labor expense in 1935/36. A girl might earn only 2 cents or maybe 3 cents for every quart of berries she picked, but the pennies added up if she put in a full day or two of work. Like other Amish boys and girls, she would automatically turn those earnings over to her parents at the end of the day. Until Amish children turned 21, their wages belonged to their families.[7]

The experiences of Fannie Esch on her farm near Lancaster County's New Holland community is illustrative of some women's contributions on the farm and those women's perceptions of gendered work. In recalling the early years of her marriage 70 years later, Fannie spoke of working side-by-side with her husband in the tobacco and potato fields and in the dairy barn, even reciting how much they made on their tobacco, wheat, and potato crops in 1930. She also recalled that sometimes she and her oldest daughter milked the 20 dairy cows alone "without the men." Nevertheless, in recollecting that labor, she also said that she "helped milk," and she similarly characterized her work in the tobacco, potato, wheat, corn, and alfalfa fields as "help." Fannie's labors outside the house

4.1–4.2 (*Above and opposite*) An Old Order Amish husband and wife canning beef. When visiting the Amish, the photographer respected their proscription against full-face images of baptized adults. Photographs by John Collier, Jr., Chester County, 1942. (Courtesy of the Farm Security Administration / Office of War Information Collection, Library of Congress, Washington, DC)

were, it seems, in support of the family's true farmer—her husband. Thus, Fannie demonstrates that even when Amish women regularly performed outdoor farm labor, they still considered it "men's work."[8]

In characterizing the farm labor she performed as "help" rather than "work," Fannie Esch employed a rhetorical convention that was common among farm women in Lancaster County and many other locations. Even though their actions contradicted their words, women who labored alongside their husbands in New York dairy barns, Iowa cornfields, and Pennsylvania butchering sheds all adamantly insisted they were helpers rather than farmers. Their language both reflected and reinforced the patriarchal structure of farm-family life and buttressed the notion of the word *farmer* as a masculine noun. Nevertheless, in describing the diversity of their tasks, whether performed alone or in tandem with men, Amish and other farm women confirmed that interdependent male and female labor was necessary for successful family farming (figures 4.1 and 4.2).[9]

The oral history narratives of Lydia Stoltzfus, Ada Lapp, Fannie Esch, and others offer vivid descriptions of gender relations and women's farm work in Depression-era Lancaster County, and SCP records provide systematic information on the economic value of that labor. Even families that did not farm tobacco—the county's major cash crop—benefited significantly from women's cash-producing outdoor work. In mid-September 1936, Agent Viola J. Hambright visited an Old Order Amish family to gather data to supplement information recorded two months earlier by Agent Rigdon. The family, referred to here as the Kings, had received $192 for taking their tobacco land out of production as part of the New Deal's program to raise farm prices by decreasing commodity surpluses. The Kings' situation was highly unusual. While the Old Order Amish might voluntarily reduce acreage to improve farm prices, their beliefs involving labor and fair pay generally prevented them from accepting government payments to do so. As an Amish man told a Philadelphia reporter at the time, "I don't think it's right to take money that isn't earned," adding that receiving a government payment meant "that a farmer [was] being paid not to work." The reasons for the Kings' atypical acceptance of the money remain a mystery. Even in the absence of labor-intensive tobacco farming, however, the family's survey responses provide striking evidence of the mutuality of men's and women's work and the necessity of women's outdoor labor.[10]

Forty-seven-year-old Amos King and his wife, Sadie, who had just turned 51, headed a household that included six children in residence: Jacob (19), Sarah (16), Mary (15), Rebecca (13), and Samuel and Moses, who had recently turned 12 and 10.[11] The three youngest children were still in school, while the three older children were full-time participants in the farm-family economy. During the week of Hambright's investigation, the Sabbath was the only day on which Sadie could rely on household assistance from all three of her daughters. From Thursday, September 17, through Saturday, September 19, and again from Monday, September 21, through Wednesday, September 23, daughters Sarah and Mary spent eight hours a day picking tomatoes. If their father or older brother worked alongside the two girls in the tomato fields, Hambright simply subsumed this male labor under the general heading "Farming." With Sarah and Mary in the field, this left 13-year-old Rebecca as her mother's only household help on a Saturday and apparently with a weekend houseguest. The 21-year-old guest—most likely the 21-year-old daughter listed elsewhere in the survey as the family's eldest child—arrived from her week of perhaps working as the hired girl on a neighboring farm to reap the benefits of the tomato pickers' diligent labor. A typical day's menu during the time of the houseguest's visit included fried tomatoes at noon and fresh sliced tomatoes for supper.[12]

While many Lancaster County farm families sold tomatoes as a cash crop, SCP records indicate that this family did not. Instead, they processed their abundant tomatoes for use at their own table or perhaps for sale to city customers at a farmers' market or door-to-door. In total, during the week that Hambright visited the family, they consumed 17.5 pounds of tomatoes. If indeed their young visitor was the family's oldest daughter, she may even have arrived specifically to help with tomato canning. During Hambright's visit, a report published in *The Budget* noted that women in the Lancaster County community of Leola, Pennsylvania, were "busy . . . canning . . . tomatoes, and making catsup to use up the tomatoes which [were] very plentiful [that] summer." The King family also likely canned corn during the week of Hambright's visit, accounting for their consumption of 70 pounds of fresh corn in that seven-day mid-September period. The family in fact produced a significant majority of the canned vegetables and fruits they consumed that year, indicating the wisdom of their "ownership of [a] pressure cooker." In total, the Kings canned 180 quarts of fruits and vegetables during 1935/36. They also apparently dried some of their homegrown fruits and vegetables, including the three pounds of dried onions they used during the week of Hambright's visit. Perhaps they combined fresh tomatoes, a portion of the dried onions, and the three pounds of homegrown cabbage and store-bought vinegar they consumed that week to make chow-chow, a local relish dish that women typically pickled in mid-September. During the survey year, the family also produced 40 quarts of sauerkraut, 25 quarts of pickles, and 15 quarts of jams and jellies for home consumption.[13]

Potatoes were another mainstay of the family's diet, and, according to Amish scribes in *The Budget*, spuds were in large supply during Agent Hambright's visit. Fannie Beiler reported from the city of Lancaster that farmers had their hands full that week both "cutting corn and picking up late potatoes." *The Budget's* Leola scribe characterized local "men folks" as "very busy" picking tomatoes and "taking out potatoes" at a time when they were also cutting corn, filling silos, and making hay. Mrs. John K. Lapp of New Holland explained to *Budget* readers that the current abundance of both tomatoes and potatoes in Lancaster County was the result of "dry September weather, which was in favor of potato and tomato picking." Families throughout the county were soon busy eating, processing, and selling potatoes and potato products.[14]

The King family certainly took advantage of the bumper potato crop, listing fried potatoes on their sample day's breakfast and supper menus and boiled potatoes at the noon meal. Even if they had eaten potatoes at every meal for seven days, the family still could not have consumed the 84 pounds of potatoes they reported having on hand during the survey week. Rather than consuming the majority of this produce themselves, family members obviously sold potatoes as one of their cash crops. In fact, two months earlier, Agent Rigdon had ranked potatoes second only to wheat as an income-producing crop for the Kings. While the family made $120 selling their 150-bushel wheat crop at 80 cents a bushel, they earned two-thirds that amount, $80, by selling 200 bushels of potatoes at 40 cents a bushel. Amish women and children played a major role in the potato harvest. Had Hambright visited earlier in the now waning potato season, she might have recorded "taking out potatoes" among the daily activities of daughters Sarah and Mary. At another time of year, she might have described them "shocking wheat." Depending on the urgency of the harvest, the girls' mother might even have participated in these activities. On a farm that did not hire labor and instead relied entirely on its "own help," even the chief household manager necessarily took a turn in the fields.[15]

Fruits, vegetables, and grains were important to the King family's economic welfare, but SCP agents classified their farm as primarily a livestock, dairy, and poultry operation. If this family practiced the typical division of labor, the farm husband and sons were primarily in charge of the large livestock, both sexes took part roughly equitably in dairying, and the females dealt with poultry. During the survey year, the Kings sold 27 steers at $65 a head, two calves at $10 apiece, and one horse for $50, earning $1,825 in gross income for their livestock operation. They apparently raised livestock strictly for the market because the survey recorded no butchering activities or consumption of home-produced meat. Hambright instead noted that the household had patronized a local butcher shop to procure the cured ham, beef bologna, and dried beef its members consumed during the third week of September 1936.[16]

The King family's dairy and poultry enterprises were another matter. Without benefit of electric-powered milking machines or incubators, the family produced a variety of dairy and poultry products for both the market and home consumption. Although they only ran a dairy operation for half the survey year, the Kings nevertheless grossed $780 in annual milk sales. While they averaged $15 in milk sales per week, they also averaged $1.40 in milk consumption, meaning 28 quarts. Their sample meal menus listed milk as a beverage at every meal, and they ate home-produced butter on their homemade bread three times a day. The family's poultry operation, however, was the real mainstay of the farm economy. During the survey year, they sold 7,200 dozen eggs at 30 cents a dozen to gross $2,160 in egg income, and they grossed another $300 in chicken sales. In addition, the family itself consumed two chickens per month and five dozen eggs a week. Hambright in fact listed fried eggs as the main course on the family's sample supper menu.[17]

Of the two major cash-producing enterprises the King family engaged in over the entirety of the survey year, their traditionally female poultry operation clearly outstripped their traditionally male large livestock business. The annual gross profit for egg and chicken sales combined stood at $2,460, which surpassed large livestock sales by $635. Poultry production costs were significantly lower than those for cattle operations, so the net profit as well as gross income was higher for the family's poultry business than their livestock enterprise. In reporting their farming expenses for the survey year, the family noted spending $300 on chicken feed, $32.50 for five new gasoline lamps for the chicken house, and $200 for the gasoline that powered the chicken house lamps. In total, poultry production costs totaled $532.50, making a net profit of $1,927.50 for the Kings' poultry business. In contrast, livestock investments came in notably higher. According to the family's own reporting, the main monetary investment in their beef operation was the purchase of 27 steers at $37 a head for a total outlay of $999. The family listed $200 in dairy feed expenses but reported no feed costs for their beef cattle, suggesting the steers primarily ate the farm's own grains, hay, and grass. The cattle may have also had periodic access to the pastureland of a neighboring farm or farms through some type of arrangement. Once fattened, the cattle then sold for $65 a head, netting the family $756 in beef profits, $1,171.50 less than their poultry profits.[18]

In addition to poultry production requiring lower investment costs than the livestock operation, it also made better use of the family labor force. By the age of five or so, a young child could scatter chicken feed and collect eggs, whereas working with large livestock was physically impractical and dangerous for someone so young. On farms with particularly large poultry operations, such as the Kings', the family's patriarch and older sons might even lend a hand when necessary. The cost and labor efficiency of female-managed poultry operations thus made them centerpieces of the Amish farm economy. On average, poultry profits for both Old Order Amish families and those who belonged to the smaller Church Amish community outpaced those of non-Amish households throughout Lancaster County.[19]

In a list of daily activities, Agent Hambright recorded variation in every King family member's schedule save one. For wife and mother Sadie, the week was simply one long, ceaseless exercise in "housework." Household maintenance was indeed a significant component of her work. With varying levels of assistance from her also busy daughters, Sadie cleaned the house without benefit of a vacuum cleaner or indoor running water; cooked, baked, and did the laundry with old-fashioned coal, wood, or gasoline-powered equipment; mended the distinctive Old Order Amish garments she had constructed on her pedal-powered sewing machine; and tended to minor illnesses or injuries. In reality, however, Sadie's work extended far beyond keeping house. The corn and tomatoes she canned, the cows she milked, the henhouse she supervised, and the potatoes she likely harvested allowed her husband and children to live and prosper on their 78-acre family-owned farm even in the middle of an economic depression.[20]

Budget correspondents may have reported the local tomato and potato harvests as strictly work for the "men folks," and government agents may have classified the work of Old Order Amish wives and mothers as simple housekeeping, but the SCP data indicate the story of Amish family farming was much more complex. The gendered language reflected idealized work-role prescriptions, in both Anabaptist and mainstream society, but not the reality of daily farm life. The frequent collision been the ideal and reality is perhaps best demonstrated in Elizabeth Benner's comment that she was her father's "hired man," regularly performing outdoor labor that a male family member of the right age and size would have done, had one been available.

While the crossing of gendered labor lines, mainly by women and girls, was frequently necessary, managerial roles were less flexible. The recognized household head, the husband and father, managed barn and field labor. The wife and mother managed work that took place in a house—both the farmhouse and the henhouse—and in the yards around these two structures. In the farmhouse yard, she managed a garden, and in the henhouse yard she managed the flock. When Agent Hambright made her mid-September visit, she logged the weekend activities of 13-year-old Rebecca as "helps with housework," but that work could have just as easily included scattering chicken feed as dusting the furniture. Both activities fell under her mother's supervision and under the catchall rubric for her mother's realm of management—"housework."[21]

Only in a system that viewed adult women as "housework" managers and adult men as "farming" managers could Fannie Esch say that she and her daughter "helped milk" when they were the only two people at work in the barn. In characterizing the Amish division of labor as one in which the "women keep the house and the men work the farms," New Deal investigators and the Amish themselves were referring not to the reality of where labor—particularly female labor—took place, but to the primary locations where female and male decision-making took place. The realm of "housework" included all work in the farmhouse and the yard, the garden, and the henhouse and the area around it. The people who worked in these locations, primarily women and girls, engaged in "housework" or "helping with housework." "Farming" included work in the barn, livestock pens, and cash crop fields. Men supervised this labor, and men and older boys did most of the work in the livestock pens, but people of both sexes could be found in the dairy barn on a regular basis and in the farm fields on a periodic basis. Because these were male-managed spaces, however, the work that women and girls performed in them, even if men were not physically present, was simply "help."[22]

As the SCP data indicate, women's work—whether in the kitchen, poultry house, or farm field—contributed significantly to the farm-family economy. As Amish women catalogued their contributions to the family farm in laborious detail to SCP investigators, they could not help but recognize that their work had an obvious impact on the standard of living and community status of their families. That these women performed their labor within the constraints of a patriarchal family and religious system is evidenced by their insistence that they were homemakers who merely "helped" their farmer husbands even if their poultry work was the most profitable enterprise on the farm. The system in which they worked, however, had prescribed and valued roles for all members of the family as they worked toward a common goal: maintaining their sacred way of life on the land.

CHAPTER FIVE

Friends and Frolics

Having Fun but Saving Money

We played baseball with homemade bats.

—*Lydia Stoltzfus, remembering the 1930s*

For most American women and girls, commercial entertainment provided temporary respite from the emotional and psychological stresses of the Great Depression. Tuning into a favorite radio program or attending a movie after saving up for weeks to buy a ticket provided short-term relief. Old Order Amish women and girls, however, belonged to a community that rejected such worldly amusements in favor of recreation organized around the family, neighborhood, and church. The Old Order Amish had long maintained their religiously based recreational habits, but the financial advantages of their low-cost entertainment practices became vividly apparent during the Depression. Amish women and girls amused themselves in ways that were both culturally appropriate and economically practical for hard times.

For the Survey of Consumer Purchases (SCP), agents recorded families' recreational expenses in section IX, page 4, of the Expenditure Schedule—Farm. This was one of several areas in the survey that prompted SCP agents to break the rules of strict anonymity and identify Amish households by religion. Except for the occasional few dollars spent on a dog license, hunting license and supplies, or children's toys, Amish families listed no expenditures in this portion of the survey. The Kings in Salisbury Township were a typical family in listing a $1 dog license as the household's only recreational expense. Agents felt compelled to explain why they left this section—with its questions about movie attendance, athletic equipment, radio expenses, social club dues, and other entertainment expenditures—largely blank. For example, in the case of 17 different families, Agent Rigdon wrote, "Amish family who do not believe in paid for recreation" (Survey 1762). Other agents employed alternative language to explain the lack of recreational expenses for Amish families. Margaret Fratantono wrote, "No money for pleasure" (Survey 1583). Ella Veit often simply jotted the word "Amish" across the form's recreation section (Survey 1582; figure 5.1). The data agents gathered showed the Old Order Amish spending less on amusement activities than all other Lancaster County groups. Amish households averaged $9.24 for the survey year, 1935/36, while English households averaged $17.91. Most revealing was the "paid admission to" subsection for money spent on movies, plays, pageants, lectures, concerts, ball games and other spectator sports, fairs, circuses, and dances. Here, Amish households listed only zeros.[1]

SCP agents noted the lack of commercial entertainment in Amish families' lives, but they recorded other types of recreational activities elsewhere in the survey. Sections of the survey devoted to food consumption, for instance, frequently included information on Amish families hosting guests for lunches and dinners. In the Old Order Amish world of face-to-face communication, making mealtime or other visits to one another played an important role. Such visits enabled the exchange of news and information, strengthened community bonds, and provided a break from the usual household routine. *Budget* scribes reported on their local Lancaster County communities, cataloguing seemingly endless rounds of Amish visits to one another, which might include a meal or perhaps only dessert. While entire families often participated in these visits, Amish women also made such calls without men or children in tow. While at one Amish home in May 1936, Veit recorded a lunchtime visit from the wife's mother, two sisters, and two sisters-in-law. Perhaps they came to quilt or to help with the May whitewashing or some other chore, but their presence also served a valuable, purely social function: sharing a meal with the woman, her husband, and the couple's two small children—even as a lunch break during a busy day of whitewashing—was an opportunity to sit down and enjoy one another's company and conversation.[2]

Amish women frequently combined work and pleasure. In a June 11, 1934, submission to *The Budget* from the Gordonville community, Katie F. Lapp reported families visiting one another for Sunday supper and commented on

5.1 A form on which agents conducting the Study of Consumer Purchases took care to explain why the portion on recreation is largely blank for the Amish household. (Study of Consumer Purchases, Survey 1582)

a neighbor's Saturday evening gathering that she attended where the ice cream "sure was good." She also recorded events that included practical labor along with socializing. Prior to the Saturday evening ice cream party, Lapp had spent the afternoon at another neighboring farm "helping to strip straw" for what she later referred to as her friend Mary Fisher's "straw hat business." Lapp's description of the afternoon indicated that she and the other 13 women in attendance considered it an occasion for amusement as well as labor, noting, "[W]e all enjoyed it."[3]

In the same week that Lapp described making straw hats, she also noted that two nearby households had hosted quilting parties. These events could be quite large. Later that same summer, for instance, Lapp reported on a neighborhood quilting involving 30 women. Such occasions were yet another opportunity for women to socialize while producing a useful product for the family who hosted the event. As one scholar noted, Amish women engaged in "mutual help . . . [as] a festive and enjoyable activity" that conformed with their society's emphasis on family, community, and strong work ethic.[4]

In these exchanges of food, hospitality, and labor with one another, Amish women of the 1930s seemingly conducted their own version of the nineteenth-century "female world of love and ritual" that historian Carroll Smith-Rosenberg has described. Amish women provided one another with friendship, physical and material assistance, and emotional support during major events in the female life cycle, such as marriage and childbirth, as well as during the more mundane occurrences of everyday life. In contrast to Smith-Rosenberg's middle-class Victorians, however, Lancaster County Amish women did not spend their social time almost exclusively with members of their own sex. With their culture's emphasis on family, much of Amish women's recreation took place alongside husbands, potential husbands, fathers, brothers, and sons.[5]

Along with all-female working parties—such as quilting bees or "frolics" as the local Amish and Mennonites called them—women also took part in labor-sharing events that included the entire family. Women and children accompanied men when they participated in neighborhood barn raisings and other construction projects, with women providing plentiful food for the builders and other attendees. Even as agricultural professionals worried that farm residents in general did not enjoy sufficient leisure time and "play[ed] only under a work camouflage," Amish practices remained noteworthy. The frequency and scope of both Amish and Mennonite labor frolics made them highly visible. *Budget* writers in western Pennsylvania reported that an October 1934 frolic "to cement the chicken house floor" at one farm had included husbands, wives, and children from eight neighboring families, but the sizeable festivities had also grabbed the attention of traveling confidence men looking to sell faulty sewing machines to gullible Anabaptists. Mrs. Sam M. Miller reported that the con artists claimed to have "sold machines to the Amish people" elsewhere in the state, and she hoped those customers "didn't get beat on the deal."[6]

Like labor frolics, Amish reading habits reflected their devotion to farm stewardship and improvements. Whereas SCP survey data indicated that mainstream farm families typically subscribed to several popular magazines, Amish households regularly reported only one—a $1 annual subscription to the *Pennsylvania Farmer*. Along with a subscription to one or two newspapers—likely *The Budget* or a local Lancaster County paper—the *Pennsylvania Farmer* was usually an Amish family's only reading purchase. Buying and reading novels or other frivolous and worldly publications was not an option for Amish family members because their religion forbade literature that distracted from their labor and faith.[7]

Keeping family members busy and focused on household and farm duties was important, but some Amish family activities were purely recreational. Lancaster County resident Fannie Esch remembered summer canoe trips on the Conestoga River with her husband and children during the Depression. Even though SCP records indicate that the Amish made few recreational purchases, Fannie and her family bought a croquet set and played the game with neighborhood friends. Lydia Stoltzfus, in contrast, recalled playing baseball with her brothers using homemade bats and also remembered playing quoits—a ring-toss game similar to horseshoes—with equipment that family members may have also constructed themselves. Families also socialized together at farm sales, where teams of Old Order Amish boys challenged Old Order Mennonite boys to a version of team dodgeball known as "corner ball"—an inexpensive game that only required purchase of the ball—while their sisters and mothers chatted and "watched the boys" at play (figures 5.2–5.3).[8]

Young men and women of marrying age socialized together at evening events that served as courting opportunities. *Budget* scribes and diarists of the period frequently noted young people's evening suppers and hymn singings. A particularly noteworthy young people's evening might include a supper featuring the local sausage and potato delicacy known as "pig stomach" or "hog maw." An evening that included "a taffie [sic] pulling" might also deserve special mention.[9]

In contrast to the low-cost, group-oriented courting practices of the Old Order Amish, youngsters in some other Lancaster County families practiced newer, consumer-oriented dating habits. In the 1920s and 1930s, rural youth not affiliated with Plain denominations had begun, like their counterparts in urban areas, to court as heterosexual couples rather than as members of a larger peer group of boys and girls. Adoption of the automobile was key to this development because it enabled a boy and girl to pair off, removing themselves from the presence of others, including adult chaperones. While pig stomach suppers

5.2 Amish, Mennonite, and other children enjoying themselves at a farm sale candy stand. Photograph by John Collier, Jr., Lancaster County, March 1942. (Courtesy of the Farm Security Administration / Office of War Information Collection, Library of Congress, Washington, DC)

and taffy pulls took place in the host's farm home, with his or her parents presumably on the premises, non-Plain couples likely conducted their courtship in commercial spaces, away from their homes and parents. In these locations for public entertainment, young men spent cash on themselves and their dates for admission fees, refreshments, and souvenirs. The Old Order Amish, with their rejection of automobile use and worldly entertainments, of course never adopted these new courtship trends.[10]

The local movie theater was a popular commercial establishment that dating couples frequented, but the Amish did not. In fact, differences in recreational spending between Plain and non-Plain farm people appear most obviously under

5.3 Anabaptist women socializing at a farm sale while their husbands bid on equipment. Photograph by John Collier, Jr., Lancaster County, 1942. (Courtesy of the Farm Security Administration / Office of War Information Collection, Library of Congress, Washington, DC)

the SCP survey category devoted to movies. The Great Depression spurred rather than inhibited movie attendance in mainstream society, with Americans seeking escape from their economic woes by indulging in Hollywood fantasies. Forty percent of adults attended motion pictures on an at least weekly basis in the 1930s. Among Lancaster County's first-time moviegoers was a 62-year-old farm woman who reported that the dollar she had spent to take herself and her 16-year-old daughter to two movies during the 1935/36 survey period was "all she spent in her life for movies." Her detailed recounting to Agent J. I. Byler that the films had featured Shirley Temple and Will Rogers—the period's number 1 and number 2 box office stars—indicated that the movies had made a significant impression on her.[11]

Young adults particularly gravitated to the movies. While rural youth generally spent less money than their urban counterparts on commercial entertainment, movies were somewhat of an exception. Studies of the period showed that movie attendance for rural young people lagged only slightly behind that of their town-based peers, and young farm people could combine movie attendance with other activities when on a weekly trip to town for shopping or visiting friends and relatives.[12]

One young Lancaster County husband and wife were typical of their generation. When SCP Agent Shoemaker visited their farm in September 1936, the 27-year-old husband and 23-year-old wife reported that both of them had attended the movies every week during the survey year. With adult admission at movie theaters in Lancaster County ranging between 25 and 30 cents, the couple reported spending a total of $31 on movie attendance in 1935/36. Perhaps the couple, who were not affiliated with any Plain denomination, were continuing a pattern they had established years earlier when dating. The age of their oldest child indicated that they had been married for at least six years, suggesting that they had been a dating couple when the wife was in her mid-teens and the husband in his early twenties—prime ages for frequent movie attendance. Agents visiting other non-Plain farm families at the time found clear evidence of dating couples attending movies. A 40-year-old farm couple reported that they had attended a total of 12 movies during the year, spending $3, while their 18- and 20-year-old daughters had no movie expenses because "boyfriends pay for girls." The 47-year-old mother of another family reported that she had spent a total of $4 on 16 movies but that her 19- and 20-year-old daughters had no such expenses because "gentlemen friends take the daughters."[13]

In Old Order Amish families, boys did not of course pay for movie tickets or for the expense of driving a car to the theater. Instead, like their mothers and sisters, their recreational practices remained family and community centered, often focused around shared labor, and away from commercial establishments. Like other aspects of Amish life, recreational practices reinforced members' distinctive religious and cultural beliefs. Quilting frolics, barn raisings, and taffy pulls primarily solidified Amish identity and community, but these customs incidentally also saved cash resources.

In addition to the recreation section on the SCP survey, the other section that produced all zeros on Amish forms was section VI, Automobile. The section usually had a line drawn through it and often the word "Amish" written as the explanation. By way of contrast, "English" families averaged $166.74 in automobile expenses. Amish families recorded an average of $35.10 on the "horse and carriage for family use" line. The differences in transportation costs, and the related costs of leisure and recreation, were quite stark.[14]

In a submission to *The Budget*, John Renno, a member of the Amish community in central Pennsylvania's Mifflin County, summarized the reasons behind Old Order Amish resistance to modern communication and transportation technology and by extension the group's rejection of commercial entertainment. In reporting that two Amish couples from Indiana had recently hired a driver to take them by car for a visit in Mifflin County, Renno worried that Amish leaders were not sufficiently vigilant about the impact of the automobile on their community. Perhaps thinking of dating couples headed to the movies by car, Renno hoped Amish youth would push back against automobile use more effectively than their elders. As he warned *Budget* readers, "The auto is slowly and surely drifting into the [Old Order] Amish churches and till another generation has grown up there may be a great change if our young people do not see more danger of the church drifting into the world than many of our older brethren do at the present." Stating that "the hand that rocks the cradle is the hand that rules the world," Renno argued that the only solution was Amish mothers' reinforcement of home and family-based recreation. Only in that way would the next generation know that they should continue to be vigilant and resist worldly influences. Renno closed his comments in the first person plural, "wishing we all could be more careful how we and our children are spending our spare time."[15]

Renno was astute in associating automobiles with leisure and youth culture. Robert Staughton Lynd and Helen Merrell Lynd discussed the relationship of automobiles and leisure in Muncie, Indiana, in *Middletown: A Study in American Culture* (1929), a sociology classic, and in *Middletown in Transition: A Study in Cultural Conflicts* (1937).[16] The Lynds expressed amazement at the speed with which automobile culture had replaced horse culture, noting that US manufacturers had produced some 2 million horse-drawn carriages in 1909 but only 10,000 in 1923. In contrast, car makers had produced only 80,000 automobiles in 1909 but 4 million in 1923. While in 1910 fewer than 500,000 automobiles were registered in the United States, that number jumped to 15.5 million by 1924. As the Lynds commented in their 1929 study, the diffusion of automobile culture in "Middletown" (i.e., Muncie) had taken place only "within the last ten or fifteen years."[17]

The Lynds explicitly noted the impact of automobiles on teenage and young adult dating and sexuality. They reported that in 1929, of the 30 girls brought before juvenile court for "sex crimes" in the year preceding September 1, 1924, 19 had "committed the offense in an automobile." In *Middletown in Transition*, they included an anecdote, collected during their initial research in 1925 but not published in their 1929 book: a juvenile court judge, speaking to a women's club "on local moral conditions," expressed his fear that "the automobile [was] becoming a house of prostitution on wheels." The mutual reinforcement of automobile culture, leisure time, movie theaters, radio programs, and freedom from parental oversight during courtship concerned parents and moral leaders in small town Indiana as well as in rural Pennsylvania.[18]

Lancaster County Amish women who read Renno's commentary already knew that keeping children away from worldly influences was one of their many responsibilities. Nevertheless, Renno's warning, which also referenced recent urban suicide rates, served as a dramatic reminder that Amish youngsters should spend their after-chore time with members of their family, church, or neighborhood. By encouraging these entertainment boundaries, Amish mothers ensured their family's recreational time remained wholesome and served a higher practical or religious purpose.

When explaining the lack of entertainment expenses on an Amish family's survey schedule in October 1936, Agent J. I. Byler was mistaken in commenting that "religion prohibits recreation." In reality, the Amish faith encourages recreation, but only within the parameters of family, farm, and community. What Amish women and their families in the 1930s rejected was the type of commercial entertainment growing increasingly common in other parts of rural America. Amish women and girls did not buy movie tickets or novels on the bestseller list. They did, however, enjoy culturally appropriate recreational activities, and these events required minimal financial investment. In other words, Amish women knew how to have fun. They just did it without spending much money.[19]

CHAPTER SIX

Religion and Rituals
Preparing for Celebrations and Ceremonies

We washed and cleaned the church dirt away.
—*Annie Smucker, 1938*

The events of January 31, 1938, that the diarist Annie Smucker recorded described the typical Monday routine for an Amish woman whose family had just hosted Sunday worship services and the large meal that followed. Now that her family's latest turn at Sunday hosting was complete, Annie and her mother and sisters could put their farmhouse back in order until other possible gatherings were held there as the year progressed.[1]

Should a family member die, the Smucker women would open their home for mourners to view the body, attend the funeral service, and eat dinner afterward. If one of Annie's sisters married that year, they would spend months preparing for the ceremony, likely to take place in November or possibly early December, after the fall harvest. It required planting their garden with an abundance of celery to later turn into heaping bowls of creamed celery for the wedding feast. The bride's wedding dress would have to be made and her trousseau assembled. The women would once again sweep, scrub, dust, and rearrange the furniture to host the houseful of friends, neighbors, and relatives attending the celebration.

Like other Amish residents of Lancaster County, the Smucker women organized their lives around both the agricultural calendar and a recurring series of religious events and rituals. Because the Old Order Amish eschewed church buildings in favor of holding their religious ceremonies in members' homes, the labor of wives and daughters played a critical role in preserving the Amish religion and culture. Their home-produced rituals also saved the Old Order Amish limited cash resources that many other farm families paid to commercial institutions.

While men served as the formal religious authorities in the Amish faith, women's labor maintained the settings and social rituals associated with religious practice. Not having a formal, seminary trained clergy, the Old Order Amish in each church district chose their own church leaders and preachers from among the married male members who exhibited appropriate humility and good farm and family management skills. Successful management of farm and family activities was likewise important for the women whose labor accompanied the work men did in Sunday preaching and presiding at communions, baptisms, marriages, and funerals.

In the 1930s, the Old Order Amish held preaching services every other Sunday in individual church members' homes; the tradition continues today. In a typical church district, that meant each family hosted services approximately once a year, and when their turn came, the majority of the work fell to the women of the family. The mother and daughters worked diligently for days to prepare the farmhouse for what might be as many as 200 worshippers. They swept and scrubbed floors, dusted furniture, blackened stoves, and carefully rewashed china to withstand the scrutiny of other congregation members. The father and sons of the family likely assisted only in removing room partitions, if they had them, and moving the family's furniture out so they could bring in the long backless benches for the service. On Sunday itself, church members arrived early in the morning for a service that typically lasted from 9 to shortly after noon (figure 6.1). Following the service, the women of the congregation unpacked the breads and pies they had brought along and helped the household's mother and daughters serve the lunch they had prepared for those in attendance. Following lunch, worshippers remained at the hosts' home to visit for a few hours, with some even staying for supper. After the evening meal, the host family typically welcomed the congregation's young people for a hymn singing. After a Sunday of non-stop guests and activity, fathers and sons would begin removing benches the next morning and putting the family's furniture back in place. The mothers and daughters would commence cleaning the "church dirt away."[2]

Preparing a household for religious rituals and ceremonies proved particularly burdensome for women in the month of November, when most wedding celebrations took place. Women's accounts of local events published in *The*

6.1 A typical Sunday morning with buggies parked outside the barn of an Old Order Amish farm while church services take place in the farmhouse. Photograph by Irving Rusinow, Lancaster County, March 1941. (Courtesy of the Bureau of Agricultural Economics Collection, National Archives II, College Park, MD)

Budget provide a sense of their hectic November workload. Typical November reports included the news that "women folks" were "preparing for that wedding feast" or "sewing and getting ready for weddings." Reporting one November from the Lancaster County community of Leola in the mid-1930s, Mrs. M. P. Stoltzfus commented on several upcoming Amish weddings and also described the recent double wedding of sisters Lizzie and Naomi Stoltzfus at their parents' farm home. Anticipating the end of the November wedding crunch and the beginning of winter sewing, Stoltzfus reported, "Women folks will soon be busy sewing, after the weddings are over, which are quite a good many."[3]

November might be wedding season, but that did not forestall the necessity of preparing for other religious events. As Stoltzfus noted in her report from Leola, "It seems when the weddings are going on, there will also be funerals in between." For example, on the heels of Lizzie and Naomi Stoltzfus's double wedding on Thursday came the funeral of 78-year-old Isaac J. Lapp in the same church district on Friday. The local women who shared baskets of food with the Stoltzfus family for their daughters' wedding feast now contributed to the funeral dinner for Lapp's survivors. A neighboring family opened their farm home for the funeral, so Lapp's elderly widow, Nancy, did not have to host her husband's last rites. More typically, bereaved female relatives dealt simultaneously with houseguests and their grief. In November 1934 while the Amish women in Mary Lapp's Lancaster County neighborhood were "getting ready for weddings," she was dealing with the death of her son Christian in a hay wagon accident. As Mary, a widow, rested after his funeral at their farmhouse, "quite a few friends and relatives attended to give respects to the bereaved ones and also to view the corpse."[4]

Mary Lapp's farm home may have served as the setting for her son's funeral, but she and her daughter Fannie probably did little of the cleaning, arranging, and cooking necessary for holding the funeral service and dinner. Just as neighbors relieved the aged widow Nancy Lapp of her domestic responsibilities by offering their house to host her husband's funeral, Mary's friends and neighbors undoubtedly followed Amish custom and took over her household tasks at the time of her son's death. Neighbor women would have cleaned the house and rearranged the furniture both before and after the funeral and would have contributed their cooking skills and food from their own farms to prepare the funeral meal. Having previously lost her husband, Mary would have already been familiar with the generosity of her neighbors, and she and daughter Fannie would have performed the same services for neighboring Amish households when deaths occurred in those families.[5]

Mary Lapp not only benefited from the labor and emotional support of the Amish community in her time of loss, but also from the inexpensive nature of Amish funerals (figure 6.2). The widowed and "deeply bereaved mother" did not have to worry about spending money on elaborate funeral arrangements. With no flowers or other worldly accoutrements, her son's funeral expenses would have entailed little more than the cost of a wooden coffin. In contrast, according to records from the Study of Consumer Purchases, non-Amish funerals—depending on the age and size of the deceased—could be expensive. In the mid-1930s, the funeral costs for Lancaster County farm families ranged from $10 for a stillborn Amish infant to $500 for a 24-year-old man of indeterminant religion. The man's $500 funeral ($10,315 in 2022) represented more than a third of his family's annual income.[6]

Although Amish women's house cleaning and cooking were significant for funerals, nothing rivaled the time and effort expended on weddings. Funerals

6.2 A funeral procession of Old Order Mennonites. It is like the ritual practiced by Old Order Amish. John Collier, Jr., Lancaster County, March 1942 (Courtesy of the Farm Security Administration / Office of War Information Collection, Library of Congress, Washington, DC)

often followed unexpected illnesses or accidents and thus entailed minimal advanced planning and preparation. In contrast, women might spend the better part of a year preparing for a wedding, which always took precedence over funerals on the Amish calendar. As Mrs. M. P. Stoltzfus noted in her *Budget* report from Leola, when a death occurred during wedding season, the Amish scheduled the funeral "in between" the dates already reserved for nuptial celebrations.[7]

The November 14, 1929, nuptials of Lancaster County resident Fannie Esch illustrate the time and effort women expended on Old Order Amish weddings. Wearing a new homemade dress in the plain Amish style, eighteen-year-old Fannie married her young groom in a ceremony presided over by ministers from her church district and attended by scores of her neighbors and relatives as well as the groom's parents and siblings. The wedding took place at her parents' farm home and was followed by a meal of farm-raised chicken, beef, fruits, and vegetables prepared by friends and family members. Following the wedding, Fannie and her husband did not go on a honeymoon vacation but instead spent the next several months visiting the area's other young Amish couples, who provided the newlyweds with numerous wedding gifts—usually household goods and small farm tools, purchased for about a dollar apiece. In this way, their peers helped Fannie and her groom prepare to establish their new farm household during the April 1930 planting season.[8]

Deconstructing Fannie Esch's story to examine the women's work supporting her wedding celebration demonstrates the labor-intensive nature of Amish religious and family rituals. For example, making Fannie's wedding dress and the new underwear, nightwear, and everyday dresses for her trousseau amounted to extra projects amid the already voluminous amount of sewing the typical Lancaster County Amish woman performed. Fannie's mother, or perhaps even Fannie herself, spent extra hours at the treadle sewing machine making her wedding dress out of the monochromatic "Special Amish Dress Mat[erial]," available in a range of colors. While Fannie or her mother made the wedding dress and other new clothing items for her marriage, the bride's six younger sisters undoubtedly took on a larger portion of the household's other domestic responsibilities.[9]

In preparing for Fannie Esch's November 1929 wedding, the bride, her mother, and sisters also assumed additional outdoor work. Perhaps they raised a larger flock of chickens that year in anticipation of the 200 guests who would attend the wedding meal. They possibly expanded their garden that spring and planted a greater variety of fruits and vegetables and undoubtedly planted more celery to ensure that the wedding guests would enjoy plenty of creamed celery, an Amish wedding meal staple. Since Fannie's marriage would not be announced to other members of her church district until a few weeks before the wedding, the overabundance of celery in her family's garden might be the neighbors' first clue of the impending nuptials. Their larger garden meant that the family would also do more canning that year. At a time when the typical Lancaster County Amish family canned 357 quarts of fruits and vegetables a year, Fannie and her mother and sisters would have expanded their already extensive canning activities to ensure plenty of food for the wedding guests. They could rest assured, however, that if they ran short of a particular item, they could find it in at least one of the baskets of food that female wedding guests brought from their own gardens, smokehouses, orchards, and poultry houses.[10]

In many respects, Fannie Esch's wedding, held in 1929, could have taken place in a non-Amish farm setting. The research of Jane Pederson, Mary Neth, Rebecca Sharpless, and others indicates that many of the practices associated with Lancaster County Amish weddings were likewise prevalent in other rural communities during the Depression years. This scholarship reveals that many a non-Amish farm-based wedding of the period took place in the bride's home, was scheduled around major events in the agricultural season, featured a home-cooked meal, limited the guest list to members of the bridal couple's ethno-religious group, and included a round of neighborhood visits following the wedding day, with calls by the bridal couple to neighboring farms or, in the shivaree ritual, visits to the newlyweds by boisterous, noisy neighbors, who demanded treats from the young couple. In subsequent decades, however, increased levels of physical mobility, exogamy, cash income, and exposure to urban social standards eroded such wedding customs in most of rural America. Churches decorated with flowers and candles, catered receptions, and packaged honeymoon vacations replaced home-produced celebrations confined to the bridal couple's local ethnic community.[11]

Even by the standards of Depression-era farm weddings in general, Amish weddings of the period were inexpensive. Whereas Fannie Esch's family and neighbors produced all the major elements of her celebration themselves, most non-Amish nuptials entailed at least a modest cash outlay. The experiences of another Lancaster County bride, who married in December 1935, provide a notable contrast to Fannie Esch's.[12]

SCP records clearly indicate that the 20-year-old bride belonged to a Plain household. When SCP agents visited her family's farmhouse in 1935/36, they noted that the household did not have a radio or spend any money on commercial entertainment. The most obvious evidence of the family's membership in a Plain denomination, however, appears in the survey's clothing purchase section. Under the category "Hats, caps, berets," Agent Wiker carefully noted that both the bride and her 18-year-old sister piously kept their heads covered and had made several "prayer covering" purchases. While survey evidence indicates the bride and her family were Plain, it also demonstrates that they were not Old Order Amish. Their farmhouse used highline electricity, and the family had a telephone, phonograph, piano, and camera. The bride's father and younger brother made regular visits to a barbershop, and several family members had attended school beyond the one-room neighborhood schoolhouse. Most significantly, the family owned a car. They were likely members of the Church of the Brethren or the Brethren in Christ.[13]

Among the expenditures the bride's family listed for the survey year was $100 ($2,136 in 2022 dollars) categorized as a "wedding expense." Exactly what that expense entailed is unclear. Perhaps the family engaged a baker to produce a decorated wedding cake, hired a printer to create formal wedding invitations, or procured some other type of professional service. Other information on the family's SCP survey schedule, however, provides detailed information on the costs of a non-Amish wedding. For example, the bride's clothing purchases far exceeded those of other family members and included garments that were likely wedding attire and trousseau pieces. Comparing the bride's wardrobe acquisitions to those of the family member who spent the second highest amount on clothing, her 18-year-old sister, confirms that the bride purchased some singularly expensive items.[14]

While the bride spent a total of $148.29 on new clothing during the survey year, her sister spent only $42.65. Both young women spent money on sewing supplies, but those made up a larger proportion of the younger sister's clothing expenses. While the bride purchased 25 yards of cotton fabric and two spools of thread for $2.60, her sister spent $7.25 for 50 yards of cotton, two spools of thread, and four cards of new buttons. In contrast, ready-made clothing made up a much larger part of the bride's wardrobe expenses. Likely in preparation for her marriage and setting up her own household, the bride bought numerous clothing items that her sister did not, including 10 new aprons. She also purchased twice as many prayer coverings, 12 of them, as her younger sister did. In the autumn immediately prior to the wedding, the bride spent $3 on a new bonnet, $8.90 on hosiery, $10 on 10 cotton housedresses, $12 on a winter coat, and $30.85 on undergarments and nightwear. During that same period, the bride's sister never purchased a bonnet, hosiery, housedress, coat, or nightwear; her one apparent underwear purchase was a silk or rayon slip. The greatest disparity in the sisters' purchases, however, appeared in the category of "suits, skirts, blouses, dresses." The older sister listed her fall 1935 purchases as a $23 silk dress, which might well have served as her wedding dress, and a $3.50 silk blouse and $25 wool suit that might have been her going away ensemble. In contrast, the younger sister listed her total purchases for the entire year as three silk dresses, bought for $4 apiece. In sum, the bride's apparent bridal wear and trousseau purchases totaled $116.25, several dollars more than even the family's extra $100 "wedding expense."[15]

In spending generously on the bride's clothing, members of this family were typical of other non-Amish farm households of the period. A new dress or suit for the bride to wear at her wedding was a common purchase even for families that typically sewed most other women's garments at home. Cash-strapped families were willing to splurge a bit at a local department store or women's clothing shop to purchase special attire for a bride's wedding day. If additional resources were available, a bride likely also purchased new nightwear, underwear, and a few other items. In eschewing such practices, Amish brides like Fannie Esch preserved cash resources. Like other farm brides, those in Amish families spent the months prior to marriage acquiring the extensive wardrobe they would take to their new lives as young wives, but those items, along with the wedding dress itself, were homemade. Agent Rigdon frequently noted when explaining why the Amish women she interviewed had no ready-made clothing expenses: "The Amish make all their own clothing that is possible—dresses-aprons-underwear-etc." In addition, because Amish women did not follow mainstream fashion trends, their clothing never went out of style. The investment in sewing supplies and effort at the time of an Amish woman's marriage could thus pay dividends for years to come. A 27-year-old Amish woman explaining to Agent Wiker why she had not purchased clothing or sewing supplies for herself in 1936 reported that her wardrobe was still "full plenty from when she was married" several years earlier.[16]

The family of the 20-year-old Plain bride had another wedding-related expenditure alongside purchasing a new wardrobe for their daughter. Under the Gifts section of the SCP survey, Agent Schreiner noted that the family "gave daughter who married $500.00." This was a significant endowment for a family who reported $2,240 in total income for the year. They likely intended this substantial gift as a contribution toward the bridal couple's establishment of their own farm and household.[17]

A large cash dowry was yet another type of expense rarely found in an Old Order Amish household. Rather than give a couple money to establish their own farm directly, Amish parents typically provided those funds as an interest-free loan that the couple would one day repay. Agent Rigdon noted on the survey schedule for a 24-year-old Amish couple that they had borrowed $800 from one of their mothers with "no interest charged," while a 32-year-old Amish farmer reported to Agent Getz that he had recently "paid off about $700.00 to father. No interest." That same farmer and his wife informed Getz of another way in which the Old Order Amish helped young couples establish their own farm households. Along with the inexpensive household items and small tools the Amish gave as wedding presents, wedding guests might also contribute a little cash. In explaining the $10 the couple had recently given as a wedding gift, Getz noted, "When a young Amishman marries they give him money. This is called *Aus-Steuer* (house dower)." Spelled *Aussteuer* in German today, it means "dowry." As comments like the one to Getz indicate, members of the neighboring Amish community often literally invested in launching a bridal couple's new life together.[18]

For the Old Order Amish, a Depression-era wedding celebration served the same purpose it did for rural Americans in general: It marked the transition of a young man and woman into adulthood. Unlike their counterparts in mainstream society, however, the Amish largely continued their wedding practices of the 1930s in subsequent decades, with a few embellishments. In addition to the traditional homemade creamed celery, home-canned fruit, and meat raised on the family farm, Old Order Amish weddings now feature decorated cakes that women purchased from local grocery stores and bakeries. Guests also now provide more elaborate wedding gifts, such as expensive cookware sets, and they present them in decorative wrapping paper, an unthinkable luxury during the Great Depression. In their general outlines, however, Amish wedding and marriage customs continued after the Depression while those of most other Americans changed dramatically.[19]

In contrast to most other contemporary Americans, the Amish do not leave home in their late teens to attend college or pursue distant employment. They do not typically delay marriage until their middle or late twenties or consider divorce an antidote to an unhappy marriage. Instead, Amish couples commonly marry in their early twenties, move directly from their birth families to their own marital households, and consider marriage a union for life. Once married, a young couple contributes to the perpetuation of Amish culture in establishing an additional home where Sunday worship services can be held and by bearing and raising new members of the Amish faith. The entire Old Order Amish community thus holds a stake in commemorating and contributing to a couple's change of status from carefree youngsters to adults permanently committed to the Amish way of life. As was once the custom throughout rural America, wedding guests are not mere observers in the celebration of an Amish marriage, they are participants. For Amish women, this participation entails exercising what they believe is their God-given role as homemakers. Their faith prohibits women's involvement as religious officials on these occasions, but it welcomes their efforts as seamstresses, gardeners, and cooks.[20]

At the end of the twentieth century, an elderly Old Order Amish couple sitting in the kitchen of their Lancaster County farm home reminisced with the husband's brother about the many weddings they had attended over the course of their long lives. The brother's favorite wedding story, however, revolved around a ceremony that never even took place. Leaning back in his chair, the octogenarian laughingly remembered the facetious explanation the father of one bride gave for his daughter's canceled nuptials: "Our celery just froze." His hosts chuckled appreciatively at the joke, understanding the centrality of garden-grown celery on the Amish wedding menu. Every Old Order Amish wedding the storyteller had attended—including his own, in November 1932 on the day Franklin Roosevelt won his first presidential election—had featured large servings of celery that Amish women had grown in their gardens and prepared in their kitchens. For the storyteller and other Old Order Amish, a wedding day without the fruits—and vegetables—of farm women's labor was impossible to contemplate. Like all other religious celebrations and ceremonies, a successful wedding relied on the diligent efforts of Amish women.[21]

CHAPTER SEVEN

Accidents and Illness

Healing the Sick and Spreading the News

Susie Zook had the misfortune of hurting her foot a few weeks ago, while working in the fields.

—*Katie F. Lapp, 1935*

Like other residents of Lancaster County, the Old Order Amish relied on professional doctors, nurses, and healthcare facilities for many of their medical needs. Farm accidents, communicable diseases, buggy wrecks, at-home births, and other health-related events racked up noteworthy medical bills for Amish families, but they also depended on the unpaid labor of Amish women, who both tended the sick and injured and informed worried friends, neighbors, and relatives about medical emergencies and outcomes. Lacking telephones and automobiles, Amish households counted on women's letters to friends and relatives and their submissions to *The Budget* to circulate health-related information throughout the community. Thus, women's work at the time of a medical crisis served numerous practical functions and frequently saved the Old Order Amish money that otherwise would have been paid to medical professionals. These savings were important because the high Amish birthrate resulted in a greater number of doctors' house calls and therefore larger average medical bills for the Amish than for their non-Amish neighbors.

Members of the Lancaster County Amish community often received first word of local health-related matters via *The Budget* and its group of predominantly female scribes. Established in 1890 in Sugarcreek, Ohio, near the large Holmes County Amish community, the newspaper initially served a religiously mixed readership and resembled other local weekly newspapers. Plain Anabaptists of various denominations soon became its chief subscribers—attracted in part by the paper's hospitable policy toward readers' letters—and its popularity spread beyond Ohio to other areas of Anabaptist settlement. By the time of the surveys in the Study of Consumer Purchases, *The Budget* had become a primary means through which the Amish in Ohio, Pennsylvania, and elsewhere shared news of their local communities with one another. By 1938 the Old Order Amish made up more than three-fourths of the paper's letter writers, and *The Budget* was on its way to becoming a periodical exclusively composed of reader letters. Most of the letter writers—referred to as "scribes" in *The Budget* universe—were women. As in mainstream society, the Amish largely viewed letter writing and other clerical labor as women's work.[1]

Letters to *The Budget* almost always began with observations about weather- and health-related matters in the community. In a society that proscribed ownership of gasoline-powered conveyances and field equipment, *Budget* accident reports of the 1930s resembled those once common throughout rural America in the nineteenth century. Horse-related injuries were especially prevalent. The indefatigable Katie F. Lapp, *Budget* scribe from Lancaster County's Gordonville community, frequently provided readers with vivid accounts of horse-related accidents, including the time in June 1934 when Bishop Ben Beiler's son John "had the misfortune of hurting his foot when a horse he was riding fell and John's foot got tangled in the harness, throwing him off." Lapp assured her readers that the foot was not broken but was so badly bruised that John was now temporarily walking with crutches. Two weeks later, Lapp breathlessly reported that another Gordonville farmer had sustained injuries when his startled horse team pitched him from the top of his hay wagon into the road. The unfortunate man strained his arm muscles, but "otherwise he wasn't hurt much." Other horse accidents resulted in more serious injuries. In November 1934, Mrs. M. P. Stoltzfus reported from Leola that a horse had fallen on a local boy and broken the child's leg, while New Holland scribe B. F. King reported on the funeral of Christ Lapp, whose "death was caused by injuries sustained when he upset a load of hay about a week before his death."[2]

Accidents involving horse-drawn vehicles and automobiles received special attention in *The Budget* as the Amish increasingly shared Lancaster County roadways with their car-driving neighbors. Always on the lookout for dramatic stories from the Gordonville area, Katie F. Lapp reported in February 1934 that a collision with an automobile had thrown Abram and Rebecca King from their sleigh, but that the couple were "not hurt much." Others did not fare so well. When a drunk driver rammed his car into an Amish family's buggy near the town of Intercourse later that year, the Amish father did not survive.[3]

Of course, not all farm injuries involved horses or horse-drawn equipment and conveyances. Reporting from Gordonville in 1934, Katie F. Lapp wrote, "Isaac Huyard ran a hay fork partly through his arm. They gave him a few doses of anti-toxin." She announced that Enos King had received burns on his face and arms when sparks from a steam-powered threshing machine started a fire that burned down his barn and killed a portion of his livestock. She assured her readers, however, that King was recovering and now "up and around." Lapp also reported the freak accident that befell David Stoltzfus. While working in his tobacco field, a stray bullet fired from some distance struck him in the chest, resulting in a trip to the hospital for its removal. She was pleased to inform *Budget* readers that he had now returned home and was "getting along fine." Other stories did not have such happy endings. A New Holland scribe reported that a 15-year-old boy had died when the tree he and his father were sawing down fell the wrong way, and the same reporter wondered who would perform the funeral when a man who had been "expelled from the Amish church long ago and never came back" died as the result of an accident with a corn-chopping machine. Mrs. B. K. Stoltzfus reported from Gap on another father-son lumbering accident. This time, the son survived, but his 380-pound father, who neighboring farmers "had quite a bit of trouble in extricating" from under the fallen tree, died in "intense pain and agony."[4]

Although most of the reported accidents relating to farm work and the agricultural calendar involved men and teenage boys, news of women and small children also made it into *The Budget*. During the June 1935 strawberry and cherry season, for instance, Katie F. Lapp not only reported that "Samuel Esch of near Intercourse had the misfortune of breaking his arm when he fell while picking cherries," but also that "Reuben, little son of Stephen Stoltzfus [was] seriously ill . . . from eating strawberries." In mid-September of that same year, when "women folks [were] canning apples, making chow-chow and starting to clean house," Mary M. Beiler reported from Lancaster County's Ronks community that "Mattie, wife of Jonas M. Beiler, scalded her arm while canning apple sauce." Other mishaps could have taken place any month of the year. For example, Nettie M. Yoder reported from southwest Pennsylvania's Somerset County that Mrs. Milt Kinsinger was "bruised considerable" when her milk cows "pushed her in the trough." Perhaps to inform *Budget* readers their aid would not be necessary, Yoder assured them that Mrs. Kinsinger's chores would still get done because Miss Sadie Kinsinger, presumably the unfortunate woman's daughter, was "doing her work."[5]

Individual farm and transportation accidents received significant coverage in *The Budget*, but more routine medical problems also warranted mention in passing. Local outbreaks of whooping cough, scarlet fever, mumps, measles, and the flu earned mention, as did the occasional tonsillectomy and appendectomy. Gordonville's Katie F. Lapp even commented on the mental health concerns of her neighbors, mentioning by name those individuals recently "taken to the insane asylum." In her usual upbeat fashion, Lapp typically wished these unfortunate neighbors well and hoped they would "soon be able to return home."[6]

The intervention of medical professionals was required for Isaac Huyard's antitoxin therapy, David Stoltzfus's gunshot wound, the Leola boy's broken leg, the various tonsillectomies and appendectomies, and treatment for mental health issues. When the patients were released to convalesce at home, Amish wives, mothers, sisters, and daughters provided daily care, as they did when household members suffered from the flu, mumps, measles, and other communicable diseases. In the mid-1930s, as Katie F. Lapp and others reported to *The Budget* on their neighbors' health concerns and crises, SCP agents were gathering information about the healthcare work that Amish women performed and the economic value of that labor.

SCP agents recorded information about a family's "medical care" expenses as well as its "personal care" expenses on page 4 of the Expenditure Schedule—Farm. The medical care expenses appeared on the survey form directly above tell-tale comments that potentially identified households as Amish. Agents' itemization of personal care products and services, specifically in the portion devoted to hair care, was a section of the survey where they clearly stated that a household was Amish. The Amish spent little money on barbershop shaves and haircuts, and none on stylish haircuts, permanent waves, or makeup. While one Amish husband spent $4 ($83 in 2022) on haircuts, or 16 haircuts at 25 cents each, and another spent $3, most Amish husbands recorded no such expenses. Agents routinely made marginal comments explaining the lack of barbershop and beauty parlor outgoings for these households—for example, "Haircutting done in family. Amish no Exp[ense]" and "Amish. Wife does haircutting."[7]

The medical care portion of the survey asked a total of 19 questions encompassing 17 expenditure categories. With the exception of home visits by a physician, no significant differences appeared among the various Lancaster County ethno-religious groups in the amount of money spent in any medical category.

TABLE 7.1
Medical Expenses for Lancaster County Ethno-Religious Groups (in FY 1935/36 dollars)

	Old Order Amish	"English"	All Groups*
Total Costs			
Mean	$72.66	$42.00	$50.89
Median	$53.50	$24.50	$32.50
Standard deviation	$82.47	$56.06	$66.39
Maximum	$465.00	$315.00	$635.00
Home Visits			
Mean	$19.44	$10.81	$12.19
Median	$12.00	$0.00	$3.00
Standard deviation	$29.78	$24.09	$21.90
Maximum	$180.00	$180.00	$180.00

Source: Reschly-Jellison sample, "Study of Consumer Purchases: Background, Findings, and Use," appendix II, in this volume.
 *All groups combined: Old Order Amish, all other Anabaptists, and "English."

The Amish had the highest expense for home visits, at $19.44 for the year, which was proportional to the greater number of children in Amish households. In terms of total medical expenses, the Amish mean was $72.66, again the highest, likely related to the number of children, with a standard deviation of $82.47. In fact, each grouping in the revised Reschly/Jellison sample showed higher standard deviations than each mean, indicating a wide variation in expenditures. Some fortunate households spent nothing or next to nothing, while others paid out relatively high amounts, up to $465 for Amish households and $635 for the county in general (table 7.1).[8]

The survey data indicate that even when trained medical personnel were involved, much of Amish healthcare took place in the home. The families did have to purchase the occasional services of oculists and dentists. Expenses might include a $15 pair of glasses, a $50 pair of dentures, or a tooth extracted for a dollar. Information on page 4 of the Expenditure Schedule–Farm also included evidence regarding professional medical treatment for serious illnesses, ailments, and injuries. For example, when Agent Getz called at the home of a young Amish couple in August 1936, she found the 32-year-old wife with some major responsibilities on her hands. In addition to the usual tasks associated with raising five small children, she had to pay particular attention to the one suffering from tuberculosis and provide post-operative care for the child whose $40 in-home tonsillectomy constituted the family's largest medical expense of the survey year.[9]

Once again, the King family was generally representative of Old Order Amish families in the county. In the personal care section of the survey, Agent

Rigdon recorded zero expenses for personal services and explained in a note, "All hair cut by some member of family at no cost." Other than $7.70 for soap, toothpaste, and shaving supplies, about average for an Amish family, the Kings reported no expenses under the "toilet articles and preparations" portion of the personal care section. In fact, Amish households spent significantly less on personal care when compared with other ethno-religious communities in the Reschly/Jellison sample. The Kings reported $70 in medical expenses, a few dollars below average for an Amish household, and paid no money for visits to a doctor's office, but expended $28 for 14 visits, at $2 each, for "home calls." Dental care cost $14, medicines and drugs totaled $10, and eyeglasses came to $18, specified as two pairs at $9 each. The SCP records provide no indication of what conditions led to the 14 doctor visits to the King home.[10]

When Agent Rigdon visited a middle-aged Amish couple in Upper Leacock Township on May 8, 1936, she found a household with much higher medical expenses. The husband, age 45, the wife, age 48, their 21-year-old twins, and four teenagers presented a family wracked by catastrophic injury or illness. Their medical bills totaled $465, or 16 percent of their annual gross farm income. The family spent $40 for dental treatment and $25 for medical examinations and tests, including $10 for an "ex-ray" [sic]. Another $150 went to medicines and drugs, and another $50 went to medical supplies, including an "electral blanket [sic]," and 20 visits to a doctor's office at one dollar per visit. Presumably the blanket (81 x 90 inches) used batteries or a generator for a power source, since the household was not connected to the electrical grid, or perhaps the patient used the blanket strictly during those 20 doctor's office visits as some type of on-going therapy. Whatever the medical crisis, its treatment did not require inpatient hospitalization. Rigdon reported that all eight family members resided at home for the entire fifty-two weeks of the survey year. The crisis, however, did require 90 physician house calls at $2 per visit. Unless the wife and mother of the family was herself the afflicted party, she undoubtedly spent long hours seeing to the daily needs of the at-home patient or patients (figure 7.1).[11]

When a health crisis for one family member became a health crisis for all, the results could be devastating. Lacking indoor plumbing, Amish families sometimes also lacked safe drinking water, and waterborne illnesses could take a heavy emotional, physical, and financial toll. The 24-year-old woman who contracted typhoid fever in 1935 while working as her aunt's hired girl had to rely on her father to pay the $100 doctor's bill and $157.50 nurse's fee. In total, the young woman's medical bills represented 11 percent of her parents' total farm income.[12]

XII. MEDICAL CARE

Item _02719_	Check if any free	Expense for year
1. Physician:		
_020_ office visits at $____		$ _020.00_
2. _09_ home calls at $____		_180.00_
3. Dentist____		_40.00_
4. Oculist____		_0._
5. Other specialist (specify)____		_0_
6. Clinic visits: ____ at $____		
7. Hospital room or bed:		
____days at $____		_0_
8. Private nurse:		
At hospital, ____ days at $____		_0_
9. At home, ____ days at $____		_0_
10. Visiting nurse:		
____visits at $____		_0_
11. Examinations and tests (not included above) _by May 10.00_		_25.00_
12. Medicines and drugs____		_50.00_
13. Eyeglasses____		_0._
14. Medical appliances and supplies_ELECTRAL BLANKET-81X90_		_0.50_
15. Premiums on health and accident insurance____		_0_
16. Other____		_0_
17. TOTAL (1–16)____		$ _465.00_

7.1 The medical expenses section of a household's survey schedule from the Study of Consumer Purchases. It reveals an Old Order Amish family beset with health problems. (Study of Consumer Purchases, Survey 1198.)

If the young Amish woman's situation was typical, the tainted water that caused her illness also affected other members of her aunt's household, and their care would have entailed the services of both medical professionals and female relatives. The experiences a few years earlier of Mennonite neighbor Elizabeth Benner are instructive. Early in her first pregnancy, Elizabeth and her husband, David, had taken a trip to the Atlantic shore, where she contracted typhoid from tainted ice. Thinking it was only morning sickness, the young couple returned to Lancaster County, where Elizabeth soon exposed David to the illness by sharing an ice cream spoon and exposed her older sister by drinking spring water from the same tin cup. Eventually, all three young people were delirious and cared for in the Benners' home around the clock by paid nurses as well as Elizabeth's mother and another of her sisters. David's parents pitched in too, with his father caring for the couple's cattle and his mother cooking for the nursing staff. Despite such efforts, the story came to a tragic end: Elizabeth lost the baby, and her sister lost her life.[13]

Communicable diseases were financially as well as emotionally taxing for Lancaster County families, but surgeries that required hospitalization were often a household's greatest medical expense. When one young Amish couple's 9-month-old daughter required mastoid surgery in 1936, the bill came to $200. Grateful to receive their full payment in cash during hard economic times, the doctor refunded the couple $25, which they promptly used to purchase an ice box so they no longer had to store perishable food items in their springhouse.[14]

If the person needing surgery was the family's wife and mother, her husband either had to take on new tasks or accept assistance from female neighbors or extended family members. When the 26-year-old mother of two small daughters spent two weeks in the hospital for an appendectomy in 1935, her husband perhaps took on some of her household duties and likely also relied on the assistance of neighbor women and family members. At any rate, the family listed no expenses for extra household help during the wife's absence or for nursing care upon her return. The family did report, however, that a non-Amish neighbor had provided automobile transportation to and from the hospital at no cost. Free transportation must have been comforting to a young couple facing $270 in bills for doctor visits, x-rays, medical tests, medication, anesthesiology, hospital care, and surgeon's fee.[15]

Frequent pregnancies and births were the events that took the greatest toll on women's time, workload, and health and the family budget. The highest medical expense recorded in any Lancaster County farm family in the Reschly/Jellison sample was $635, for a family whose wife experienced complications in childbirth.[16] Agent Wiker interviewed the young Strasburg Township family in November 1936 to record their expenses from October 1, 1935, to September 30, 1936. Wiker wrote "Plain people" above the recreation expense section of the survey and recorded that the wife had purchased 12 white head coverings at 50 cents apiece, but the family was obviously not Old Order Amish or horse-and-buggy Mennonites because they owned a used Dodge automobile purchased for $350 in 1932. Their farmhouse also included a telephone and used highline electricity. The 33-year-old husband and 30-year-old wife had a 5-year-old daughter and sons aged 3 and 1. Evidence that the 1-year-old's birth had been difficult includes Wiker's notation that the wife had been away from home for four weeks during the survey year. In the survey's medical care section, Wiker noted a 25-day hospital stay totaling $125 and 50 hours of private nursing care in the hospital at $6 per hour for a total of $300. The cost for a "prenatal & kidney specialist" came to $150, with additional expenses of $15 for medical tests, $30 for medications, and $15 for medical supplies. At a time when the average medical expenditure for farm families in Lancaster County was about $51, this family's medical payments were enormous, consuming 21 percent of their $2,980 gross farm income. Still, the family managed to spend $25 on personal care: haircuts for the husband, soap, toothpaste, shaving supplies, and "cold cream and powder." Another recorded expense was a $10 layette for the child whose birth had been so difficult for his mother.[17]

Although Amish women and their families viewed childbirth as a blessing rather than a potential health crisis, they, like other twentieth-century Americans, had adapted to the medicalization of childbirth and sought trained medical assistance with their in-home births. With a high birthrate, the Old Order Amish sustained higher medical expenses on average than any other Lancaster County group. SCP records reveal that the cost of routine obstetrical care was dependent on the number of $2 house calls the attending physician believed necessary to provide sufficient prenatal care, assist in delivery, and monitor the new mother and infant. A healthy 30-year-old Amish woman required only 10 visits from the physician who presided over the birth of her seventh child in March 1936, while a 46-year-old Old Order Mennonite woman giving birth for the final time required twice as many visits from her doctor. The latter birth apparently proceeded normally and required no hospital time or additional nursing care, but when complications occurred, costs rose accordingly. Agent Ella Veit reported that the birth of a 33-year-old Amish woman's fifth child required at least 25 physician house calls and the services of a practical nurse who stayed with the family for two weeks, eating three meals a day and charging them $10 for her services. Still, the family paid a total of only $105 in medical bills for the 1935/36 survey year.[18]

The women who provided paid nursing services to mothers and newborns were likely persons with little formal training but plenty of practical experience caring for their own family members. Fannie H. Sauder, for example, was a Mennonite widow who supported her family with fees from the maternity cases a sympathetic local physician sent her way. Typically serving the families who hired her from 10 days to two weeks, she was able to save enough money to buy a row house in the city of Lancaster that also provided a home for her two unmarried sisters and two unmarried daughters during the Depression years. While maternity nurse fees benefited Sauder and other women who marketed their time and skills in this way, the families who had to pay these costs frequently viewed them as burdensome. A 35-year-old Amish woman reported to Agent Rigdon that she and her husband had paid for 10 doctor's calls when their sixth child was born in September 1935, but she gratefully acknowledged that her own mother had assumed any additional childbirth-related nursing or housekeeping duties "at no cost."[19]

As noted in the situation of the Strasburg Township Plain woman described above, serious complications in childbirth could have a significant effect on a family's budget and welfare. Events surrounding the birth of her fourth child landed both a 31-year-old Amish mother and her newborn son in the hospital for four full weeks in midsummer 1935, leaving her husband and three other small children on their own. The only clue to their survival strategy is Agent Rigdon's notation about the additional meals provided to "extra help." Since the family reported no household labor costs, and the husband's neighboring father and brothers assisted him with free farm labor, the extra meals were not provided to hired help. One might reasonably surmise, therefore, that visiting neighbor women and female family members cooked as well as consumed these additional meals as they assisted the young family during the woman's hospitalization and recovery. The woman and her husband undoubtedly appreciated this assistance as they faced a $358 bill for six doctor's office visits, 25 house calls, medication, additional medical examinations and tests, the four-week hospital stay, and the cost of an operation—perhaps an emergency caesarian section—during the medical crisis. In all, these bills accounted for 16 percent of the family's total gross farm income.[20]

While SCP medical treatment data reveal much about the expense and household labor involved in childbirth and infant and maternal care, they offer little to no information about the care that Amish women and their families provided for their eldest members. Like other farm women of the period, Amish women undoubtedly expended notable time and effort caring for elderly relatives, but SCP methodology prevented gathering much data about these experiences. The survey planners wanted to focus on the "economic family," those living under the same roof and participating directly in the farm-family economy, so they ignored older children no longer living at home and elderly fam-

7.2 A "fine Old-Order Amish farm house." The original caption for this photograph noted that the structure had been "enlarged by the addition of a fourth floor and also a *Grossdawdyhaus*" (grandfather's house). Photograph by Irving Rusinow, Lancaster County, March 1941. (Courtesy of the Bureau of Agricultural Economics Collection, National Archives II, College Park, MD)

ily members living in separate housing. Occasionally, the widowed parent of a household's wife or husband appeared in the records because that person resided in the main farmhouse. More often, however, elderly parents resided in their own separate structure on the farm of one of their children in what the Amish referred to as the *Grossdawdyhaus* (grandfather's house). Even if, as was frequently the situation, the *Grossdawdyhaus* was attached directly to the main farmhouse, the SCP agents asked no questions about its elderly inhabitants and their possible medical challenges (figure 7.2). Thus, while the records reveal significant information about a great variety of healthcare concerns, they are largely silent about Amish women's eldercare labor.[21]

The medical experiences of 1930s Old Order Amish were not altogether unique. Throughout rural America, neighbors assisted one another in times of crisis, and sympathetic physicians refunded portions of medical bills. What set the Lancaster County Amish apart was the way they negotiated through health emergencies with minimal reliance on the twentieth-century technologies many other rural northerners increasingly viewed as vital to weathering medical crises: telephones, automobiles, and electric-powered devices. In a society in which people received only a one-room schoolhouse education, connection to the electric grid was forbidden, and ownership of modern communication and transportation equipment disallowed, the Amish necessarily engaged with the outside world when the lives and health of family members were at risk. They sought the services of physicians trained in modern medical schools and friendly neighbors willing to phone for medical assistance or provide car transportation to the hospital or to a doctor's office for therapeutic use of an electric blanket. In the interstices, however, the Amish relied on members of their own community— particularly wives, mothers, and sisters—to perform many of the additional nursing and household tasks required for at-home care. Such assistance was particularly valuable during the frequent childbirths that characterized Amish family life and alone caused their average medical costs to exceed those of other Lancaster County populations. Without the unpaid labor of Amish women at the time of a new baby's arrival, the medical costs of introducing a new "little dish washer" or "woodchopper" to the world would have been even higher.[22]

In announcing the outcomes of local childbirth stories, the scribes of *The Budget* provided another free service to their community. They also performed necessary communication labor in reporting the outcomes to other medical stories. Katie F. Lapp wrote that although Menno Beiler's wife had remained too ill to attend church services, a few members of the congregation had dropped by her home on a Sunday afternoon to perform an abbreviated worship service just for her. When a young woman from a nearby county was released from the Lancaster Hospital after an appendectomy, Lapp informed worried family members and other *Budget* readers that the woman was now recuperating "at the home of Christ King's girls and is getting along fairly well." If the results of a crisis proved tragic, *Budget* scribes were also there to provide words of comfort. When Katie Y. Beiler reported from the Ronks community about the deaths of two pneumonia patients in February 1936, she assured her readers it was all part of God's plan, stating, "We are again reminded that our abiding place is not here on earth."[23]

Within their culturally prescribed roles as care providers, social communicators, and keepers of the faith, Amish women enabled their community to survive and cope with medical concerns during the hard times of the Great Depression. As with the other labor they provided to their families and neighbors, the health-related work that Amish women performed enhanced community cohesion and stability. Whether providing physical aid or spreading the news during times of medical concern, women's health-related work helped Amish farm families maintain their way of life in Depression-era Lancaster County.

CHAPTER EIGHT

Insiders and Outsiders

Telling the Story of the Amish Farm Family

Neither on the family level nor on the community level does the
wife initiate or direct important activities.

—Walter M. Kollmorgen, 1942

In a report for the Bureau of Agricultural Economics (BAE), cultural geographer
Walter M. Kollmorgen argued that the Old Order Amish of Lancaster County
had so masterfully weathered the Great Depression that they were undoubtedly
the most stable and successful rural community in the nation. Kollmorgen, the
organizers of the Study of Consumer Purchases (SCP), and other government
investigators recognized the patriarchal system under which Old Order Amish
farmers and homemakers functioned, but their statistical data and awareness of
Amish gender role prescriptions often obscured an important reality: Women's
labor, sometimes conducted under direct male supervision and sometimes performed autonomously, was key to Amish success. One need look no further than
the diaries of one Lancaster County Amish woman whose Depression-era entries
record such diverse economic activities as sewing and mending, ironing, making butter, baking, butchering, making soap, planting and hoeing the garden,
washing feedbags, whitewashing, making noodles, canning, hooking rugs, dry-
ing apples, husking corn, cooking for field workers, making jelly, making catsup,
cleaning the yard, hauling corn, making potato chips, dying cloth, and stripping
tobacco. The addition of Amish women's voices to the government study evidence reveals the vital nature of their work.[1]

Kollmorgen undertook his Lancaster County research as a member of the team of social scientists working under the direction of rural sociologist Carl C. Taylor in the BAE's Division of Farm Population and Rural Welfare. Within the US Department of Agriculture, the BAE—particularly Taylor's team of social scientists—maintained a vision of US agriculture at odds with the philosophy and focus of most USDA policies and projects of the era. While most USDA efforts in the 1930s benefited large farmers and landowners, the BAE, along with the Farm Security Administration, looked to improve conditions for agrarians lower on the socioeconomic ladder. At a time when most USDA agencies continued to push for the greater capitalization and mechanization of farming—with an eye toward the agribusiness model that would come to dominate US agriculture in the second half of the twentieth century—BAE personnel continued to champion family farming and the idea that farming was more a way of life than a business. To Taylor, in fact, family farming was unquestionably the *best* way of life. In a 1937 letter to his BAE colleague O. E. Baker, Taylor extolled the virtues of farm life in contrast to the forces of agribusiness: "There are inherently good traits in the rural way of life, . . . there are spiritual, cultural, esthetic, and social values which attach themselves to . . . the closer association of family and community which are typical of the simpler rural cultures." He further stated that as a society "grows more complex, becomes more mechanical and mercenary, it tends to lose its spiritual, cultural, esthetic, and creative nature."[2]

Taylor's allegiance to what was in essence the Jeffersonian ideal of the United States as a nation of yeoman farmers found expression in his ambitious series of research studies, Culture of a Contemporary Rural Community, in the early 1940s. A major purpose of the project was to gauge the impact of New Deal programs on six geographically, economically, and culturally diverse rural communities and to provide guidance for future planning. From the beginning, however, Taylor envisioned the six communities lying along a continuum ranging from stability to instability, from the stable yeoman farm families of Lancaster County's Old Order Amish community to the unstable, highly mechanized wheat farmers of the Kansas Dust Bowl community of Sublette. In between these two extremes on the spectrum lay the communities of El Cerrito, New Mexico; Irwin, Iowa; Harmony, Georgia; and Landaff, New Hampshire. The centerpiece of Taylor's research design was the assignment of a participant-observer to each of the six communities for a three- to five-month period. The New Mexico and Georgia studies focused on communities of color, and all six studies included analysis of women's activities, but all of the participant-observers were white men. In assigning Kollmorgen as the participant-observer for the

Lancaster County Amish community, Taylor entrusted the study to a scholar whose Columbia University doctoral research on a Swiss-German community in Tennessee (along with much of his other scholarship) had made him an expert on German-speaking cultural "islands" in rural America.[3]

During his 1940 fieldwork, which took place primarily in the area surrounding the town of Intercourse, Leacock Township, the 33-year-old Kollmorgen immediately ran into issues of trust with his Amish informants. Largely disregarding the fieldwork manual that the BAE had prepared for its participant-observers, Kollmorgen followed his instincts in eliciting information about the Amish without resorting to lengthy written questionnaires and other recommended procedures. In candid correspondence with Taylor in March and April 1940, Kollmorgen reported that two recent developments—the introduction of the 1940 long-form census schedule and publication of an error-filled article about Lancaster County Amish life in the *Saturday Evening Post*—had made his informants highly suspicious of nosey outsiders. Kollmorgen informed Taylor that asking his Amish contacts to complete a lengthy survey form would "mark [him] as a government man" and perhaps mean that his "cordial relations with the people would come to an end." Taylor advised Kollmorgen to reassure the Amish that the BAE was undertaking its research not for prurient reasons but to set them forward as role models for other farmers, telling the geographer, "Try to convince these Amish people that we believe that many of their characteristics are praiseworthy and that rather than pry into their individual beliefs, we are anxious to discover the good things in their whole system and reveal these good things to other people."[4]

Ultimately, Kollmorgen was able to build a strong rapport with members of the Old Order Amish. In addition to following Taylor's advice, Kollmorgen managed to connect with the subjects of his research by emphasizing characteristics he held in common with them. Like the Amish, Kollmorgen had grown up speaking German in a large rural family. Rather than a farmer, his father had been a teacher in a Lutheran parochial school, but Kollmorgen's childhood experiences with his 10 siblings in rural Nebraska nevertheless approximated those of his Amish informants. That Kollmorgen knew German and could understand Pennsylvania Dutch—although he could not speak it well—also helped win the trust of the local Amish. Finally, he, like the Amish, was an outsider in the nation's mainstream culture. As a polio survivor, Kollmorgen walked with a leg brace and cane, a disability that had to that point prevented him from securing an academic teaching position. His younger sister Johanna, also a polio survivor, accompanied him for some portion of his research and provided clerical support. With their culture's emphasis on family relationships, the Amish likely also warmed to Kollmorgen's devotion to his disabled sibling.[5]

Kollmorgen's working relationship with the subjects of his study proved successful and resulted in a report that pleased both the Amish themselves and his supervisors back in Washington. Agricultural economist and sociologist Charles P. Loomis, one of the major architects of the stability-instability studies, participated in a portion of the Lancaster County fieldwork and reported to Taylor in late April 1940 that he was "pleasantly surprised" that Kollmorgen had "worked up such good rapport with quite a large number of [Amish] families." Loomis attributed Kollmorgen's success to his German language skills and his familiarity with "the details of farming operations in the area, particularly dairying." The positive portrayal of Amish farming that Kollmorgen assured his informants would be presented in his final report also undoubtedly contributed to their spirit of cooperation. Loomis reported that when he and Kollmorgen talked with the Amish about the other communities in the study and mentioned that people in El Cerrito, Harmony, and elsewhere were not weathering the Depression as well as the Amish, Kollmorgen's informants had a ready prescription for them: "If the Mexicans, negroes [*sic*], and other people followed the Bible, worked hard, didn't give their children too much schooling, and weren't interested in worldly things, there would be no difficulties."[6]

Loomis's report to Taylor indicates that the social scientists of the community stability-instability studies recognized from the outset that the Old Order Amish viewed their agricultural success as a product of their biblically based way of life. Shortly before the report, Kollmorgen had reported to Taylor that although he tried to talk with the Amish only about farm matters, that was a difficult task in a society that practiced farming as a biblical mandate. As he told Taylor, "Trouble is that church matters and agricultural matters are so interrelated and overlap in so many ways that little unmixed agriculture remains that can be discussed freely." The intertwined nature of religious belief and agricultural practice would be a central theme of Kollmorgen's final published study.[7]

Two years after Kollmorgen completed his fieldwork, the BAE published his final report, *Culture of a Contemporary Rural Community: The Old Order Amish of Lancaster County, Pennsylvania*. In it, the geographer attributed the group's agricultural success and high level of community cohesion to their religiously motivated adherence to nonconformity and separation from the world. He closed his study of community stability among them with a summary of their formula for success: "A group that has survived centuries of persecution in

Europe and has so far resisted many of the onslaughts of factories, with their standardized products, and the appeals of higher education must have qualities that make for survival. Important among these qualities are a tradition of hard work, a willingness to make sacrifices for the good of others, and an enviable tradition of constructive diversified agriculture."[8]

Noted throughout Kollmorgen's study was another key to Amish success—women's work. Respecting Amish gender norms, the geographer received all first-hand information from local bishops and other male community members and did not converse at length with their wives, daughters, and sisters. Nevertheless, Kollmorgen recognized that women were "very important in farming" and frequently observed them at their daily labor. He reported, "[The women] did their work quietly, unassumingly, and were occupied, but they never really took notice of me."[9]

While acknowledging that Amish women lived and worked within a patriarchal system that granted ultimate authority and decision-making to men, Kollmorgen reported their community's dependence on women's labor. Noting that "women continued to take care of the garden and the chickens, assisted with milking, and took care of dairy products," Kollmorgen also recorded how men were taking on a larger role as dairy and some poultry operations significantly expanded. Even as women ceded some of their customary responsibilities in the dairy barn and poultry house, however, they remained vital field workers. Kollmorgen reported that they raked hay and planted tobacco, potatoes, and tomatoes alongside their male relatives. He also highlighted their work in harvesting potatoes and tomatoes.[10]

Echoing the findings of the Study of Consumer Purchases during 1935/36, Kollmorgen emphasized women's food preservation activities, reporting that women frequently canned 500 to 700 quarts of fruits and vegetables a year, made gallons of apple and pear butter, canned and preserved "much" meat, prepared "great quantities" of jellies, and stored "impressive quantities" of dried apples, beans, and corn. He also recorded that young brides brought cash resources to their marital households with money they had earned working as hired girls, harvesting potatoes on a neighbor's farm, picking fruit at a commercial orchard, or raising and selling their own chickens or calves.[11]

Kollmorgen devoted particular attention to Amish women's needle skills. Again echoing SCP findings from the mid-1930s, Kollmorgen found that women's sewing activities saved Amish families significant cash outlays. Noting that the Amish commitment to nonconformity necessitated that "housewives and grown daughters" construct most of their families' unique clothing, he further observed that the practice meant "a considerable saving in the cost of the finished product." He also reported that since Amish clothing styles never changed, the Amish only discarded clothes when they were completely worn out, making for further "economy." The principle of nonconformity also meant that the Amish rejected the purchase of commercial carpeting, instead relying on women to save rags and sew them into strips for rag rugs that became "cheap but durable carpet." Kollmorgen additionally referenced the many hours Amish women spent constructing quilts and pillowcases and doing embroidery work. As he summarized the situation in his report, "It is doubtful that rural women anywhere in this country do more needlework and sewing than the women and girls of the Amish families."[12]

Kollmorgen's descriptions and SCP statistics indicate that Amish women's needlework was the labor that most dramatically set their experiences apart from that of other farm women, including other Anabaptist farm women, and most obviously saved their families cash resources to be reinvested in the farm or used elsewhere. Kollmorgen's commentary on Amish women's needlework reinforces the centrality of that labor as expressed in Lydia Stoltzfus's comment that she made "twenty or more pairs of pants every winter" and SCP agent Shoemaker's notation that the women of one family made "all clothing including men's overalls & suits." In acknowledging the importance of women's sewing work near the end of his report, Kollmorgen also raised an interesting question: What did Amish women think about the extensive time and effort they spent with needle in hand or feet on the pedal of the treadle sewing machine? To Kollmorgen, the answer was unknowable. In his words, "Just what the Old Order Amish housewife thinks about this required task cannot be said, for matters like this are not discussed freely with outsiders."[13]

One logically wonders whether women of the Old Order Amish community would have been so reticent to share their thoughts about their work if the person observing their labor had been a female rather than a male investigator. After all, as reflected in their marginal comments, the predominantly female SCP agents had somehow managed to draw out Lancaster County Amish women to discuss their concerns about buying extra meat to feed a threshing crew or weathering a medical crisis that required 90 visits from a physician. That Kollmorgen's descriptions of women's work were so insightful suggests that he perhaps gained greater proximity to women's daily experiences than he later recalled. In fact, in Carl C. Taylor's introduction to Kollmorgen's published report, Taylor suggested that Johanna Kollmorgen played more than a clerical role in her brother's fieldwork and thus may have gained greater access

to the women. Taylor emphasized the bona fides of both siblings in his introduction, stating, "Walter Kollmorgen and his sister, both of whom speak High
German, lived in the community for 4 months and probably came as near to
developing the status of participant observers as is possible without being members of the Amish church." If Johanna did indeed talk with Amish women and
convey their information to her brother, the official record remains silent.[14]

Kollmorgen had completed his fieldwork by the time anyone at the BAE suggested hiring a female researcher to spend significant time with Amish women
and record their thoughts and words. Not until July 1940 did agricultural economist Conrad Taeuber suggest that the stability-instability team add "at least
one woman and at least one Negro" to its personnel "in order to provide materials which your present workers are not likely to get," but no evidence suggests
that the study's organizers followed this advice. Even in the face of Taeuber's
report that "some good persons in both these categories [were] available through
the Civil Service," Black and female researchers seemingly remained absent from
the study. Perhaps other BAE social scientists did not see the important racial
and gender perspectives such personnel would have brought to the study or the
significance of the data they might have elicited from interview subjects reluc-
tant to speak to white men. In other words, Taeuber may have been ahead of
his time in voicing concerns that would be uppermost to social scientists today
but not so obvious in 1940. Rumors of war may have also prevented the hiring
of any new personnel, regardless of race or gender, as the United States prepared
for possible entrance into World War II. Even as Taeuber suggested hiring a
more diverse research staff, in a July 1940 memo, he recognized that new ap-
pointments might not be possible in the coming year. A month before Pearl
Harbor, with his staff and resources dwindling, Taylor prodded those involved
in the stability-instability studies to bring them to a close. As he reported to
Charles P. Loomis, "I am anxious to move the whole thing along because every
day brings a heavier impact of defense activities. I feel pretty sure that it will
not be long until we have to justify everything we do by defense implications
and will have to stop doing things that don't contribute to defense."[15]

By the time the BAE published Kollmorgen's report and the other five community studies in 1942, the United States was indeed at war. In fact, among
those who wrote to the BAE complimenting Kollmorgen's study was Charles
Suter, assistant director of a wartime Mennonite Civilian Public Service (CPS)
camp in Howard, Pennsylvania. He reported that among the conscientious objectors he supervised were several Amish men who believed Kollmorgen's work
to be "the best and most sensible evaluation of their sect that has ever been pub-

lished" and were "loud in their praise of the man who has done such a remarkable job in recording [the] innermost feelings of the 'Plain People' who are so often misunderstood." In his letter, Suter also requested a dozen copies of the report to distribute among camp residents. As director of economic information, Peter H. DeVries informed him, "We regret that the supply is now exhausted and that there is no possibility of having a rerun before the end of the war."[16]

By 1943, the year of Suter's and DeVries's correspondence, the United States had, in the words of President Franklin Roosevelt, definitively shifted care of its national health from "Dr. New Deal" to "Dr. Win-the-War." With that shift came changes in plans for the stability-instability studies. In addition to the war limiting printing and distribution of the six individual community studies, it also halted publication of a planned seventh volume in the series that would have synthesized the findings of the six studies. Wartime priorities likewise ended plans for publishing an extensive volume of photographs to accompany each of the reports. As the nation turned its eyes from overcoming the Depression to defeating the Axis powers, the lessons that the Taylor team hoped to impart about the merits of traditional family farming were somewhat muted. Without the synthetic volume or presentation of their wide-ranging photographic evidence, those involved in the studies had greater difficulty demonstrating how dramatically agricultural success and stability differed between the labor-intensive, diversified family farming of the Pennsylvania Amish to the mechanized monoculture of the Kansas Wheat Belt. At the same time, government wartime spending and high demand for farm products by the US military and allies abroad brought an end to the agricultural Depression and inherent interest in reading about its possible causes and solutions.[17]

Even with its limited wartime distribution, Kollmorgen's study became well known to other social scientists interested in rural communities and in the Amish. Following the initial 1942 publication, the government eventually ordered two more printings. In total, the BAE sold 15,000 copies of Kollmorgen's report, making it the agency's "most popular for-sale item." Rural sociologists particularly found Kollmorgen's study useful for its insights into the connection between the Amish community's traditional agrarian values and its relative economic success. To Kollmorgen's chagrin, the successful reception his study received erroneously "branded" him as a sociologist and did nothing "to enhance [his] standing as a geographer."[18]

Among those interested in Kollmorgen's findings was budding sociologist Grant M. Stoltzfus. As a 27-year-old conscientious objector residing at a Civilian Public Service camp in Clear Spring, Maryland, Stoltzfus wrote to the BAE in September 1943 asking about the protocol for reproducing some of the pictures that photographer Irving Rusinow had taken early in 1941 to illustrate Kollmorgen's study. Rusinow, the BAE's head field photographer, had in fact taken nearly a thousand photos over the course of a fourth-month period in which he visited all six communities featured in the stability-instability studies. With the war ending plans for publication of extensive photo essays to accompany the six written reports, the BAE ended up publishing only a small portion of Rusinow's voluminous catalog. While Rusinow had taken 92 photographs during his several days in Lancaster County, only 13 of those ultimately appeared alongside Kollmorgen's text in the published study. Most of the published photographs were of buildings and buggies. Only three of the pictures included any people, and these were of children in a schoolroom and men discreetly photographed in profile. One presumes that the BAE chose to include only pictures of this type out of respect for Amish proscriptions against baptized adults appearing in full-face photographs.[19]

No adult women appeared in any of the photos that illustrated Kollmorgen's study, but it was a photograph of Anabaptist women that specifically drew Stoltzfus's praise in his 1943 letter. Stoltzfus, who had assisted Kollmorgen during the geographer's 1940 fieldwork, had already requested and received copies of several of Rusinow's unpublished Lancaster County photos. In his follow-up correspondence, the young scholar now looked ahead to reproducing those images in a future "article or feature on Amish life," but he also expressed a personal interest in one of the photos. As he informed DeVries, "One picture is especially valuable and treasured since it was taken in my home and shows my mother and my aunt at work quilting. Since these people are camera-shy for the most part, I feel that the pictures are unexcelled and I cannot express too strongly my joy in having them in my possession" (figure 8.1).[20]

As art historian Elizabeth L. Bennett notes in her study of Rusinow's Lancaster County photographs, his pictures "told many stories." In particular, they gave further voice to the women's stories only partially told in Kollmorgen's narrative. In attempting to illustrate women's work, Rusinow scrupulously avoided offending Old Order Amish proscriptions against personal photographs by instead photographing women, such as Stoltzfus's mother and aunt, who were members of neighboring Church Amish and Plain Mennonite communities. Rusinow also circumvented religious proscriptions by photographing the landscapes and the exteriors of the buildings where Old Order Amish women labored. In photographing interior spaces where women's work took place, he relied again on the willingness of Mennonite and Church Amish women to

8.1 Grant M. Stoltzfus's normally "camera-shy" Church Amish mother and aunt constructing a quilt. Photograph by Irving Rusinow, Lancaster County, March 1941. (Courtesy of the Bureau of Agricultural Economics Collection, National Archives II, College Park, MD)

oblige. Regardless, as previously noted, none of Rusinow's representations of women ultimately appeared in Kollmorgen's published study. Nevertheless, as Stoltzfus's correspondence with DeVries indicates, subsequent scholars and others have frequently employed Rusinow's Lancaster County pictures for their own purposes.[21]

At the time Rusinow took his Lancaster County photos and those for the other five communities, he was 26 years old and filling some big shoes. His immediate predecessor as the BAE's head field photographer was the legendary Dorothea Lange. His position with the BAE, which he assumed in late 1940, was not his first time working for a USDA agency. He had worked as a photographer for the Soil Conservation Service in the late 1930s, and both there and in his assignment with the BAE, Rusinow took photos that in style and subject matter closely resembled those of the era's famous Farm Security Administration (FSA) photographic unit. Like Lange, Arthur Rothstein, Marion Post Wolcott, Marjory Collins, and the other FSA photographers, Rusinow focused his camera primarily on agriculture, landscapes, housing, churches, and people. Among the people Rusinow photographed was Church Amish woman Hannah Beiler Smoker as she performed typical Amish women's chores, including baking bread and milking a cow. As noted in chapter 2, he also took pictures of her farmhouse parlor, recording the furnishings and knickknacks displayed there.[22]

Rusinow's photos and their captions, which BAE anthropologist Kenneth MacLeish likely wrote, provide a glimpse of what the fully realized stability-instability series would have looked like if the war had not intervened. Had the BAE been able to publish a full volume of photographs illustrating Kollmorgen's study, the plan was obviously to connect individual pictures to specific lines from the geographer's text. A close examination of the photos of Hannah Beiler Smoker and their captions clearly reveals this intention.[23]

Rusinow's first picture of Smoker made economical use of just one image to illustrate several of Kollmorgen's observations about Amish women, including information about their piety, home production efforts, and consumer practices. The picture showed Smoker in profile, with her white prayer covering prominently displayed, placing two huge loaves of fresh baked bread on the cloth-covered countertop of a kitchen cabinet (figure 8.2). The image's caption reads, "This Church Amish housewife is engaged in the rapidly disappearing practice of baking bread. Note the devotional head-covering which is worn in accordance with I Cor. 11: 1–16." The two-sentence caption directly echoed information in Kollmorgen's report. Early in the study, Kollmorgen listed the plethora of Bible verses that lay behind distinctive Old Order Amish practices, including the admonition in I Corinthians 11: 1–16 that women should pray with their heads covered as a sign of their submission to God and their husbands. The caption's reference to the "disappearing practice of baking bread" directly referred to Kollmorgen's statement that an increasing number of Amish women found buying bread more cost efficient than baking it themselves, a trend that SCP pantry inventories also confirmed. Both SCP agents and Kollmorgen found that while women still baked large numbers of pies, cakes, and pastries, they were beginning to rely more frequently on commercial bakeries for their bread supply. Kollmorgen reasoned that women found locally produced flour sufficient for baking desserts and breakfast pastries but preferred higher quality,

8.2 Church Amish member Hannah Beiler Smoker baking bread in her farm home. Photograph by Irving Rusinow, Lancaster County, March 1941. (Courtesy of the Bureau of Agricultural Economics Collection, National Archives II, College Park, MD)

and more expensive, western Wheat Belt flour for baking bread. Under these circumstances, many had started patronizing one or more of the five local bakeries that made bread truck deliveries in Amish neighborhoods.[24]

Rusinow's second picture of Smoker illustrated one of Kollmorgen's chief observations about Amish dairy farming: Amish farm families did not use milking machines and instead employed the labor of every able and available family member. Captioned "Milking is a family enterprise in the absence of milking machines," this photo of Smoker portrayed the stout farm woman, then in her late forties, as the antithesis of the urban housewife. Here was a woman who by necessity left the cozy kitchen where Rusinow pictured her baking bread to engage in labor as a farm producer (figure 8.3).[25]

In addition to Rusinow's pictures of Hannah Beiler Smoker and Grant M. Stoltzfus's mother and aunt, the only other Anabaptist women who appeared

8.3 Church Amish member Hannah Beiler Smoker in the dairy barn milking "in the absence of milking machines." Photograph by Irving Rusinow, Lancaster County, March 1941. (Courtesy of the Bureau of Agricultural Economics Collection, National Archives II, College Park, MD)

in his Lancaster County photos were women selling their farm products at the city of Lancaster's Southern Market and a Plain Mennonite woman pictured in profile as she cooked on her kitchen range (figures 8.4 and 8.5). While the pictures taken at the Southern Market were apparently candid shots, the picture of the Mennonite woman was necessarily planned and part of Rusinow's effort to enter and photograph Church Amish and Mennonite interiors as a substitute for images of Old Order Amish interiors. As with the captions for most of Rusinow's farmhouse interiors, this one clearly delineated the ways in which the pictured objects resembled or differed from those in an Old Order Amish home. In this instance, the caption noted, "The most characteristic thing about this kitchen (in a [c]onservative Mennonite home) is its extreme cleanliness. The colorful kitchen range shown in this picture would not be acceptable to the Old Order Amish." No one looking at the black and white print would have ever

8.4 Anabaptist women selling farm products at the Southern Market. Photograph by Irving Rusinow, Lancaster County, March 1941. (Courtesy of the Bureau of Agricultural Economics Collection, National Archives II, College Park, MD)

known that the cooking range was "colorful," but the caption nevertheless scrupulously documented this deviation from Amish practice.[26]

While all these photos portrayed Anabaptist farm women at their traditional tasks—quilting, baking, milking, marketing, and cooking—two of Rusinow's photos without women perhaps best represented their labor. One showed a cellar in which a Church Amish woman had stored 800 quarts of home-preserved food in the autumn of 1940, and the other captured a sewing room that a Church Amish woman had quickly fled when Rusinow arrived with his camera (figures 8.6 and 8.7).

Rusinow's photo of the cellar, with what its caption characterized as "typical" white-washed walls, showed what remained of 1940's canning efforts by the end of winter 1941. The simple shelving, constructed of cinderblocks and boards, now held only a few dozen glass jars of fruits, vegetables, and other

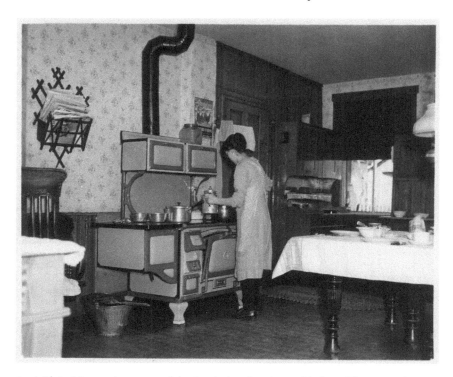

8.5 A Plain Mennonite woman laboring in her farmhouse kitchen. The original caption noted that her "colorful kitchen range . . . would not be acceptable to the Old Order Amish." Photograph by Irving Rusinow, Lancaster County, March 1941. (Courtesy of the Bureau of Agricultural Economics Collection, National Archives II, College Park, MD)

home-canned foods. When summer and fall rolled around again, however, the farm woman would begin restocking her family's supply of canned goods, and the cellar would be full once more. Rusinow's photograph provided vivid proof of what Amish women had reported to SCP agents five years earlier—that their home-produced and processed foods were the mainstay of the Amish family diet.[27]

Rusinow's photo of the abandoned quilt-making scene, unlike the picture of Grant M. Stoltzfus's mother and aunt doing quilting handwork, showcased the treadle sewing machine's role in the quilting process. The woman who had been sitting at the machine left her chair askew, the quilt top lying on the floor, and fabric scraps strewn about the room. Rusinow obviously interrupted her work, but in doing so, he revealed the extent to which her farm home was some-times also a messy workshop. Without a chance to clean up her work space be-

8.6 A Church Amish fruit cellar with what remains of 800 quarts of food a farm woman canned the previous fall. Photograph by Irving Rusinow, Lancaster County, March 1941. (Courtesy of the Bureau of Agricultural Economics Collection, National Archives II, College Park, MD)

fore Rusinow photographed it, the woman had left behind the evidence of her diligent labor.

Old Order Amish women's work at the treadle sewing machine represented their labor more so than their work preparing food at the stove, milking on a stool, or tending to the pressure cooker during canning season. As the SCP data showed, by the mid-1930s, 97 percent of Old Order Amish women owned treadle machines and used them to outpace the sewing efforts of all other Lancaster County groups. SCP agents described Old Order Amish women as making all the "clothing & repairs possible" for their families, and Amish women described themselves as "patching all day." Of all the pieces of equipment Old Order Amish women put to use in the New Deal era, the sewing machine arguably best symbolized their labor.[28]

Sewing was in fact the only type of women's work represented, albeit obliquely,

8.7 A quilt in process in the sewing room of a Church Amish farm home. The quilter fled the scene so the photograph could be taken. Photograph by Irving Rusinow, Lancaster County, March 1941. (Courtesy of the Bureau of Agricultural Economics Collection, National Archives II, College Park, MD)

in the thirteen Rusinow photos and captions that actually made it into Kollmorgen's published study. Rusinow's interior shot of a one-room Amish schoolhouse showed a half-dozen boys standing to recite while a smaller boy and several girls listened at their desks. Its caption remarked on the pupils' unique hairstyles, drew attention to two girls ducking the camera, and noted, "With the exception of 2 boys' sweaters, all the [children's] outer clothes were made at home" (figure 8.8). Although the caption writer's use of the passive voice may have obscured the fact, the children's mothers were the laborers who had constructed all their "made at home" clothing.[29]

Publication of a full volume of Rusinow's photos would have highlighted the importance of women's work to the Amish success story. In its absence, several of Kollmorgen's observations about women's labor remained relatively muted.

8.8 Amish children in a one-room schoolhouse. The original caption for this photograph read, "With the exception of 2 boys' sweaters, all the [children's] outer clothes
were made at home." Photograph by Irving Rusinow, Lancaster County, March 1941.
(Courtesy of the Bureau of Agricultural Economics Collection, National Archives II,
College Park, MD)

Visual evidence, such as the messy sewing room scene, would have enhanced
the argument that women's diligent effort went into projects that saved cash
resources and contributed to the family economy. Likewise, when the war dis-
rupted plans to publish a volume synthesizing the findings of all six community
studies, the comparative advantages of Amish women's economic contributions
were lost.

The importance of women's work to Amish success would have been most
evident when comparing their experiences to those of their counterparts in the
Dust Bowl community of Sublette, Kansas, which the BAE designated the nation's least stable agricultural community. With the exception of the area's small
Mennonite community, these residents of southwestern Kansas invested in expensive mechanized farm equipment, focused almost exclusively on farming

wheat, and relied only minimally on unpaid family labor. As a result, at a time when Lancaster County Amish families annually averaged $1,444 in the sale, trade, and use of agricultural products, one-fourth of Sublette area families sold, traded, or consumed less than $250 worth. Climate, soil quality, and local market factors certainly contributed to the economic disparity between the two communities, but women's differing levels of participation in the agricultural economy also played a role. For instance, in contrast to the ubiquity of gardening among Lancaster County Amish women, only 13 percent of Sublette area women raised vegetable gardens. The author of the Sublette community case study in fact questioned whether the women in most area farm families even identified themselves as agriculturalists at all, noting that many of them drove to town every weekday to work as office or retail clerks.[30]

Without the originally planned comparative and photo essay volumes, Kollmorgen's 105-page report stood on its own in making the case that the Old Order Amish of Lancaster County were the nation's most stable and successful rural community. Readers both inside and outside the Amish community praised the thoroughness and factual accuracy of Kollmorgen's research and his assessment of Old Order Amish cultural and economic stability. Although he dutifully documented women's work at several points in the report, the centrality of that labor to Amish stability remained underemphasized. That the photos and comparative analysis that would have enhanced Kollmorgen's discussion of women's labor never appeared in their originally intended form further obscured the vital role that women's toil played in the Amish success story. Most significantly, the absence of women's voices in Kollmorgen's report and the other community studies prevented a full appreciation of rural women's labor throughout the stability-instability project.

Kollmorgen's study remains important for understanding many aspects of Lancaster County Amish life at the end of the Great Depression. A complete understanding of women's part in the story, however, requires the addition of their voices and information that only they could provide, through their diaries, newspaper submissions, oral history narratives, and survey responses for the SCP. Such evidence reveals not only the full significance of Amish women's work, but also the greater complexity of the gender system that Kollmorgen encountered in the early 1940s.

As Amish women catalogued their contributions to the family farm in laborious detail to SCP investigators, they could not help but recognize that their work had an obvious impact on the standard of living and community status of their families. As evidenced by their insistence that they were homemakers who merely "helped" their farmer husbands, Amish women performed their labor within the constraints of what Kollmorgen accurately characterized as a patriarchal family and religious system. The system in which they worked, however, had prescribed and valued roles for all members of the family as they worked toward a common goal: maintaining their sacred way of life on the land.

Conclusion

The Study of Consumer Purchases and other research by the Bureau of Agricultural Economics in the 1930s and early 1940s revealed the relative success of Old Order Amish farming methods and labor arrangements. While many of the nation's other agricultural communities faltered during the Great Depression, the Lancaster County Amish survived and remained on the land their ancestors had been farming for generations. The published reports of the New Deal investigators, while justifiably lauded, fell short in not fully envisioning the significance of women's work to the Amish sustainability story. In filling that gap, the retrieval and examination of women's own voices exposes an important truth: Women's work was an essential glue in holding the Old Order Amish community together and attached to the land.

The meticulous diary that one woman kept in the late 1930s provides a window into the range of chores an Old Order Amish woman performed on a Lancaster County farm. On Fridays, the woman baked bread, pies, and cakes for the weekend. On Saturdays, she thoroughly cleaned the farmhouse, sometimes in anticipation of hosting Sunday worship service or Sunday visitors. During the other days of the week, she performed a varied list of farm and household activities, depending on the season and the work that needed to be done. Her tasks ranged from sewing and mending to canning garden produce to hauling corn. Sixty years later, the collector who acquired the woman's diary marveled at the diversity of her labor and mused about America's agrarian past: "You know, all women were once Amish women."[1]

Amish women's labor of the 1930s indeed looked like the work that all farm women had once performed, and the Amish were not alone in continuing many of these time-honored activities. Other families who successfully sustained their farming operations during the Depression also relied significantly on the labor of wives, mothers, and daughters. These women gardened, raised poultry, made clothing out of feed sacks, and engaged in many of the other activities that sustained Old Order Amish farm households. Many of these women, whether residing in Lancaster County or elsewhere in the United States, did this work without the modern equipment that would become common in non-Amish farm households following World War II. Even if their families owned a few key pieces of equipment, such as a telephone or a farm truck, most farm women of the 1930s labored under material conditions that in numerous ways resembled those of their Amish counterparts. In examining the lives of Old Order Amish farm women, then, one gains clearer insight into the best practices for sustaining family farming in general during the Great Depression.

Whether expressed in diaries, oral history narratives, submissions to *The Budget*, or information shared with SCP agents, Amish women told stories of everyday labor that contributed to their families' ability to remain intact and on the farm. Old Order Amish women's contributions to commodity production, clothing construction and repair, food production and processing, low-cost religious celebrations and recreational activities, and home-based medical care significantly benefited their families. Their efforts earned profits and kept consumer spending to a minimum at a crucial time in the nation's economic history. Motivated by their commitment to a faith that required an agrarian, community-based way of life, Amish women kept up the practices they had always known, but those activities were more important than ever to the survival of family farming during the Depression.

Amish women's labor, like other women's, was vital to the physical survival of their families on the land, but for the former it was also imperative to the maintenance of Amish solidarity and the imagined community beyond Lancaster County borders. In reports to *The Budget*, Lancaster County Amish women described local events—quilting parties, religious rituals, gardening activities—that Amish women elsewhere in Pennsylvania and in Ohio, Indiana, and other locations could relate to and appreciate. In this sharing of Amish ways and values across county and state boundaries, Lancaster County women reinforced a collective religious and cultural identity that undoubtedly strengthened the morale of Depression-era Amish farm families around the country. Surely, when Amish women in Lancaster County read the accounts that Amish women from elsewhere submitted to *The Budget*, they felt a similar sense of encouragement and solidarity.

SCP and BAE research and that of subsequent scholars all point to the qualities and practices that kept US family farming viable during the Depression years and poised to help feed the free world during World War II and its aftermath. A family farming operation had its greatest chance for success when all family members, regardless of gender, were dedicated to working on the land as a permanent, sustainable commitment. Although Lancaster County Amish women were members of a distinctive ethno-religious community, they and their households vividly illustrated the specific characteristics necessary for family farms around the country to survive the Depression years: a dependence on diversified agriculture rather than cash-crop monoculture, a greater reliance on family labor than paid labor, limited consumer spending, women's involvement in farm production, and a commitment to farming as a way of life rather than as a business. While other farming communities followed this blueprint for agricultural success in hard times, none hewed so closely to it as the Old Order Amish. Amish history and religious beliefs predisposed their families to whole-heartedly embrace the practices and mindset necessary to farm successfully when confronted with harsh economic conditions.[2]

In the post–World War II era, the Lancaster County Amish continued functioning within the familiar structures of their religion and culture to maintain their connection to the land, even as many other farm families found it increasingly difficult to do so. By the closing decades of the twentieth century, circumstances had made it impossible for all Old Order Amish to live primarily as farmers in Lancaster County. Their continued high birthrate as well as urban and suburban sprawl meant there simply was not enough available farmland to accommodate every Amish household. As a result, Amish families developed two major survival strategies. One solution was to establish new farming settlements elsewhere in Pennsylvania or in another state. The other solution was to remain in Lancaster County on a small plot of land that allowed for gardening and perhaps a few other small-scale agrarian activities but primarily earn a living in a family-owned business, such as a woodworking shop or a neighborhood grocery store. By the twenty-first century, entrepreneurship rather than farming was the major economic activity of Old Order Amish families in Lancaster County. The basic principles, however, remained the same: commitment to diligent, family-based work in the countryside. The husband and father remained the head of the family, but the wife and mother played a recognized, appreciated, and crucial role in the enterprise. In those businesses that centered primarily on the products of women's labor, such as a bake shop or a quilt shop, the twenty-first-century granddaughter of a 1930s farm woman might enjoy a greater level of influence than her grandmother had known. Nevertheless, the granddaughter owed a measure of her success to the hard-working Amish grandmother who kept the family intact and in place in Lancaster County during the 1930s. Looking back at that difficult time, Lydia Stoltzfus spoke for other Amish of her generation when she noted, "Yes, we struggled some during the Depression. . . . [But] we worked hard. . . . On our farm, I did whatever needed to be done. I stripped tobacco. I mixed donuts. I papered the house. Whatever needed to be done, I did it."[3]

The Study of Consumer Purchases: Survey 1903

Of all the surveys conducted for the New Deal–era Study of Consumer Purchases, Survey 1903 provides the most detailed account of life in an Amish farm family. It undoubtedly concerns an Old Order Amish family, includes all five of the study's survey schedules, and is the only Amish survey, and one of the few completed in Lancaster County in general, that includes the fifth schedule. Of the 1,266 farm surveys that Lancaster County families completed, only 83 include the fifth schedule, and only 55 include all five schedules. Two Old Order Amish households completed the fifth schedule, but only one of those two completed all five schedules. Therefore, SCP Survey 1903 is unique. It is not, however, representative.

SCP 1903 documents one farm household in Salisbury Township and is a revealing sample in many ways. Agent Rigdon, employed by the Works Progress Administration (WPA) and working under the auspices of the Department of Agriculture's Bureau of Home Economics, oversaw completion of the first four schedules, including a clothing record for seven members of the family, all on July 14, 1936. Agent Viola J. Hambright returned in September to complete the seven-day Food Record, dated September 17–24, and Agent R. Groome returned October 21 to complete the clothing record for the eighth family member, the 13-year-old daughter. For purposes of identifying the anonymous family members for this study, they are assigned arbitrary but appropriately Old Order Amish names: Amos King (age 47), his wife Sadie (50), and children Jacob (19), Sarah (16), Mary (15), Rebecca (13), Samuel (11), and Moses (9). In total, the survey schedules and related notes add up to 28 pages of forms filled in by hand (figures A1.1–A1.28).

Why is it so clear that this survey represents an Old Order Amish farm household? Agent Rigdon was particularly assiduous in providing explanatory notes in the margins and between survey sections. Most often, she wrote beside, above, or within the Recreation category, section IX on page 4 of the second schedule. In the case of SCP 1903, she wrote in all capital letters, "THIS IS AN AMISH FAMILY

WHO'S [*sic*] RELIGION DOES NOT PERMIT PAID FOR RECREATION."
Her comment is fairly sophisticated because it acknowledges that while the Amish
certainly believed in fun and games, they did not condone "paid for" recreation,
such as movies or sporting events. In the Personal Care category, section XIII on
page 4, Rigdon wrote, "ALL HAIR CUT BY SOME MEMBER OF FAMILY AT
NO COST." On page 5, section XV, Equipment Owned by Family, she noted that
the household contained a motor-driven washing machine and pedal sewing machine but no piano and no phonograph, radio, or other electric-powered equipment.
When completing the survey's clothing schedules, Rigdon wrote on the first page
of five of the eight schedules, "This is an Amish family who make all their own
clothing possible," or a similar phrase. Of course, there are no automobile expenses,
only $250 in horse-and-buggy expenditures.

The five survey schedules in SCP 1903 contain a remarkable amount of information: family finances; crops produced and sold; farm operation expenses; food
produced, sold, and consumed; contents of the house (such as the type of stove used
for heating and cooking); education; travel; medical expenses; income and debt;
and much more. It is almost difficult to think of a household issue not examined.
Comparisons of quantitative data from SCP 1903 with those from other farm surveys appear in various chapters of this book. This one survey serves to demonstrate
the richness and diversity of the information gathered in Lancaster County during
1935/1936.

U.S. DEPARTMENT OF AGRICULTURE
BUREAU OF HOME ECONOMICS
IN COOPERATION WITH:
NATIONAL RESOURCES COMMITTEE
WORKS PROGRESS ADMINISTRATION
AND
DEPARTMENT OF LABOR
WASHINGTON

STUDY OF CONSUMER PURCHASES
A FEDERAL WORKS PROJECT

FAMILY SCHEDULE—FARM

CONFIDENTIAL—The information requested in this schedule is strictly confidential. Giving it is voluntary. It will not be used for any except sworn agents of the cooperating agencies and will not be available for taxation purposes.

VI. MONEY EARNINGS OF FAMILY FROM EMPLOYMENT OTHER THAN OPERATION OF FARM during schedule year

A	B	C	D	E	F	G
Relationship	Line number from II–A	Age	Occupations during year (give kind of work and nature of industry, such as laborer on road work)	Rate of earnings per unit of time	Time employed (same time unit as in E)	Total money earnings from employment

Members of family gainfully employed

1.
2.
3.
4.
5.
6.
7.
8.
9. Total. (1–9)

VII. OTHER MONEY INCOME during schedule year

	Total for year
1. From roomers and boarders (gross)	$
2. From sale of home-made products	
3. From work in home not entered in VI above (specify)	
4. Interest and dividends from bonds, stocks, bank accounts, trust funds, etc.	
5. Profits not included in VI above, less expenses	
6. Rents from property, less expenses	
7. Pensions, annuities, benefits	

VII. OTHER MONEY INCOME during schedule year—Continued

	Total for year
8. Gifts in cash for current use from persons not members of economic family	$
9. Other money income	
10. Total (1–9)	
11. Losses from business not deducted above	0
12. Difference (10 minus 11)	
13. Has family received direct relief (in cash or kind) during schedule year? a. ☐ Yes. b. ☐ No.	
14. Has any member of family had work relief during schedule year? a. ☐ Cash. b. ☐ Kind. c. ☐ None.	

VIII. VALUE OF PRODUCTS FURNISHED BY FARM FOR FAMILY'S OWN USE during schedule year

		Total value for year
1. Milk for drinking and cooking:		$
Quarts per week		
Number of weeks	52	
2. Cream for table use and for butter:	0	
Quarts per week		0
Number of weeks		
3. Eggs:		
Fall and winter: Dozen per week		39.00
Number of weeks		
Spring and summer: Dozen per week		
Number of weeks		
4. Poultry for meat:		
Winter and spring: Number per month		
Number of months		
Summer and fall: Number per month		
Number of months		
5. Pork, dressed weight: Pounds for year		0
6. Other meats, dressed weight: Pounds for year		0
7. Potatoes (white): Bushels for year		
8. Value of other food from farm garden		
9. Value of fruits		
10. Value of other food (sirups, grain products, etc.)		
11. Value of fuel		
12. Value of other products (wool, tobacco, etc.)		
13. Total		

IX. TOTAL INCOME (III–13 minus IV–13 plus IV–13 plus VI–9 plus VII–12 plus VIII–13) ...... $

X. COLOR: a. ☐ White. b. ☐ Negro.

CONFIDENTIAL

The information requested in this schedule is strictly confidential. Giving it is voluntary. It will not be seen by any except sworn agents of the cooperating agencies and will not be available for taxation purposes.

U. S. DEPARTMENT OF AGRICULTURE
BUREAU OF HOME ECONOMICS
IN COOPERATION WITH
NATIONAL RESOURCES COMMITTEE
WORKS PROGRESS ADMINISTRATION
DEPARTMENT OF LABOR
WASHINGTON

STUDY OF CONSUMER PURCHASES
A FEDERAL WORKS PROJECT
EXPENDITURE SCHEDULE—FARM

Code No. _____
Family Schedule No. _____
Expenditure Schedule No. 1903
Inc. _____ County _____
Clr. _____ State _____
Agent _____ M. C. D. _____
Date of interview _____, 1936

YEAR COVERED BY SCHEDULE
12 months beginning _____, 1935
and ending _____, 1936

I. COMPOSITION OF ECONOMIC FAMILY

	A	B	C	D	E
	Members of family	Sex	Age	Number of weeks— At home	Away
1. Husband		M	47	52	0
2. Wife		F	50	52	0
3. Son		M	19	52	0
4. Daughter		F	16	52	0
5. Daughter		F	15	52	0
6. Daughter		F	13	52	0
7. Son		M	11	52	0
8. S.		M	9	52	0

II. FAMILY DWELLING

1. Total number of rooms (exclude bathroom)...... 7
2. Total number of persons occupying these rooms (include family, paid help, roomers, others)...... 8

	A For kitchen	B For bathtub or shower
3. Water supply, indoors:		
a. Running hot and cold		
b. Running cold only		
c. Hand pump, only		
d. None		

4. Kitchen sink with drain pipe:
   a. ☐ Yes. b. ☑ No.
5. Toilet (check one):
   a. ☐ Indoor, flush.
   b. ☐ Indoor, other.
   c. ☑ Outdoor (privy).
   d. ☐ None.
6. Cooking fuel (check one):
   a. ☐ Wood, coal, cobs.
   b. ☐ Kerosene or gasoline.
   c. ☐ Electricity.
   d. ☐ Gas.
   e. ☑ Both a and b.
   f. ☐ Other combinations.

7. Heating, principal method (check one):
   a. ☐ Central furnace.
   b. ☑ Stoves other than kitchen. Number 2
   c. ☐ Fireplace.
   d. ☐ Kitchen stove only.
   e. ☐ None.
8. Lighting (check one):
   a. ☐ Kerosene. Electricity:
   b. ☐ Power line.
   c. ☐ Home plant.
   d. ☑ Other. Gasoline

8-9554

III. HOUSING EXPENSE DURING SCHEDULE YEAR

	Expense for year
1. Structural additions to home during year...... $	X X X
2. Repairs and replacements paid for by family	0122.00
3. Insurance premiums on house (fire, tornado, other)	017.00
3a. Sub Total 2-3	0139.00
4. Vacation home owned: Net expense	0
5. Vacation home rented (rent and repairs)	0
6. Lodging while traveling or on vacation	0
7. Rent at school (transfer from IV, 12)	0
8. Other	
8a. Sub Total 4-8	
9. TOTAL (2-8)	$0139.00
10. Money value of housing received without direct money payment...... $	

IV. EDUCATION

	A	B	C	D	E
School attended during schedule year		Members attending (Give line number from IA) Public	Private	Expense for year Tuition fees	Books and supplies
1. Kindergarten; nursery school				$ 0	$ 0
2. Elementary school				0	0
3. High or prep. school				0	0
4. Business or tech. school				0	0
5. College, graduate, or professional school				0	0

	F Item of expense	G Expense for year	H Previous education
6. Total: Tuition (1–5D)	$ 0	Highest grade completed by:
7. Total: Books and supplies (1–5E)	0	13. Husband 8
8. Special lessons	0	14. Wife
9. Other (exclude board and rent)		15. Son or daughter over 16 years with most schooling
10. TOTAL (6–9)	0	a. Sex: ☐ M.
11. Board at school		b. Age 21
12. Rent at school	0	c. Member of economic family: ☐ Yes. ☑ No.
(Transfer board at school to food, VIII 20; rent to housing, III, 7)		

V. HOUSEHOLD OPERATION

FUEL, LIGHT, REFRIGERATION	B Quantity purchased in year	C Price per unit	D Expense for year
1. Coal purchased:			
Winter (DJF)____tons	x x x		x x x
Fall (SON)____tons	x x x		x x x
Summer (JJA)____tons	x x x		x x x
Spring (MAM)____tons	x x x		x x x
Total____tons	x x x		
2. Coke, briquettes			
3. Wood and kindling			
4. Kerosene for fuel and light	____gal.		
5. Gasoline for fuel and light	____gal.		
6. Fuel oil	____gal.		

AVERAGE EXPENSE PER MONTH

	Winter Dec.-Feb.	Fall Sept.-Nov.	Summer June-Aug.	Spring March-May
7. Electricity (purchased)				
8. Gas				
9. Ice (purchased)				
10. Total (1–9)	x x x	x x x	x x x	x x x
11. Money value of fuel and ice obtained without direct money payment				

PAID HOUSEHOLD HELP	B Persons customarily employed (number)	C Meals usually furnished to each person (number daily)	D Total time of service in year and wage rate	E Expense for year
12. By hour			____hrs. @ $____	
13. By day			____days @ $____	
14. By week			____wks. @ $____	
15. By month			____mos. @ $____	
16. Aprons furnished and other gifts to paid help				
17. Total (12–16)				$
18. Living quarters furnished to:	Yes	No		
a. Help paid by hour	☐	☐		
b. Help paid by day	☐	☐		
c. Help paid by week	☐	☐		
d. Help paid by month	☐	☐		

OTHER HOUSEHOLD OPERATION

	Expense for year
19. Telephone: Number mos.____ Per mo., $____	
20. Laundry soap and other cleaning supplies	
21. Laundry sent out: Number wks.____ Per wk., $____	
22. Stationery, postage, telegrams	
23. Express, freight, drayage, moving	
24. Water rent	
25. Other	
26. Total (18–25)	$
27. Total for household operation (sum of 10, 17, and 26)	$

VI. AUTOMOBILE
Owned at any time during schedule year

1. How many months during year did you own:
a. 1 auto____mos.; b. 2 autos____mos.
c. 3 autos____mos.; d. No auto____mos.

AUTOMOBILE OWNED AT END OF SCHEDULE YEAR

A YEAR BOUGHT	B New (check)	C Used (check)	D Make	E Price
2. 19__				$
3. 19__				
4. 19__				

5. Gross price of car bought during year. $____
6. Trade-in allowance on used car____ $____
7. Net price of car bought (5 minus 6)__ $____
8. Terms: a. ☐ cash; b. ☐ installments.
9. Month bought ____
10. Total miles driven during year (all cars owned)____miles.
11. Average miles per gallon of gasoline____miles.

GASOLINE FOR AUTO	Miles per quarter	Number gallons bought	Expense for quarter	Expense for year
12. Winter			$	x x x
13. Fall				x x x
14. Summer				x x x
15. Spring				x x x
16. Total for year (12–15)				$

17. Oil: Number of quarts____ $
18. Tires, tubes: Purchase
19. Repairs, replacements, service
20. Garage rent, parking
21. Licenses, including registration fees
22. Fines, damages paid others
23. Automobile insurance (all types)
24. Tolls (bridge, ferry, tunnel)
25. Accessories (include automobile radio)
26. Other (include association dues)
27. Total (7 plus 16 plus 17–26) $
28. Proportion of automobile expense chargeable to business____ x x x

VII. OTHER TRAVEL AND TRANSPORTATION

	Expense for year
Local—to work, school, stores:	
1. Bus, trolley, taxi, train, ferry, boat, rent of auto	$
Other travel (exclude business travel):	
2. Railroad (include Pullman)	
3. Interurban bus and trolley	
4. Other (specify vehicle)	
Purchase and upkeep during year:	
5. Of motorcycle	
6. Of horse and carriage for family use	
7. Of boat or other conveyance	
8. Total (1–7)	
9. Proportion of motorcycle, horse and carriage, or other vehicle expense chargeable to business	

VIII. FOOD

USUAL EXPENSE FOR FOOD AT HOME DURING EACH SEASON OF SCHEDULE YEAR

THIS IS AN AVERAGE WEEKLY FOOD COST FOR EACH WEEK OF YEAR.

A ITEM	B Winter 1935-36 Dec., Jan., Feb.		C Fall 1935 Sept., Oct., Nov.		D Summer 1935 June, July, Aug.		E Spring 1936 March, Apr., May	
	Per week	Per month	Per week	Per month	Per week	Per month	Per week	Per month
EXPENSE AT—								
1. Grocery or general store (exclude soap and other supplies included as household operation)	$2.25	$	$2.25	$	$2.25	$	$2.25	$
2. Meat, fish: Market or farm	2.00		2.00		2.00		2.00	
3. Dairy farm or creamery 4 # Butter @ 25¢	1.00		1.00		1.00		1.00	
4. Vegetable and fruit: Market or farm			0		0		0	
5. Bakery MAKE OWN BREAD	0		0		0		0	
ADDITIONAL EXPENSE FOR FOOD AT HOME								
6. Ice cream, candy	0		0		0		0	
7. Soft drinks, beer, other drinks	0		0		0		0	
8. Other food at home	0		0		0		0	
9. TOTAL FOR WEEK OR MONTH	5.25		5.25		5.25		5.25	
10. TOTAL FOR SEASON	299.00	$ 74.75	$ 74.25		$ 74.25		$ 74.75	

FOOD AWAY FROM HOME
(Exclude board while away at school and meals carried from home)

A ITEM	B Amount per week	C Number of weeks in year	D Total for year
11. Meals at work	$		$
12. Lunches at school			
13. Meals while traveling or on vacation			
14. Other meals away from home			
15. Ice cream, candy			
16. Soft drinks, beer, etc.			
17. TOTAL (11–16)	x x x	x x x	$ 0

TOTAL FOOD EXPENSE DURING SCHEDULE YEAR

18. Food at home (add line 10)	$
19. Food away from home (line 17)	0
20. Board at school (transfer from education)	0
21. TOTAL (18–20)	299

MONEY VALUE OF FOOD RAISED AT HOME OR RECEIVED AS GIFT OR PAY DURING SCHEDULE YEAR

Value for year

22. Food received as gift or pay	$
23. Food raised for family's own use	
24. TOTAL (22–23)	

FOOD CANNED AT HOME DURING SCHEDULE YEAR

25. Vegetables	Quarts	180
26. Sauerkraut	Gallons	
27. Fruit	Quarts	050
28. Jellies, jams	Pints	015
29. Pickles, relishes	Quarts	025
30. Poultry, meats	Quarts	
31. Other	Quarts	060

32. Of food canned at home, what proportion was home produced:

More than half	Less than half	
☐	☐	Vegetables.
☐	☐	Fruits.
☐	☐	Poultry, meats.

(8)

127

THIS IS AN AMISH FAMILY WHO'S RELIGION DOES NOT PERMIT PAID FOR RECREATION. u 7

IX. RECREATION

PAID ADMISSION TO—

	Expense for year
1. Movies: Adults	$
2. Children	
3. Plays, pageants, lectures, concerts	0
4. Ball games, other spectator sports	0
5. Fairs, circuses, dances, other	0
6. TOTAL (1-5)	$ 0

GAMES AND SPORTS

Equipment, supplies, fees, licenses (Enter year's expense for each item)

7. Hunting.... $.....; fishing.... $.....;
   camping.......... $.......; trapping
   (sport)...... $.......; hiking.... $.....;
   riding.... $.....; boating.... $.....;
   tennis........ $.....; golf...... $.....;
   baseball..... $.....; bicycles.. $.....;
   skates, sleds, skis............ $.....;
   billiards and bowling........... $.....;
   cards, chess, other games..... $.....;
   other............ $.....;
8. TOTAL (all items of 7).... $ 0

OTHER RECREATION

9. Radio: Purchase (exclude auto radio)	$ 0
10. Batteries, tubes, repairs	0
11. Musical instruments: Kind	0
12. Sheet music, phonograph records	0
13. Cameras, films, photo supplies	0
14. Children's toys, play equipment	0
15. Pets (purchase and care) Dog License	01
16. Entertaining in and out of home (exclude family meals)	0
17. Dues to social and recreational clubs	
18. Other (specify)	
19. TOTAL (9-18)	$ 1 X X
20. TOTAL recreation (6, 8, and 19)	$ 1 X

X. READING

1. Newspapers: Daily	$ 0
2. Weekly	0
3. Magazines (subscriptions and single copies) 2 YEARLY	05 1 00
4. Books (not school books) bought during year: Number	0
5. Book rentals and library fees (public and rental libraries)	0
6. Books borrowed from public and rental libraries: Number 0	X X X X X
7. TOTAL (1-5)	$ 0 1 00

8-9575   (4)

XI. TOBACCO

	Expense for year
1. Cigarettes: Packages per week, ...; price ...... cents	$ 0
2. Cigars: Number per week, 4; price 3 FOR cents 5T	005 520
3. Tobacco: All other Chewing ST 50 WK	026 26 180
4. Smokers' supplies	0
5. TOTAL (1-4)	$ 031

XII. MEDICAL CARE

Item 02609

	A	B Check if any free	C Expense for year
1. Physician: office visits at $			$ 0
2. home calls at $	0/4		005 028 00
3. Dentist	04		014 00
4. Oculist			0
5. Other specialist (specify)			0
6. Clinic visits: 0 at $			0
7. Hospital room or bed: 0 days at $			0
8. Private nurse: At hospital, 0 days at $			0
9. At home, 0 days at $			0
10. Visiting nurse: 0 visits at $			0
11. Examinations and tests (not included above)			0
12. Medicines and drugs EST			010 00
13. Eyeglasses 2 Pc			18 00
14. Medical appliances and supplies			0
15. Premiums on health and accident insurance			
16. Other			0
17. TOTAL (1-16)			070 00

XIII. PERSONAL CARE

ALL HAIR CUT SERVICES BY SOME MEMBER OF FAMILY AT NO COST

	Expense for year
1. Wife: Haircuts, shampoos, waves, manicures, facials, other	$ 0
2. Husband: Haircuts, shaves, shampoos, other	0
3. Children under 16 years of age: Haircuts, other services	0
4. Other members of family: Haircuts, other services	0
5. TOTAL (1-4)	$ 0

TOILET ARTICLES AND PREPARATIONS

6. Toilet soap cakes at 5 cents	$ 02 00
7. Tooth paste, tooth powder, mouthwash	05 00
8. Shaving soap and cream EST	01 00
9. Cold cream, powder, rouge, perfume, nail polish	0
10. Brushes, combs, razors, files, other toilet articles	10 00
11. Other	
12. TOTAL (6-11)	00
13. TOTAL personal care (5 plus 12)	$ 00

128

XIV. GIFTS, COMMUNITY WELFARE, TAXES

	Expense for year
1. Gifts (Christmas, birthday, other) to persons not members of economic family (non-charity)	$ 0
2. Contributions to support of relatives not members of economic family	0
3. Donations to other individuals	
4. Community chest and other welfare agencies	
5. Church, Sunday school, missions	225.00
6. Taxes payable in schedule year: Poll, income (except back taxes)	004.00
7. Other	0
8. TOTAL (1-7)	

XV. EQUIPMENT OWNED BY FAMILY
(At end of schedule year)

A Item	Owned at end of schedule year Yes	No	D Price if purchased in schedule year
1. Radio		✓	x x x x
2. Piano		✓	x x x x
3. Phonograph		✓	x x x x
4. Pressure cooker		✓	0
5. Refrigerator: Mechanical		✓	0
6. Ice		✓	0
7. Washing machine: Motor driven	✓		0
8. Other			0
9. Ironing machine		✓	0
10. Vacuum cleaner		✓	0
11. Sewing machine: Electric		✓	0
12. Other Pedal	✓		0
13. TOTAL (4-12)	x x x x		$ 0

XVI. FURNISHING SAND EQUIPMENT (Purchased during schedule year and not included in 4 to 12 above)
(Do not fill out if check list is used)

SEE CHECK LIST

	Expense for year
1. Kitchen, cleaning, laundry equipment	024.00
2. Glass, china, silver	003 3.00
3. Household linens, blankets, curtains, other textiles	0208.50
4. Floor coverings	0
5. Furniture	
6. Other	0121.25
7. TOTAL (1-6)	$ 55.75

XVII. CLOTHING EXPENSE (During schedule year)
(Do not fill out if check list is used)

SEE CHECK LIST

A	Wife Age 50	Husband Age 47	2-3 Age 19	2-4 Age 16	2-5 Age 15	2-6 Age 13	2-7 Age 11	2-8 Age 9
1. Hats, caps, berets	$ 0	$ 2.00	$ 3.25	$ 0	$ 0	$ 0	$ 0	$ 0
2. Coats, raincoats, jackets, sweaters, furs	0	8.95	0	0	0	0	0	0
3. Women's suits, dresses, skirts, blouses, aprons	0		0	0	0	0	0	0
4. Men's suits, trousers, overalls, shirts	0		0	0	0	0	0	0
5. Bathing suits, beach kimonos, riding habits, other special sportswear	0	0	0	0	0	0	0	0
6. Underwear, nightwear, bathrobes, hose	4.50	4.50		4.50	5.00	5.00		2.00
7. Footwear, including repairs	6.00		10.00		7.00	7.00	6.00	6.00
8. Gloves, handkerchiefs, umbrellas, purses, ties, jewelry, other accessories		1.55						1.00
9. Materials, paid help for sewing	17.00	11.45						
10. Cleaning and pressing								
11. TOTAL (1-10)	22.00	30.25		25.00	25.00			$ 18.00
12. Money value of clothing received as gifts	0	0	0	0	0	0	0	0

8-9554

(5)

129

XVIII. OTHER FAMILY EXPENSE
During schedule year

	Expense for year
1. Interest on debts incurred for family living (other than mortgages on own home)	$ 0
2. Did family have checking account at any time during schedule year? a. ☑ Yes	
b. ☐ No.	
3. Bank service charges, safe deposit box	0
4. Legal expense (not business)	0
5. Losses other than business losses	0
6. Funeral, cemetery	0
7. Other	0
8. TOTAL (1-7)	$ 0

XIX. OCCUPATIONAL EXPENSE
Not reported as business expense or as deductions from gross income

	Expense for year
1. Union dues	$
2. Professional or business association dues	
3. Technical books and journals	
4. Supplies and equipment (business)	
5. Other	
6. TOTAL (1-5)	$ 0

XX. PREVIOUS OCCUPATION OF HUSBAND

1. Was husband's occupation same during schedule year as in 1929? a. ☑ Yes b. ☐ No
2. If not, his occupation in 1929 was

XXI. CHANGES IN FAMILY ASSETS AND LIABILITIES DURING SCHEDULE YEAR ____, 1935, TO ____, 1936
(Exclude changes due to increases or decreases in the value of property which has not changed hands)

CHANGES IN PROPERTY OWNED BY FAMILY AND AMOUNTS DUE FAMILY

CHANGES IN DEBTS OWED BY FAMILY

A	B	C	D	E	F
MONEY, STOCKS, REAL ESTATE, OTHER ASSETS	Changes in assets during schedule year		LIABILITIES	Changes in liabilities during schedule year	
	Net amount of increase	Net amount of decrease		Net amount of increase	Net amount of decrease
1. Money in savings accounts	0	0	21. Mortgages on owned home farm	0	175.00
2. In checking accounts	2650	0	22. Mortgages on other real estate	0	0
3. On hand		0	23. Notes due to banks, insurance companies, small loan companies	0	0
4. Investments in business	1399.50		24. Notes due to individuals	0	0
5. Real estate: Purchased		x x x	25. Back rents (due before schedule year)	x x x	0
6. Sold	x x x	0	26. Rents due in schedule year, unpaid	0	x x x
7. Stocks and bonds: Purchased		x x x	27. Back taxes (due before schedule year)	x x x	0
8. Sold	x x x	0	28. Taxes due in schedule year, unpaid	0	x x x
9. Other property: Purchased	0	x x x	29. Charge accounts due	0	0
10. Sold	x x x	0	30. Other bills due	0	0
11. Improvements on owned home farm	0	x x x	31. Payments on installment purchases made prior to schedule year (specify goods purchased):		
12. Improvements on other real estate	0	x x x	a.	x x x	0
13. Insurance premiums paid (life, endowment, annuity)	0	x x x	b.	x x x	0
14. Frequency of payment:			c.	x x x	0
15. Insurance policies surrendered	x x x	0	32. Balance due on installment purchases made in schedule year (specify goods purchased):		
16. Insurance policies settled	x x x	0	a.	0	x x x
17. Loans made by family to others during schedule year (balance not repaid)	0	x x x	b.	0	x x x
18. Repayments to family on loans made before schedule year	x x x	0	c.	0	x x x
19. Other (specify)	2048 2048		33. Other (specify)		
20. TOTAL (1-19)	2049.50	0	34. TOTAL (21-33)	0	175.00

INVESTMENT + 2223
5-GASOLINE LAMPS FOR CHICKEN HOUSE @ 6 ea. 32.50 (32.50) 258T-0 2049.50
9 HORSES 66.00 175
3-REGISTERED CALVES @ 50 each 100.00 +222.50
8-COWS @ 75 " 600.00
1399.50

U.S. GOVERNMENT PRINTING OFFICE 8-9554

2223

BOX 1296.2   1903   9

F 2004

U. S. DEPARTMENT OF AGRICULTURE
BUREAU OF HOME ECONOMICS
IN COOPERATION WITH
NATIONAL RESOURCES COMMITTEE
WORKS PROGRESS ADMINISTRATION
AND DEPARTMENT OF LABOR
WASHINGTON
STUDY OF
CONSUMER PURCHASES
A FEDERAL WORKS PROJECT
CLOTHING PURCHASES
DURING SCHEDULE YEAR
(Check list)
MAN OR BOY

CONFIDENTIAL
The information requested in this schedule is strictly confidential. Giving it is voluntary. It will not be seen by any except sworn agents of the cooperating agencies and will not be available for taxation purposes.

Year covered by schedule:
12 months beginning ___ 1, 1935
and ending ___ 3, 193 6
Family member (check):
1 Husband: Age 47 years. 9
2. Other male (over 2 years).
Age ___ years.
No. weeks in economic family 52

Code No. 61 - X137
Expenditure schedule No. 3435
Town, village ___
County ___ State ___
E. D. or M. C. D. ___
Agent ___
Date of interview ___ 14, 1936
Number persons in economic family 8
Occupation of husband FARMER
Clr. ___ Inc. 3818

	A	B	C	D	E	A	B	C	D	E
	ITEM	Number	Price	Expense for schedule year	Season purchased	ITEM	Number	Price	Expense for schedule year	Season purchased
	Hats, caps:			3.50		39. Underdrawers: Cotton	0	$	$	
1.	Hats: Felt	1	$3.50	3.50		40. Cotton and wool	0			
2.	Straw	0				41. Rayon, silk	0			
3.	Caps: Wool	0				42. Pajamas, nightshirts	0			
4.	Other	0				43. Bathrobes, lounging robes	0			
	Coats, jackets, sweaters:			0		44. Hose: Cotton, dress	0			
5.	Overcoats	0				45. Cotton, heavy	0			
6.	Topcoats	0				46. Rayon, silk	0			
7.	Raincoats	0				47. Wool	0			
8.	Jackets: Wool	0				48. Other	12	20	2.40	
9.	Leather	0				Footwear:	0		4.48	
10.	Other	0				49. Shoes: Work				
11.	Sweaters: Wool	0				50. Work	1	1.98	1.98	
12.	Other	0				51. Street	0			
	Suits, trousers, overalls:	0		0		52. Street	1	2.50	2.50	
13.	Suits: Heavy-wool					53. Sport	0			
14.	Light-wool	0				54. Other	0			
15.	Cotton, linen	0				55. Boots: Rubber	0			
16.	Palm-beach	0				56. Leather	0			
17.	Child's sun suit	0				57. Arctics	0			
18.	Other	0				58. Rubbers	0			
19.	Trousers: Wool	0				59. Shoe shines, repairs	0			
20.	Cotton					Gloves, handkerchiefs, other accessories:			1.35	
21.	Other					60. Gloves: Cotton, work				
22.	Overalls, coveralls	0				61. Other, work				
	Shirts:					62. Leather, street				
23.	Shirts and blouses: Cotton, work					63. Other, street				
24.	Cotton, other					64. Handkerchiefs				
25.	Rayon, silk					65. Ties				
26.	Wool					66. Collars				
27.	Other					67. Belts, garters, suspenders			1	
	Special sports wear:			0		68. Jewelry	0			
28.	Bathing suits					69. Other accessories	0		17.00	
29.	Other special sports clothes: Cotton					Home sewing:				
30.	Other			3.90		70. Yard goods: Cotton		30	3.00	
31.	Union suits: Cotton, knit	1	1.50	1.50		71. Other materials and findings		2.50		
32.	Cotton, woven	0				72. Paid help for sewing	xx	xx		xx
33.	Cotton and wool					Upkeep:			0	
34.	Rayon, silk					73. Cleaning, pressing	0			
35.	Undershirts: Cotton					Other clothing expense:	0		0	
36.	Cotton and wool					74. (Specify)				
37.	Rayon, silk					75. TOTAL	1	xx	xx	$39.23	xx
38.	Underwaists					76. Money value of clothing received as gift or pay $				

(8)   8—9877

131

1903

Case no. 61 - N37
Expenditure Schedule No. 34335
Grp. Salisbury
County fame. State Pen...
M.C.B. - 36 - 112
Agent. Rigdon
Date of Interview July 14 - 1936
Number in Econ. Fam. - 8

ITEM	Number	Price	Expense for schedule year	Season purchased	ITEM	Number	Price	Expense for schedule year	Season purchased
Hats, caps:			3.00		39. Underdrawers: Cotton	0	$		
1. Hats: Felt	1	$2.50	$2.50	1	40. Cotton and wool	0			
2. Straw	1	.50	.50		41. Rayon, silk	0			
3. Caps: Wool					42. Pajamas, nightshirts	0			
4. Other	0				43. Bathrobes, lounging robes	0			
Coats, jackets, sweaters:			198		44. Hose: Cotton, dress	0			
5. Overcoats	0				45. Cotton, heavy	0			
6. Topcoats	0				46. Rayon, silk	0			
7. Raincoats	0				47. Wool	0			
8. Jackets: Wool					48. Other 47 Cotton	12	15	185	
9. Leather	0				Footwear:				
10. Other					49. Shoes: Work	1	1.75	1.75	S
11. Sweaters: Wool					50. Work	1	2.00	2.00	
12. Other Cotton	1	1.75	1.75 F		51. Street	1	2.50	2.50	Su
Suits, trousers, overalls:			0		52. Street	0			
13. Suits: Heavy-wool	0				53. Sport	0			
14. Light-wool	0				54. Other	0			
15. Cotton, linen	0				55. Boots: Rubber	1	3.75	3.75	W
16. Palm-beach	0				56. Leather	0			
17. Child's sun suit	0				57. Arctics	0			
18. Other	0				58. Rubbers				
19. Trousers: Wool	0				59. Shoe shines, repairs				
20. Cotton	0				Gloves, handkerchiefs, other accessories:			1.20	
21. Other	0				60. Gloves: Cotton, work	0			
22. Overalls, coveralls	0				61. Other, work	0			
Shirts:					62. Leather, street	0			
23. Shirts and blouses: Cotton, work					63. Other, street	0			
24. Cotton, other					64. Handkerchiefs				
25. Rayon, silk					65. Ties				
26. Wool					66. Collars				
27. Other					67. Belts, garters, suspenders				
Special sports wear:			0		68. Jewelry				
28. Bathing suits	0				69. Other accessories			1.50	
29. Other special sports clothes: Cotton					Home sewing:				
30. Other					70. Yard goods: Cotton				
Underwear, nightwear, hose:			1.90		71. Other materials and findings				
31. Union suits: Cotton, knit					72. Paid help for sewing	xx	xx	0	xx
32. Cotton, woven					Upkeep:				
33. Cotton and wool					73. Cleaning, pressing	0		0	
34. Rayon, silk					Other clothing expense:				
35. Undershirts: Cotton					74. (Specify)	0		0	
36. Cotton and wool	0				75. TOTAL		xx	xx	$31.18	xx
37. Rayon, silk					76. Money value of clothing received as gift or pay	$ 0			
38. Underwaists									

(4)

8—9577

132

1903

2009

B. H. E. Form 106

CONFIDENTIAL

The information requested in this schedule is strictly confidential. Giving it is voluntary. It will not be seen by any except sworn agents of the cooperating agencies and will not be available for taxation purposes.

U. S. DEPARTMENT OF AGRICULTURE
BUREAU OF HOME ECONOMICS
IN COOPERATION WITH
NATIONAL RESOURCES COMMITTEE
WORKS PROGRESS ADMINISTRATION
AND DEPARTMENT OF LABOR
WASHINGTON

STUDY OF

CONSUMER PURCHASES
A FEDERAL WORKS PROJECT

CLOTHING PURCHASES
DURING SCHEDULE YEAR
(Check list)
WOMAN OR GIRL

Year covered by schedule:
12 months beginning ___/___, 1935
and ending ___/___, 1936

Family member (check): ___
☑ Wife: Age 50 years ___
☐ Other female (over 2 years).
Age ___ years.
No. weeks in economic family 52

Code No. 61 - X137
Expenditure schedule No. ___
Town, village ___
County ___ State Cal.
E. D. or M. C. B. ___
Agent C. SIMON
Date of interview ___, 1936
Number persons in economic family 8
Occupation of husband FARMER
Clr. White ___ Inc. 3918

White
M. Inc - 30

A	B	C	D	E	A	B	C	D	E
ITEM	Number	Price	Expense for schedule year	Season purchased	ITEM	Number	Price	Expense for schedule year	Season purchased
Hats, caps, berets:			0		34. Dresses: Cotton, street	0	$	$	
1. Hats: Felt	2	$	$ 0		35. Cotton, street	0			
2. Felt	0				36. Cotton, house	0			
3. Straw	2				37. Cotton, house	2			
4. Fabric	2				38. Other	0			
5. Caps, berets: Wool	2				39. Child's sun suit	2			
6. Other	2				40. Aprons, smocks	0			
Coats, raincoats, jackets, sweaters, furs:					41. Coveralls	0			
7. Coats: Heavy, with fur	0		0		Special sportswear:			0	
8. Heavy, no fur	0				42. Bathing suits	0			
9. Fur	0				43. Beach pajamas	0			
10. Light-wool	0				44. Knickers, breeches, shorts	0			
11. Cotton	2				45. Other special sports clothes: Cotton	0			
12. Rayon, silk	0				46. Other	0			
13. Raincoats	0				Underwear, nightwear, hose:			3.50	
14. Jackets: Wool	0				47. Slips: Cotton	0			
15. Leather	2				48. Rayon, silk	0			
16. Other	0				49. Corsets, girdles	0			
17. Sweaters: Wool	0				50. Brassieres	0			
18. Other	0				51. Union suits, combinations: Cotton	0			
19. Furs	0				52. Rayon, silk	0			
Suits, skirts, blouses, dresses:			0		53. Wool	0			
20. Suits: Wool, with fur	0				54. Underwaists, shirts: Cotton	0			
21. Wool, no fur	0				55. Rayon, silk	0			
22. Rayon, silk	0				56. Bloomers, panties: Cotton	0			
23. Other	0				57. Rayon, silk	0			
24. Skirts: Wool	0				58. Other	0			
25. Other	0				59. Nightgowns, pajamas: Cotton flannel	0			
26. Blouses, waists: Cotton	0				60. Cotton, other	0			
27. Linen	0				61. Rayon, silk	0			
28. Rayon, silk	0				62. Bathrobes	0			
29. Other	0				63. Kimonos, negligees	0			
30. Dresses: Wool	0								
31. Wool	0								
32. Rayon, silk	0								
33. Rayon, silk	0								

(1)

8—9577

133

1903   12

CLOTHING PURCHASES, WOMAN OR GIRL—Continued					CLOTHING PURCHASES, CHILDREN UNDER 2 YEARS				
A	B	C	D	E	A	B	C	D	E
ITEM	Number	Price	Expense for schedule year	Season purchased	ITEM	Number	Price	Expense for schedule year	Season purchased
64. Hose: Rayon, silk	0	$	$		Ready-to-wear:				
65. Cotton	1/0	35	3.20		1. Caps, hoods, bonnets		$	$	
66. Wool	0		6.00		2. Coats				
Footwear:					3. Snow or sweater suits				
67. Shoes: Street	1/1	2.00	2.00		4. Sweaters, sacques				
68. Street	0				5. Dresses, rompers				
69. Dress	X/1	3.00	3.00	F3	6. Sun suits				
70. Dress	0				7. Skirts, gertrudes				
71. Sport	0				8. Shirts, bands				
72. Other	0				9. Diapers				
73. Other	0				10. Sleeping garments				
74. House slippers	0				11. Stockings				
75. Arctics, gaiters	X/1	1.20	1.00		12. Bootees, shoes				
76. Rubbers	0				13. Layette				
77. Shoe shines	0				14. Other				
78. Shoe repairs	0				Yard goods:				
Gloves, handkerchiefs, other accessories:			50		15. Diaper cloth				
79. Gloves: Cotton	0				16. Other cotton				
80. Silk, rayon	0				17. Other				
81. Leather	0				18. Wool				
82. Wool	0				19. Rayon, silk				
83. Handkerchiefs	1/0	25	.50		20. Paid help for sewing	x x	x x		x x
84. Handbags, purses	0				21. TOTAL	x x	x x	$.0	x x
85. Umbrellas	0				22. Money value of clothing received as gift, $				
86. Jewelry	0								
87. Other accessories	0				II. 2d child: Age, ... months; no. wks. in econ. family				
Home sewing:			14.00		Ready-to-wear:				
88. Yard goods: Cotton	3.00				1. Caps, hoods, bonnets		$	$	
89. Cotton	X 2.5	1.8	4.50		2. Coats				
90. Cotton	0				3. Snow or sweater suits				
91. Linen	0				4. Sweaters, sacques				
92. Rayon	0				5. Dresses, rompers				
93. Rayon	0				6. Sun suits				
94. Silk	0				7. Skirts, gertrudes				
95. Silk	0				8. Shirts, bands				
96. Silk	0				9. Diapers				
97. Wool	X		2.10		10. Sleeping garments				
98. Other	0				11. Stockings				
99. Findings	X ENIT		1.50		12. Bootees, shoes				
100. Paid help for sewing	x x	x x	2	x x	13. Layette				
Upkeep:			0		14. Other				
101. Cleaning, pressing	0				Yard goods:				
Other clothing expense:			0		15. Diaper cloth				
102. (Specify)	0				16. Other cotton				
103. TOTAL	1	x x	x x	$22.00	x x	17. Other				
104. Money value of clothing received as gift or pay $			0		18. Wool				
					19. Rayon, silk				
					20. Paid help for sewing	x x	x x		x x
					21. TOTAL	x x	x x	$.0	x x
					22. Money value of clothing received as gift $.0				

(2)

8—9577

134

1903

F 2009

13

B. H. E. Form 108
CONFIDENTIAL

The information requested in this schedule is strictly confidential. Giving it is voluntary. It will not be seen by any except sworn agents of the cooperating agencies and will not be available for taxation purposes.

U. S. DEPARTMENT OF AGRICULTURE
BUREAU OF HOME ECONOMICS
IN COOPERATION WITH
NATIONAL RESOURCES COMMITTEE
WORKS PROGRESS ADMINISTRATION
AND DEPARTMENT OF LABOR
WASHINGTON

STUDY OF
CONSUMER PURCHASES
A FEDERAL WORKS PROJECT
CLOTHING PURCHASES
DURING SCHEDULE YEAR
(Check list)
WOMAN OR GIRL

Year covered by schedule
12 months beginning ____, 1935
and ending ____, 1936

Family member (check):
Wife: Age ____ years.
Other female (over 2 years).
Age 16 years.
No. weeks in economic family ____

Code No. 61 - X137
Expenditure schedule No. ____
Town, village S. Salisbury
County ____ State ____
E. D. or M. C. D. 36-112 Salisbury
Agent A. Googn
Date of interview ____-14, 1936
Number persons in economic family 8
Occupation of husband Farmer
Clr. White Inc. 3918

A	B	C	D	E	A	B	C	D	E
ITEM	Number	Price	Expense for schedule year	Season purchased	ITEM	Number	Price	Expense for schedule year	Season purchased
Hats, caps, berets:					34. Dresses: Cotton, street	0	$	$	
1. Hats: Felt	0	$	$ 0		35. Cotton, street	0			
2. Felt	0				36. Cotton, house	0			
3. Straw	0				37. Cotton, house	0			
4. Fabric	0				38. Other	0			
5. Caps, berets: Wool	0				39. Child's sun suit	0			
6. Other	0				40. Aprons, smocks	0			
Coats, raincoats, jackets, sweaters, furs:			0		41. Coveralls	0			
7. Coats: Heavy, with fur	0				Special sportswear:			0	
8. Heavy, no fur	0				42. Bathing suits	0			
9. Fur	0				43. Beach pajamas	0			
10. Light-wool	0				44. Knickers, breeches, shorts	0			
11. Cotton	0				45. Other special sports clothes: Cotton	0			
12. Rayon, silk	0				46. Other	0			
13. Raincoats	0				Underwear, nightwear, hose:			4.50	
14. Jackets: Wool	0				47. Slips: Cotton	0			
15. Leather	0				48. Rayon, silk	0			
16. Other	0				49. Corsets, girdles	0			
17. Sweaters: Wool	0				50. Brassieres	0			
18. Other	0				51. Union suits, combinations: Cotton				
19. Furs					52. Rayon, silk				
Suits, skirts, blouses, dresses:			0		53. Wool	0			
20. Suits: Wool, with fur					54. Underwaists, shirts: Cotton				
21. Wool, no fur					55. Rayon, silk				
22. Rayon, silk	0				56. Bloomers, panties: Cotton	0			
23. Other					57. Rayon, silk	0			
24. Skirts: Wool	0				58. Other	0			
25. Other					59. Nightgowns, pajamas: Cotton flannel	0			
26. Blouses, waists: Cotton					60. Cotton, other	0			
27. Linen					61. Rayon, silk	0			
28. Rayon, silk					62. Bathrobes	0			
29. Other					63. Kimonos, negligees	0			
30. Dresses: Wool									
31. Wool									
32. Rayon, silk	0								
33. Rayon, silk	0								

8—9577

135

CLOTHING PURCHASES, WOMAN OR GIRL—Continued					CLOTHING PURCHASES, CHILDREN UNDER 2 YEARS I. 1st child: Age, _____ months; no. wks. in econ. family _____				
A.	B	C	D	E	A	B	C	D	E
ITEM	Number	Price	Expense for schedule year	Season purchased	ITEM	Number	Price	Expense for schedule year	Season purchased
64. Hose: Rayon, silk	0	$	$		Ready-to-wear:		$	$	
65. Cotton	1		30°	4.50	1. Caps, hoods, bonnets				
66. Wool	0			4.48	2. Coats				
Footwear:					3. Snow or sweater suits				
67. Shoes: Street	1		1.98	1.98	4. Sweaters, sacques				
68. Street	1		2.00	2.00	5. Dresses, rompers				
69. Dress	1		2.50	2.50	6. Sun suits				
70. Dress	0				7. Skirts, gertrudes				
71. Sport	0				8. Shirts, bands				
72. Other	0				9. Diapers				
73. Other	0				10. Sleeping garments				
74. House slippers	0				11. Stockings				
75. Arctics, gaiters	0				12. Bootees, shoes				
76. Rubbers	0				13. Layette				
77. Shoe shines	0				14. Other				
78. Shoe repairs	0				Yard goods:				
Gloves, handkerchiefs, other accessories:			.50		15. Diaper cloth				
79. Gloves: Cotton	0				16. Other cotton				
80. Silk, rayon	0				17. Other				
81. Leather	0				18. Wool				
82. Wool	0				19. Rayon, silk				
83. Handkerchiefs	1		65	1.50	20. Paid help for sewing	x x	x x		x x
84. Handbags, purses	2				21. TOTAL	x x	x x	$	x x
85. Umbrellas	0				22. Money value of clothing received as gift, $				
86. Jewelry	0				II. 2d child: Age, _____ months; no. wks. in econ. family _____				
87. Other accessories	0				Ready-to-wear:				
Home sewing:					1. Caps, hoods, bonnets		$	$	
88. Yard goods: Cotton	1	15	18°		2. Coats				
89. Cotton	1	25	30	2.50	3. Snow or sweater suits				
90. Cotton	0				4. Sweaters, sacques				
91. Linen	0				5. Dresses, rompers				
92. Rayon	0				6. Sun suits				
93. Rayon	0				7. Skirts, gertrudes				
94. Silk	0				8. Shirts, bands				
95. Silk	0				9. Diapers				
96. Silk	0				10. Sleeping garments				
97. Wool	1	40°	2.00		11. Stockings				
98. Other	0				12. Bootees, shoes				
99. Findings	1		1.50		13. Layette				
100. Paid help for sewing	x x	x x	0	x x	14. Other				
Upkeep:			0		Yard goods:				
101. Cleaning, pressing	0				15. Diaper cloth				
Other clothing expense:			0		16. Other cotton				
102. (Specify)	0				17. Other				
103. TOTAL	1	x x	x x	$25.18 x x	18. Wool				
104. Money value of clothing received as gift or pay	$	0			19. Rayon, silk				
					20. Paid help for sewing	x x	x x		x x
					21. TOTAL	x x	x x	$	x x
					22. Money value of clothing received as gift. $				

8—9577

136

1903

15

F2000

B. H. E. Form 106

CONFIDENTIAL

The information requested in this schedule is strictly confidential. Giving it is voluntary. It will not be seen by any except sworn agents of the cooperating agencies and will not be available for taxation purposes.

Year covered by schedule:

12 months beginning _____, 1935

and ending _____, 1936

5. Family member (check): (6)

_____ Wife: Age _____ years.

_____ Other female (over 2 years).

Age __15__ years. (7)

No. weeks in economic family __2__ (12)

U. S. DEPARTMENT OF AGRICULTURE
BUREAU OF HOME ECONOMICS
IN COOPERATION WITH
NATIONAL RESOURCES COMMITTEE
WORKS PROGRESS ADMINISTRATION
AND DEPARTMENT OF LABOR
WASHINGTON

STUDY OF
CONSUMER PURCHASES
A FEDERAL WORKS PROJECT
CLOTHING PURCHASES
DURING SCHEDULE YEAR
(Check list)
WOMAN OR GIRL

Code No. _____ 61 - X137

Expenditure schedule No. _____ 3423

Town, village _____

County _____ State _____

E. D. or M. C. D. _____ 36-112

Agent _____

Date of interview _____ July 14, 1936

Number persons in economic family _____

Occupation of husband _____ FARMER

Chr. _____ Inc. 381.

White   M.ING.

A	B	C	D	E	A	B	C	D	E
ITEM	Number	Price	Expense for schedule year	Season purchased	ITEM	Number	Price	Expense for schedule year	Season purchased
Hats, caps, berets:			0		34. Dresses: Cotton,				
1. Hats: Felt	0	$	$		street	0	$	$	
2. Felt	0				35. Cotton, street	0			
3. Straw	0				36. Cotton, house	0			
4. Fabric	0				37. Cotton, house	0			
5. Caps, berets: Wool	0				38. Other	0			
6. Other	0				39. Child's sun suit	0			
Coats, raincoats, jackets, sweaters, furs:			0		40. Aprons, smocks	0			
7. Coats: Heavy, with fur	0				41. Coveralls	0			
8. Heavy, no fur	0				Special sportswear:			0	
9. Fur	0				42. Bathing suits	0			
10. Light-wool	0				43. Beach pajamas	0			
11. Cotton	0				44. Knickers, breeches, shorts	0			
12. Rayon, silk	0				45. Other special sports clothes: Cotton	0			
13. Raincoats	2				46. Other	0			
14. Jackets: Wool	2				Underwear, nightwear, hose:			4.80	
15. Leather	2				47. Slips: Cotton	0			
16. Other	2				48. Rayon, silk	2			
17. Sweaters: Wool	2				49. Corsets, girdles	0			
18. Other	2				50. Brassieres	2			
19. Furs	0				51. Union suits, combinations: Cotton	0			
Suits, skirts, blouses, dresses:			0		52. Rayon, silk	0			
20. Suits: Wool, with fur	0				53. Wool	0			
21. Wool, no fur	0				54. Underwaists, shirts: Cotton	0			
22. Rayon, silk	2				55. Rayon, silk	0			
23. Other	2				56. Bloomers, panties: Cotton	2			
24. Skirts: Wool	2				57. Rayon, silk	2			
25. Other	2				58. Other	2			
26. Blouses, waists: Cotton	2				59. Nightgowns, pajamas: Cotton flannel	0			
27. Linen	2				60. Cotton, other	0			
28. Rayon, silk	2				61. Rayon, silk	0			
29. Other	2				62. Bathrobes	2			
30. Dresses: Wool	2				63. Kimonos, negligees	0			
31. Wool	2								
32. Rayon, silk	2								
33. Rayon, silk	0								

(1)   8-9577

137

1903

16

CLOTHING PURCHASES, WOMAN OR GIRL—Continued

	A	B	C	D	E
	ITEM	Number	Price	Expense for schedule year	Season purchased
64.	Hose: Rayon, silk	0	$	$	
65.	Cotton	1/2	35¢	4.20	S
66.	Wool	0			
	Footwear:			7.60	
67.	Shoes: Street	1/1	2.00	2.00	Spg
68.	Street	x /	2.00	2.00	F
69.	Dress	x /	3.00	3.00	Sp
70.	Dress	0			
71.	Sport	0			
72.	Other	0			
73.	Other	0			
74.	House slippers	0			
75.	Arctics, gaiters	0			
76.	Rubbers	0			
77.	Shoe shines	0			
78.	Shoe repairs	0			
	Gloves, handkerchiefs, other accessories:			50	
79.	Gloves: Cotton	0			
80.	Silk, rayon	0			
81.	Leather	0			
82.	Wool	0			
83.	Handkerchiefs	1/0	5¢	.50	S
84.	Handbags, purses	0			
85.	Umbrellas	0			
86.	Jewelry	0			
87.	Other accessories	0			
	Home sewing:			13.80	
88.	Yard goods: Cotton	1/10	10¢	1.00	Spg
89.	Cotton	x 15	25¢	3.75	Spg
90.	Cotton	x /2	20¢	3.60	F
91.	Linen	0			
92.	Rayon	0			
93.	Rayon	0			
94.	Silk	0			
95.	Silk	0			
96.	Silk	0			
97.	Wool	7	35¢	3.15	F
98.	Other	0			
99.	Findings	x 2 A.T.		1.50	S/F
100.	Paid help for sewing	x x	x x	0	x x
	Upkeep:			0	
101.	Cleaning, pressing	0			
	Other clothing expense:			0	
102.	(Specify)	0			
103.	TOTAL	/ x x	x x	$25.50	x x
104.	Money value of clothing received as gift or pay		$	0	

CLOTHING PURCHASES, CHILDREN UNDER 2 YEARS

I. 1st child: Age, ... months; no. wks. in econ. family ....

	A	B	C	D	E
	ITEM	Number	Price	Expense for schedule year	Season purchased
	Ready-to-wear:				
1.	Caps, hoods, bonnets		$	$	
2.	Coats				
3.	Snow or sweater suits				
4.	Sweaters, sacques				
5.	Dresses, rompers				
6.	Sun suits				
7.	Skirts, gertrudes				
8.	Shirts, bands				
9.	Diapers				
10.	Sleeping garments				
11.	Stockings				
12.	Bootees, shoes				
13.	Layette				
14.	Other				
	Yard goods:				
15.	Diaper cloth				
16.	Other cotton				
17.	Other				
18.	Wool				
19.	Rayon, silk				
20.	Paid help for sewing	x x	x x		x x
21.	TOTAL	x x	x x	$ 0	x x

22. Money value of clothing received as gift, $ 0

II. 2d child: Age, ... months; no. wks. in econ. family ....

	A	B	C	D	E
	Ready-to-wear:				
1.	Caps, hoods, bonnets		$	$	
2.	Coats				
3.	Snow or sweater suits				
4.	Sweaters, sacques				
5.	Dresses, rompers				
6.	Sun suits				
7.	Skirts, gertrudes				
8.	Shirts, bands				
9.	Diapers				
10.	Sleeping garments				
11.	Stockings				
12.	Bootees, shoes				
13.	Layette				
14.	Other				
	Yard goods:				
15.	Diaper cloth				
16.	Other cotton				
17.	Other				
18.	Wool				
19.	Rayon, silk				
20.	Paid help for sewing	x x	x x		x x
21.	TOTAL	x x	x x	$ 0	x x

22. Money value of clothing received as gift.... $ 0

(2)

8—9077

138

1403   12

F2009

B. H. E. Form 108

CONFIDENTIAL

The information requested in this schedule is strictly confidential. Giving it is voluntary. It will not be seen by any except sworn agents of the cooperating agencies and will not be available for taxation purposes.

U. S. DEPARTMENT OF AGRICULTURE
BUREAU OF HOME ECONOMICS
IN COOPERATION WITH
NATIONAL RESOURCES COMMITTEE
WORKS PROGRESS ADMINISTRATION
AND DEPARTMENT OF LABOR
WASHINGTON

STUDY OF

CONSUMER PURCHASES

A FEDERAL WORKS PROJECT

**CLOTHING PURCHASES
DURING SCHEDULE YEAR**

(Check list)

WOMAN OR GIRL

Code No. _____ 61-137
Expenditure schedule No. 3422
Town, village _____
County _____ State _____
E. D. or M. C. D. 26
Agent _____
Date of interview _____ Oct 21 _____, 1936
Number persons in economic family _____
Occupation of husband _____ Farmer
Clr. _____ Inc. 3818.13
M INC

Year covered by schedule:
12 months beginning _____, 1935
and ending _____, 1936
Family member (check): _____
_____ Wife: Age _____ years.
_____ Other female (over 2 years).
Age _____ years.
No. weeks in economic family _____ 52

ITEM	Number	Price	Expense for schedule year	Season purchased	ITEM	Number	Price	Expense for schedule year	Season purchased
Hats, caps, berets:					34. Dresses: Cotton, street	0	$	$	
1. Hats: Felt	0	$	$	0	35. Cotton, street	0			
2. Felt	0				36. Cotton, house	0			
3. Straw	0				37. Cotton, house	0			
4. Fabric	0				38. Other	0			
5. Caps, berets: Wool	0				39. Child's sun suit	0			
6. Other	0				40. Aprons, smocks	0			
Coats, raincoats, jackets, sweaters, furs:					41. Coveralls	0			
7. Coats: Heavy, with fur	0			2	Special sportswear:				0
8. Heavy, no fur	0				42. Bathing suits	0			
9. Fur	0				43. Beach pajamas	0			
10. Light-wool	0				44. Knickers, breeches, shorts	0			
11. Cotton	0				45. Other special sports clothes: Cotton	0			
12. Rayon, silk	0				46. Other	0			
13. Raincoats	0				Underwear, nightwear, hose:			420	
14. Jackets: Wool	0				47. Slips: Cotton	0			
15. Leather	0				48. Rayon, silk	0			
16. Other	0				49. Corsets, girdles	0			
17. Sweaters: Wool	0				50. Brassieres	0			
18. Other	0				51. Union suits, combinations: Cotton	0			
19. Furs	0				52. Rayon, silk	0			
Suits, skirts, blouses, dresses:			5		53. Wool	0			
20. Suits: Wool, with fur	0				54. Underwaists, shirts: Cotton	0			
21. Wool, no fur	0				55. Rayon, silk	0			
22. Rayon, silk	0				56. Bloomers, panties: Cotton	0			
23. Other	0				57. Rayon, silk	0			
24. Skirts: Wool	0				58. Other	0			
25. Other	0				59. Nightgowns, pajamas: Cotton flannel	0			
26. Blouses, waists: Cotton	0				60. Cotton, other	0			
27. Linen	0				61. Rayon, silk	0			
28. Rayon, silk	0				62. Bathrobes	0			
29. Other	0				63. Kimonos, negligees	0			
30. Dresses: Wool	0								
31. Wool	0								
32. Rayon, silk	0								
33. Rayon, silk	0								

8—9577

1405

18

A	B	C	D	E
CLOTHING PURCHASES, WOMAN OR GIRL—Continued				
ITEM	Number	Price	Expense for schedule year	Season purchased
64. Hose: Rayon, silk	0	$	$	
65. Cotton	1 / 12	.35	4.20	all
66. Wool	0			
Footwear:				
67. Shoes: Street	1	2.00	2.00	SP
68. Street	1	2.00	2.00	7..
69. Dress	1	3.00	3.00	Su..
70. Dress	0			
71. Sport	0			
72. Other	0			
73. Other	0			
74. House slippers	0			
75. Arctics, gaiters	0			
76. Rubbers	0			
77. Shoe shines	0			
78. Shoe repairs	0			
Gloves, handkerchiefs, other accessories:			.50	
79. Gloves: Cotton	0			
80. Silk, rayon	0			
81. Leather	0			
82. Wool	0			
83. Handkerchiefs	1 / 10	.5	.50	all
84. Handbags, purses	0			
85. Umbrellas	0			
86. Jewelry	0			
87. Other accessories	0			
Home sewing:			3.00	
88. Yard goods: Cotton	18 yds	1.0	1.80	Sp
89. Cotton	15 "	.25	3.75	Sp
90. Cotton	12	.30	3.60	F
91. Linen	0			
92. Rayon	0			
93. Rayon	0			
94. Silk	0			
95. Silk	0			
96. Silk	0			
97. Wool	9 yds	.35	3.15	F
98. Other	0			
99. Findings	2.57		1.50	Sp F
100. Paid help for sewing	x x	x x	0	x x
Upkeep:			0	
101. Cleaning, pressing	0			
Other clothing expense:				
102. (Specify)	0		0	
103. TOTAL	x x	x x	$25.50	x x
104. Money value of clothing received as gift or pay			$ 0	

A	B	C	D	E
CLOTHING PURCHASES, CHILDREN UNDER 2 YEARS				
I. 1st child: Age, ... months; no. wks. in econ. family				
ITEM	Number	Price	Expense for schedule year	Season purchased
Ready-to-wear:				
1. Caps, hoods, bonnets		$	$	
2. Coats				
3. Snow or sweater suits				
4. Sweaters, sacques				
5. Dresses, rompers				
6. Sun suits				
7. Skirts, gertrudes				
8. Shirts, bands				
9. Diapers				
10. Sleeping garments				
11. Stockings				
12. Bootees, shoes				
13. Layette				
14. Other				
Yard goods:				
15. Diaper cloth				
16. Other cotton				
17. Other				
18. Wool				
19. Rayon, silk				
20. Paid help for sewing	x x	x x		x x
21. TOTAL	x x	x x	$ 0	x x
22. Money value of clothing received as gift, $ 0				
II. 2d child: Age, ... months; no. wks. in econ. family ...				
Ready-to-wear:				
1. Caps, hoods, bonnets		$	$	
2. Coats				
3. Snow or sweater suits				
4. Sweaters, sacques				
5. Dresses, rompers				
6. Sun suits				
7. Skirts, gertrudes				
8. Shirts, bands				
9. Diapers				
10. Sleeping garments				
11. Stockings				
12. Bootees, shoes				
13. Layette				
14. Other				
Yard goods:				
15. Diaper cloth				
16. Other cotton				
17. Other				
18. Wool				
19. Rayon, silk				
20. Paid help for sewing	x x	x x		x x
21. TOTAL	x x	x x	$0	x x
22. Money value of clothing received as gift. $ 0				

S—9577

BHE Form 168

DEPARTMENT OF AGRICULTURE
BUREAU OF HOME ECONOMICS
IN COOPERATION WITH
NATIONAL RESOURCES COMMITTEE
WORKS PROGRESS ADMINISTRATION
AND DEPARTMENT OF LABOR
WASHINGTON

STUDY OF

CONSUMER PURCHASES
A FEDERAL WORKS PROJECT

CLOTHING PURCHASES
DURING SCHEDULE YEAR
(Check list)

MAN OR BOY

Year covered by schedule:
12 months beginning _____, 1935
and ending ___ 21, 1936

Family member (check): _____
_____ Husband: Age _____ years.
_____ Other male (over 2 years),
Age __11__ years.
No. weeks in economic family ___

Code No. _____
Expenditure schedule No. 34333
Town, village _____
County _____ State _____
E. D. or M. C. D. _____
Agent _____
Date of interview _____ 14, 1936
Number persons in economic family ___
Occupation of husband _____
Clr. _____ Inc. 3818

ITEM	Number	Price	Expense for schedule year	Season purchased		ITEM	Number	Price	Expense for schedule year	Season purchased
Hats, caps:			50			39. Underdrawers: Cotton		$	$	
1. Hats: Felt		$				40. Cotton and wool				
2. Straw	1	.50	.50			41. Rayon, silk				
3. Caps: Wool						42. Pajamas, nightshirts				
4. Other						43. Bathrobes, lounging robes				
Coats, jackets, sweaters:			0			44. Hose: Cotton, dress				
5. Overcoats						45. Cotton, heavy				
6. Topcoats						46. Rayon, silk				
7. Raincoats						47. Wool				
8. Jackets: Wool						48. Other		20	300	
9. Leather					Footwear:					
10. Other						49. Shoes: Work	1	1.50		
11. Sweaters: Wool						50. Work	1	1.25		
12. Other						51. Street	1	2.00	2.00	
Suits, trousers, overalls:			0			52. Street				
13. Suits: Heavy-wool						53. Sport				
14. Light-wool						54. Other				
15. Cotton, linen						55. Boots: Rubber				
16. Palm-beach						56. Leather				
17. Child's sun suit						57. Arctics	1	1.00	1.00	
18. Other						58. Rubbers				
19. Trousers: Wool						59. Shoe shines, repairs				
20. Cotton					Gloves, handkerchiefs, other accessories:			1.10		
21. Other						60. Gloves: Cotton, work				
22. Overalls, coveralls						61. Other, work				
Shirts:						62. Leather, street				
23. Shirts and blouses: Cotton, work						63. Other, street				
24. Cotton, other						64. Handkerchiefs				
25. Rayon, silk						65. Ties				
26. Wool						66. Collars				
27. Other						67. Belts, garters, suspenders		35	.72	
Special sports wear:			0			68. Jewelry				
28. Bathing suits						69. Other accessories		33		
29. Other special sports clothes: Cotton					Home sewing:					
30. Other						70. Yard goods: Cotton				
Underwear, nightwear, hose:			5.00			71. Other materials and findings				
31. Union suits: Cotton, knit	1	1.00	2.00			72. Paid help for sewing	xx	xx		xx
32. Cotton, woven					Upkeep:					
33. Cotton and wool						73. Cleaning, pressing				
34. Rayon, silk					Other clothing expense:					
35. Undershirts: Cotton						74. (Specify)				
36. Cotton and wool						75. TOTAL	xx	xx	$	xx
37. Rayon, silk						76. Money value of clothing received as gift or pay			$	
38. Underwaists										

8—9577

1903

20

AGE 9 YEARS

NoWKS, IN FAM, 52

Case no 61-X137

Expenditure schedule no. 34035

County Lancaster State Penn.

M.O.D. 36-112

Agent. Rigdon

Date/Interview July 14-1936

ITEM	Number	Price	Expense for schedule year	Season purchased	ITEM	Number	Price	Expense for schedule year	Season purchased
1 Hats, caps:			0		39. Underdrawers: Cotton	0	$	$	
1. Hats: Felt	0	$	$		40. Cotton and wool	0			
2. Straw	0				41. Rayon, silk	0			
3. Caps: Wool	0				42. Pajamas, nightshirts	0			
4. Other	2				43. Bathrobes, lounging				
2 Coats, jackets, sweaters:	0		0		robes	0			
5. Overcoats					44. Hose: Cotton, dress	2			
6. Topcoats	2				45. Cotton, heavy	0			
7. Raincoats					46. Rayon, silk	0			
8. Jackets: Wool	2				47. Wool	0			
9. Leather	2				48. Other	17	871	1244	
10. Other					Footwear:				
11. Sweaters: Wool					49. Shoes: Work	1	175	175	
12. Other					50. Work	1	200	200	
4 Suits, trousers, overalls:			0		51. Street		250	250	
13. Suits: Heavy-wool					52. Street	0			
14. Light-wool					53. Sport	0			
15. Cotton, linen					54. Other	0			
16. Palm-beach					55. Boots: Rubber	0			
17. Child's sun suit					56. Leather	0			
18. Other					57. Arctics	2			
19. Trousers: Wool					58. Rubbers	2			
20. Cotton					59. Shoe shines, repairs	2			
21. Other					Gloves, handkerchiefs, other accessories:				
22. Overalls, coveralls					60. Gloves: Cotton, work			100	
Shirts:					8 61. Other, work				
23. Shirts and blouses:					62. Leather, street				
Cotton, work					63. Other, street				
24. Cotton, other					64. Handkerchiefs	2			
25. Rayon, silk					65. Ties	0			
26. Wool					66. Collars	0			
27. Other					67. Belts, garters, suspenders			70	
5 Special sports wear:			0		68. Jewelry	0			
28. Bathing suits					69. Other accessories	75	250	375	
29. Other special sports					Home sewing:				
clothes: Cotton					70. Yard goods: Cotton	20	20	400	
30. Other					71. Other materials and findings			125	
6 Underwear, nightwear, hose:			240		72. Paid help for sewing	xx	xx	0	xx
31. Union suits: Cotton, knit					Upkeep:				
32. Cotton, woven					73. Cleaning, pressing	0			
33. Cotton and wool	0				Other clothing expense:				
34. Rayon, silk	0				74. (Specify)	0			
35. Undershirts: Cotton					75. TOTAL	1	xx	xx	$1840	xx
36. Cotton and wool					76. Money value of clothing received as gift or pay $			0	
37. Rayon, silk									
38. Underwaists									

142

Balances 13 F02009

BHE 110
CONFIDENTIAL
The information requested in this schedule is strictly confidential. Giving it is voluntary. It will not be seen by any except sworn agents of the cooperating agencies and will not be available for taxation purposes.

U. S. DEPARTMENT OF AGRICULTURE
BUREAU OF HOME ECONOMICS
IN COOPERATION WITH
NATIONAL RESOURCES COMMITTEE
WORKS PROGRESS ADMINISTRATION
AND DEPARTMENT OF LABOR
WASHINGTON

STUDY OF
CONSUMER PURCHASES
A FEDERAL WORKS PROJECT

FOOD CONSUMED
during last 7 days
(Check list)

Number persons in economic family _____

Occupation of husband __FARMER__

Chr. WHITE Inc. 3791 (13)

Code No. F6INC-8127
10-6-13 32433
Expenditure Schedule No. 32433

Town, village SALISBURY TWP
County Lancaster State Cal 240
E. D. or M. C. D. Salisbury
Agent RIGDON
Date of interview JULY 14, 1936
Seven days covered 5 To 11 INCL

ITEM	Quantity used last 7 days (give unit)	Price or value (give unit)	Expense or money value	Check (✓) if home-produced, gift, or pay	ITEM	Quantity used last 7 days (give unit)	Price or value (give unit)	Expense or money value	Check (✓) if home-produced, gift, or pay
I. MEATS, POULTRY					33. Ham: Sliced	0.15	lbs	$0.40 0.60	
Beef:					34. Whole ☐ half ☐	0			
1. Steak: Round	02.0	2 lb	$.30 0.60		35. Picnic	0			
2. Sirloin	0				36. Salt side: Dry cured	0			
3. Other	0				37. Pickled	0			
4. Pot roast: Rump	0				38. Other	0			
5. Chuck	0				Other meat:				
6. Lower round	0				39. Bologna, etc	0			
7. Roast: Loin	0				40. Canned meats	0			
8. Rib	0				41. Cooked meat	0			
9. Other	0				42. Other	0			
10. Boiling: Plate	0				Poultry:				
11. Other	0				43. Chicken: Roasting	0			
12. Ground	0				44. Stewing None used	0			
13. Liver	0				45. Other	0			
14. Corned beef	0				46. Other poultry	0			
15. Dried beef	00.5	lb	00.00 0.20		**II. SEA FOOD**				
16. Other	0				Fish:				
Veal:					1. Fresh	0			
17. Chops	0				2. Canned salmon: Pink	0			
18. Cutlet	0				3. Red	0			
19. Roast	0				4. Other, canned	0			
20. Stew	0				5. Cured	0			
21. Other	0				Sea food (not fish):				
Lamb:					6. Canned	0			
22. Chops	0				7. Other	0			
23. Leg	0				**III. DAIRY PRODUCTS AND FATTY FOODS**				
24. Breast	0				1. Eggs	0.3		0.38	X
25. Chuck, shoulder	0				2. Milk: Whole, bottled	0			
26. Other	0				3. Whole, loose	28.0		0.68	X
Pork, fresh:					4. Buttermilk	0			
27. Chops	02.0	3 lb	25 0.75		5. Skimmed	0			
28. Loin roast	0				6. Dry, skimmed	0			
29. Sausage	0				7. Evaporated	0			
30. Other	0				8. Other	0			
Pork, smoked or cured:									
31. Bacon: Sliced	0								
32. Strip	0								

143

FOOD CONSUMED during last 7 days—Continued

A	B	C	D	E	A	B	C	D	E
ITEM	Quantity used last 7 days (give unit)	Price or value (give unit)	Expense or money value	Check (√) if home-produced, gift, or pay	ITEM	Quantity used last 7 days (give unit)	Price or value (give unit)	Expense or money value	Check (√) if home-produced, gift, or pay
9. Cheese	00.5	½ LB	$ 30	00.15	Fruits, fresh:		$	$	
10. Ice cream (purchased and consumed at home)	0				30. Oranges	0			
					31. Grapefruit	0			
11. Cream	0				32. Lemons	0			
12. Butter	½ LB	25¢	1.00		33. Apples	0			
13. Other table fats	0				34. Bananas	0			
14. Lard	01.5	½ LB	13¢	00.20	35. Berries	0			
15. Lard compound	0				36. Melons	0			
16. Vegetable shortening	0				37. Peaches	0			
17. Salad and cooking oil	0				38. Pears	0			
18. Mayonnaise	0				39. Other	0			
19. Cod liver oil	0				Fruits, canned:	4.13			
IV. VEGETABLES, NUTS, FRUITS					40. Peaches	34	2.5 LB		00.24	X
Vegetables, fresh:					41. Pears	0			
1. Potatoes, white	600	1.30	63	00.6	X	42. Pineapple	0			
2. Sweetpotatoes, yams	0				43. Fruit juices	0			
3. Tomatoes	0				44. Other	0			
4. Cabbage	03.0	5 LB	63	00.10	X	Fruits, dried:				
5. Lettuce	0				45. Apricots	0			
6. Spinach	0				46. Peaches	0			
7. Asparagus	0				47. Prunes	0			
8. Carrots	0				48. Raisins	01.9	2 BOXES	10	00.20	
9. Beets & turnips □	07.0	3 LB	03	00.09	X	49. Other	0			
10. Celery	0				**V. GRAIN PRODUCTS** BAKE OWN				
11. Snap beans	06.0	6 LB		00.18	X	1. Bread: White	0			
12. Peas	06.0	6 LB		00.24	X	2. Whole wheat	0			
13. Onions	0				3. Rye	0			
14. Other	0				4. Crackers	01.0	1	22	00.22	
Vegetables, canned:					5. Cake	0			
15. Asparagus	0				6. Other baked goods			33	00.30	
16. Green beans	0				7. Flour: White	10.5	12		00.76	X
17. Baked beans	02.0	2 cans	2	00.15		8. Graham	0			
18. Corn	0				9. Rye	0			
19. Peas	0				10. Corn meal	0			
20. Tomatoes	0				11. Hominy grits	0			
21. Tomato juice	0				12. Rice	01.0	1 LB	12	00.10	
22. Other	0				13. Rolled oats	0			
Vegetables, dried:					14. Wheat cereals, uncooked	0			
23. Navy beans	0				15. Other uncooked cereals	0			
24. Lima beans	03.0	3	10	00.30		16. Corn flakes	01.7	24 oz	2 LB	8	00.24	
25. Peas □ lentils □	0				17. Other ready-to-eat cereals	0			
26. Other	0				18. Macaroni □ spaghetti □ noodles □	0			
Nuts:					19. Other	0			
27. Shelled	0								
28. In shell	0								
29. Peanut butter	02.5	2 cans	19	00.38						

(right margin notes)
4 cu
mins
23.5
21.0
23.9
27.2
21.7
20.4
40.6
19.1

USE ABOUT 20 LBS FLOUR A WEEK
½ OF WHICH IS HOME PRODUCED
½ " " " BOUGHT

1704

144

Totals entered & &   (13930)

FOOD CONSUMED during last 7 days—Continued					FURNISHINGS AND EQUIPMENT purchased during schedule year				
A	B	C	D	E	A	B	C	D	E
ITEM	Quantity used last 7 days (give unit)	Price or value (give unit)	Expense or money value	Check (✓) if home-pro-duced, gift, or pay	ITEM	Number	Price	Expense for year	Season pur-chased
VI. SWEETS AND MISCEL-LANEOUS					Kitchen equipment:				
Sweets:					1. Tables		$	$	
01. Sugar: Granulated	10.0	$	00.50		2. Cabinets				
2. Brown					3. Refrigerator: Electric ☐ gas ☐ ice ☐ other ☐				
03. Other			02.00.08		4. Stove, heating plates		$	$	
04. Molasses			2.00.30		(a) Kind of fuel				
5. Sirup: Corn ☐ other ☐					5. Canning equipment				
06. Jellies ☐ jams ☐			00.60	X	6. Pressure cooker				
07. Preserves			01.80	X	7. Pots, pans, bowls	1			(5)
8. Candy					8. Cutlery strainers				
9. Other					9. Dishmops, dishcloths				
Miscellaneous:					10. Small electric equip-ment (specify kind):				
10. Chocolate					11. Other				
11. Cocoa					12. Other				
12. Coffee			2.50.25		Cleaning equipment:				
13. Tea					13. Vacuum cleaners				
14. Packaged desserts					14. Carpet sweepers				
15. Baking powder ☐ soda ☐ yeast ☐			00		15. Brooms, brushes, mops	6		1.00	(5)
16. Salt	X		00		16. Dustpans, pails, cans				
17. Vinegar	X		00		17. Other				
18. Spices, extracts	X		00		Laundry equipment:				
19. Pickles ☐ olives ☐ relishes ☐			00	X	18. Washing machine: Power ☐ other ☐				
20. Canned soups (specify)					19. Ironing machine				
21. Canned foods, not specified elsewhere					20. Irons: Electric ☐ other ☐				
22. Soft and other drinks consumed at home					21. Washtub ☐ board ☐				
23. Other					22. Wringer ☐ boiler ☐				
24. Total LESS H.P.	xxx	xxx	62	xxx	23. Ironing board, clothes basket, rack				
					24. Other				
					Glass, China, Silver:				
					25. China, or porcelain tableware			1.50	(5)
					26. Glassware: Kitchen				
					27. Table			1.60	(5)
					28. Flatware: Sterling				
					29. Other				
					30. Hollow ware: Sterling				
					31. Other				
					32. Other				

VII. NUMBER OF MEALS FURNISHED FROM FAMILY FOOD SUPPLY DURING LAST 7 DAYS

PERSON			Breakfast	Noon meal	Evening meal
	Sex	Age			
1. Husband	M	47	7	7	7
2. Wife	F	50	7	7	7
3. Son	M	19	7	7	7
4. Daughter	F	10	7	7	7
5. Daughter	F	15	7	7	7
6. Daughter	F	13	7	7	7
7. Son	M	11	7	7	7
8. Son	M	9	7	7	7
9.					
10.					

(3) No. 15. Brooms purchased for household Used first in house and then taken to bar

FURNISHINGS AND EQUIPMENT purchased during schedule year—Continued

ITEM	Number	Price	Expense for year	Season purchased	ITEM	Number	Price	Expense for year	Season purchased
Household linens, blankets, curtains, other textiles:					71. Desks		$	$	
33. Kitchen towels: Linen		$	$		72. Bookcases, book-shelves				
34. Cotton					73. Tables: Dining, living room				
35. Hand towels: Linen					74. Other				
36. Cotton					75. Chairs: Upholstered				
37. Bath towels	12	25	3.00	S	76. Other				
38. Table cloths: Linen					77. Benches, stools				
39. Cotton	5	75	3.75	S	78. Porch and garden furniture				
40. Other					79. Other				
41. Napkins: Linen					Miscellaneous:				
42. Other					80. Electric light bulbs				
43. Table runners, scarfs, doilies					81. Heating stoves and heaters (specify fuel)				
44. Sheets			3.50		82. Fans, electric				
45. Pillowcases			1.75	F	83. Sewing machine: Electric ☐ other ☐				
46. Bedspreads					84. Clocks: Electric ☐ other ☐	2	1	2.00	W
47. Couch covers					85. Lamps ☐ lamp shades ☐	2	6.50	13.00	F
48. Comforters, quilts					86. Mirrors, pictures				
49. Blankets: All wool ☐ other ☐	3	2.50	7.50	W	87. Vases, ornaments				
50. Pillows					88. Baby carriages, go-carts				
51. Mattresses: Inner-spring					89. Hand baggage ☐ trunks ☐				
52. Other					90. Window shades ☐ venetian blinds ☐			2.40	S
53. Draperies ☐ curtains ☐					91. Wire screens, storm windows				
54. Slip covers					92. Lawn mowers, garden equipment				
Floor coverings:					93. Household tools, hardware				
55. Carpets					94. Other				
56. Rugs					95. Insurance on furnishings	x x x	x x x		x x x
57. Linoleum, inlaid (sq. yds.)					96. Repairs and cleaning of furnishings and equipment	x x x	x x x		x x x
58. Felt-base floor covering (sq. yds.)					97. Paid help for sewing	x x x	x x x		x x x
59. Other					98. Total		x x x		x x x
Furniture:					99. Money value of furnishings and equipment received as gifts or pay			$	0
60. Suites: Living room									
61. Dining room									
62. Bedroom									
63. Beds: Wood ☐ metal ☐									
64. Cots, cribs: Wood ☐ metal ☐									
65. Bedsprings: Box ☐ other ☐									
66. Davenports, settees									
67. Daybeds, couches									
68. Dressers, dressing tables									
69. Chiffoniers, chests									
70. Sideboards, buffets									

U. S. GOVERNMENT PRINTING OFFICE   8—9560   (4)

$55.95

1903

25

CONFIDENTIAL

The information requested in this schedule is strictly confidential. Giving it is voluntary. It will not be seen by any except sworn agents of the cooperating agencies and will not be available for taxation purposes.

U. S. DEPART...
BUREAU OF HOME
IN COOPER...
NATIONAL RESOURCES COMMI
ADMINISTRATION, DE...
WASHIN...

STUDY OF CONSUM...
A FEDERAL WOR...
FOOD RECO...

SUPPLEMENTARY DATA: SCHEDULE YEAR BEGINNING _____ AND ENDING _March 31_ '36

Numbers in ( ) refer to items on Family Schedule (F), Expenditure Schedule (E), or Summary of Receipts and Disbursements (S).

1. Income (S–13)................................ $ 3818.
2. Money value of goods received without direct money payment (S–18)........................
3.   Total (1 plus 2)........................ $
4. Money value of food home-produced or received as gift or pay (E VIII 24)........................
5. Expenditure for food during schedule year (S–30)........................
6. Total person-meals in household during schedule year. (Compute from F II as directed in instructions for use of food record.)........................

.0703
.0.54
.0342
.0317

MENUS SERVED ON THIRD DAY OF WEEK'S FOOD	
BREAKFAST	NOON MEAL
Cereal	Fried Tomato
Creamed Beef	Boiled Potatoes
Fried Potatoes	Stewed Fish
Bread + Butter	Bread + Butter
Coffee	Apple Pie
Milk	Milk

RECORD OF PERSONS FED FROM FAMILY FOOD SUPPLY DURING

PERSONS	Sex	Age	Height¹	Weight¹	NUMBER OF MEALS FURNISHED			SUNDAY		MONDAY	
					Break-fast	Noon meal	Evening meal	Kind of work	Hours	Kind of work	
1. Husband	M	47	5-3	120	7	7	7	odd jobs	7	Farming	
2. Wife	F	51	5-3	165	7	7	7	housework	7	housework	
OTHER MEMBERS OF ECONOMIC FAMILY (Give relationship)											
3. Son	M	19	5-3	140	7	7	7		7	Farming	
4. Daughter	F	16	5-	120	7	7	7		7		
5. Daughter	F	13	5-	130	7	7	7		7		
6. Son	F	12	5-1	115	7	7	7		1		
7. Son	M	12	5-	70					7		
8. Son	M	10	4-5	75			7		7		
OTHERS											
9. Sons or daughters boarding at home											
10.											
11. Paid help											
12. Boarder											
13. Tourists and transients			x x x x	x x				x x x x x x	x x	x x x x x x x	x x
14. Guest	F	21	x x x x	x x	3	3	3	x x x x x x	x x	x x x x x x x	x x
15. Guest			x x x x	x x				x x x x x	x x	x x x x x x	x x

¹ Without shoes.

U. S. GOVERNMENT PRINTING O

OF AGRICULTURE
ME ECONOMICS
TION WITH
MITTEE, WORKS PROGRESS
ARTMENT OF LABOR
GTON

MER PURCHASES
RKS PROJECT
RD—FARM

Code No. ~~FETM-8137~~   Food record No. 34335

Previous food records: Nos. _____

Expenditure schedule No. 1903

County _Lancaster_   State _Penna._

Clr. _White_   M. C. D. 36-112

Period covered by _Sept 17_ to _Sept 24_, 1936

Agent _Mira J. Hammaker_

OD RECORD EVENING MEAL	LANGUAGES SPOKEN	IN FAMILY CIRCLE	BY HOMEMAKER'S PARENTS	BY HUSBAND'S PARENTS
Fried Ham	1. English	_Yes_	_Yes_	_Yes_
Fried Potatoes	2. Other	_No_	_No_	_No_
Sliced Tomatoes				
Bread & Butter				
Milk				

TYPE OF STORE FROM WHICH FOOD WAS PURCHASED DURING WEEK

FOOD	GROCERY Chain store	GROCERY Independent Cash and carry	GROCERY Independent Service	OTHER STORE (specify) Chain store	OTHER STORE Independent Cash and carry	OTHER STORE Independent Service	Milk dealer or dairy (delivery)	Other (specify)
1. Meat					_butcher shop_		x x	
2. Groceries		✓					x x	
3. Milk								H.P.
4. Baked goods					_bakery_		x x	H.P.
5. Fruits, vegetables							x x	H.P.

NG WEEK ENDING _Sept 24, 1936_

PRINCIPAL OCCUPATION FOR EACH DAY, AND NUMBER OF HOURS WORKED

Hours	TUESDAY Kind of work	Hours	WEDNESDAY Kind of work	Hours	THURSDAY Kind of work	Hours	FRIDAY Kind of work	Hours	SATURDAY Kind of work	Hours	meals
T	Farming	T	Farming	T	Farming	T	Farming	T	Farming	T	2520
T	Housework	T	Housework	T	Housework	T	Housework	T	Housework	T	3465
T	Farming	T	Farming	T	Farming	T	Farming	T	Farming	T	2940
T	Tomato picking	T	Tomato picking	T	Tomato picking	T	Tomato picking	T	Tomato picking	T	2919
T	Tomato picking	T	Tomato picking	T	Tomato picking	T	Tomato picking	T	Tomato picking	T	2730
T	School	T	School	T	School	T	School	T	Helps with Housework	T	2355
T	School	T	School	T	School	T	School	T	Farming etc.	T	1890
T	School	T	School	T	School	T	School	T	Farming etc.	T	1785
x x	x x x x x x	x x	x x x x x x	x x	x x x x x x	x x	x x x x x x	x x	x x x x x x	x x	
x x	x x x x x x	x x	x x x x x x	x x	x x x x x x	x x	x x x x x x	x x	x x x x x x	x x	1056
x x	x x x x x x	x x	x x x x x x	x x	x x x x x x	x x	x x x x x x	x x	x x x x x x	x x	21657

÷6.6
Kg days = 3281.

BAE 192
11-3-36

SUMMARY OF QUANTITY AND VALUE OF FOOD CONSUMED

Town, Village or County _Lancaster Co. Pa._

Food Record No. _34/35_

Code No. _T 6 M ~ 8137_

Date of Record _Sept - 27__ to _Sept 24, 1936_

Done by _____ Time ____ -10

Verified by _____ Time ____

Kind of food	H.P.S.G. or P.	Quantity			Money value		
		Pur-chased lb.	Inv. Differ-ence lb.	Net lb.	Ex-pend-iture $	Inv. Differ-ence $	Net $
Grain products							
Bread (White)		1975	125	2000	501	121	192
White Bread flour			275	-275		-475	-475
Fancy Cereal		200	200		401	401	
Cake (uncooked)			50	50	021	021	
Graham (cracker)		200	200		121	121	171
Shredded wheat		2000	2000	100	601	601	100
Flour		200	200		451	161	671
Corn meal		400	400		521		521
Rice		100	100		091	091	091

Vegetables, other

Kind of food	H.P.S.G. or P.	Quantity			Money value		
		Pur-chased lb.	Inv. Differ-ence lb.	Net lb.	Ex-pend-iture $	Inv. Differ-ence $	Net $
Tomatoes		1750		1750	251		244-11
Corn fresh		1000		1000	100		116-5
Cabbage, fresh		200		200	101		190-19
Potatoes, sweet		300		300	153		116-23

Fruit, fruit juice

Apples, fresh | | 300 | | 300 | 101 | | 299-9

Milk, cheese

Milk, whole, fresh		300		400			
Cream, fresh		100	200	200	201	241	121

Eggs

Eggs, fresh		300		400		201	201
Fats, oils		300	100	400	201	201	201
Butter							

1903

										Fruits, dried			$45°$ $8°0°$ $45°$ $8°/3.36$		

Meats, fish, poultry

Sweets

Miscellaneous

Potatoes

Vegetables, dried; nuts

TOTAL FOR WEEK

$\dfrac{16.11}{180} = 0.895 - 3.$

The Study of Consumer Purchases: Background, Findings, and Use

One of the legacies of President Franklin Delano Roosevelt's time in office is the wealth of primary source material left to historians by investigators who worked for various New Deal agencies. Writers employed by the Federal Writers Project left behind priceless interviews with elderly persons who were formerly enslaved. During the Great Depression, photographers working for the Farm Security Administration (FSA) took dramatic photographs of rural life. Social scientists from the Bureau of Agricultural Economics (BAE) created a series of classic farm community studies. Since that time, urban and rural historians alike have benefited from the efforts of these New Deal intellectuals and others to record and document life in the United States during the Great Depression.

A lesser-known product of the New Deal research efforts is the Study of Consumer Purchases (SCP), a massive survey conducted during 1935/36. The Department of Labor's Bureau of Labor Statistics and the Department of Agriculture's Bureau of Home Economics (BHE) organized the study as a Works Progress Administration (WPA) project. The organizers selected families in large and small cities, villages, and farming communities throughout the country for exhaustive data collection using five detailed questionnaires. Results of the study were later published in a series of government reports designed to provide state and federal agencies, civic organizations, and business and labor groups with information about living expenses and consumer practices nationwide.[1]

Among the 66 areas chosen as "farm counties" for the study was Lancaster County, Pennsylvania, representing rural households engaged in diversified, general farming, while other farm counties across the country exemplified agricultural economies based on corn, wheat, cotton, livestock, produce, and other commodities. Workers collected questionnaires from 1,266 farm families in Lancaster County, including 74 Old Order Amish families and nearly 300 families affiliated with other Mennonite or Plain religious groups. As was their practice around the country, investigators approached the women in these families to gain information about spending habits within their households. Their interviews with farm women also yielded information about farm crops and income, farm and household equipment, family size, home production, recreational practices, and dietary habits. Lancaster County investigators thus collected invaluable evidence about the production and consumption activities of Old Order Amish women and their families, as well as information about the practices of their neighbors in the county.

Exploring these distinctions, the investigation by the Departments of Labor and Agriculture is a model of professional thoroughness and rational planning. The Consumption Research Staff of the National Resources Committee, Department of the Interior, stated the goals of the project in an unpublished interim report from January 1936:

> The need for an investigation into the manner in which American families spend their incomes has long been recognized, both by government agencies and by private organizations. In 1929 the Social Science Research Council emphasized this need in its outline of a proposed study of "Consumption According to Income: A Suggested Plan for an Inquiry into the Economic and Social Well-Being of the American People." During the past five years, the maladjustment between the nation's producing power and its actual consumption has stressed still further the importance of basic data on the consumption habits and needs of the population.
>
> The survey outlined in this report will make such data available for the first time in American statistical history. Although numerous studies of family expenditures have been made during the past fifty years, they have usually covered only very small samples of families, and the few large investigations which have been undertaken have been restricted to certain groups of the population . . . . No studies have ever been made covering representative samples of the village population, or of the urban business groups. Since the studies which are available have used very diverse methods of collecting and analyzing the data, it is impossible to fit the results together to give a satisfactory indication of the consumption habits of the population. For this, simultaneous studies of large and representative samples of urban and rural families are required. The present survey is planned to meet this need.
>
> The data which the study will provide are required by Government agencies to meet a wide variety of needs, both in connection with their current work and in formulating long-time policies and progress.
>
> Thus, the Bureau of Labor Statistics needs data on family expenditures as a basis for wage and salary negotiations.
>
> The Bureau of Home Economics needs similar data as a basis for preparing nor-

mative budgets for families at different income levels, for use by welfare agencies, extension workers and other agencies concerned with improving the level of living of various groups of the population.[2]

To fulfill these objectives, the planning agencies chose communities of various sizes in five geographic regions: New England, North Central, Southeast, Rocky Mountain, and Pacific Northwest. Within each region, agents conducted interviews in six large cities (population 252,000 to 302,000); 14 middle-sized cities (30,000 to 72,000); and 29 small cities (8,000 to 19,000). Two metropolises, Chicago and New York, were also included to measure living conditions in urban areas with more than 1 million inhabitants. The Bureau of Labor Statistics organized these interviews.

Within the same five regions, families from two or more groups of villages (population 500 to 3,200) as well as two or more groups of farm counties were also surveyed. The agencies selected farm counties that specialized in a particular type of farming because they were interested in studying and comparing the spending and consumption patterns of farm families who produced different agricultural products. In all, surveys were conducted in 30 states, 51 cities, 140 villages, and 66 farm counties (figure A2.1 and accompanying geographical categories and locations list). The BHE conducted the village and farm interviews.

The study began with a brief screening sample form assessing 700,000 families from a variety of regions and communities. Workers employed by the WPA then selected 300,000 of these families for the next stage. It was required that families include at least two members, with husband and wife married for at least one year, and with no more than the equivalent of 10 boarders for the survey year. For comparative purposes, some one-parent households and foreign-born families were included. All the families were selected without restrictions in terms of occupation, income, employment status, or whether they had drawn relief benefits during the year. Only white families were included, except in New York City, Columbus, Ohio, and the South, where a proportionate sample of native-born Black families was selected and interviewed. Farm families had to live in a setting that met the census definition of a farm, and the family itself had to operate the farm (or in the Southeast be sharecroppers) and undertake farming activities for at least a year. These 300,000 selected families were given the next, two-page questionnaire, the Family Schedule, with about 140 variables.

Following these first two "waves" of interviews, study organizers selected 61,000 families from the group of 300,000 for exhaustive analysis. To reach this stage, non-farm families must have had at least one wage earner in a clerical, professional, or business occupation, and a minimum income for the survey year of $500 in the large and midsize cities and $250 in smaller cities and rural areas. There were no upper limits on income. Families that had received relief were excluded, as were those with more than one boarder or one guest. Families were required to have at the least a husband-and-wife couple that "kept house" for at least nine months, and couples married for less than a year were excluded; therefore, the survey excluded families residing in hotels, institutions, and lodging houses. Farmers had to be full-time farmers, except in Oregon. Having already completed the Family Schedule, the families chosen for exhaustive analysis were asked to complete four additional schedules, consisting of some 3,000 specific items on expenditures. The five schedules were linked by a household number. The survey resulted in the collection of extraordinarily detailed information concerning the income, expenditures, and lifestyle choices of a large number of families all over the United States. The Departments of Labor and Agriculture published numerous volumes in the 1930s analyzing aggregate data from the surveys.

Every household selected on the basis of study criteria, in addition to the already completed Family Schedule, filled out the six-page Expenditure Schedule, tuned to an urban, small town, or farm setting. This schedule alone contains nearly 800 separate items asking respondents to provide complete information on family composition, living quarters, housing expenses, fuel and other utility expenses, medical care, recreational activities, tobacco use, purchase of reading materials, educational expenses, miscellaneous occupational expenses, gifts presented, taxes paid, automobile expenses, personal care costs, and all changes in family assets and liabilities over the survey year. There were also sections that summarized family expenses on clothing and furnishings and requested an inventory of all household equipment—including radios, refrigerators, washing machines, telephones—owned by the family. The schedule also recorded a detailed summary of food purchases, comprising the family's weekly, monthly, and seasonal expenditures for nine general categories of food commodities.

If a family proved willing to continue the process, interviewers filled out one or more of the other three schedules: Clothing Purchases; Food Consumed and Furnishings and Equipment; and the Food Record, which required the wife to record what the family ate for an entire week and complete menus for one day. She also had to describe the work, school, or other activities for every member of the family for every day of the week. For the Food Consumed portion, housewives were asked about the family's consumption of 681 specific foods during the seven days prior to the interview.

In Lancaster County, survey workers collected questionnaires from 1,266 farm families, including 74 Old Order Amish families and 56 horse-and-buggy Plain families, 14 of whom they labeled "Mennonite" and leaving 42 unspecified. As elsewhere in the farm counties, survey investigators approached the women in participating families to gain information about their households' spending habits as well as data about farm crops and income, farm and household equipment, family size, home production, recreational practices, and dietary habits. In Lancaster County, only 85 farm households of the 1,266, or 6.7%, completed the Food Record, while 275 answered the Clothing Purchases schedule and 276 the Food Consumed and Furnishings and Equipment schedule. Fifty-four farm women in Lancaster County consented to be interviewed for all five questionnaires. The SCP provides invaluable evidence about the production and consumption activities of Old Order Amish women and their families as well as comparative data about the practices of their Lancaster County neighbors and, indeed, farm households around the country.

This book primarily focuses on the first two survey schedules. The Family Schedule—Farm yielded 80 variables in the following categories: Family and Household Composition; Gross Money Income from Farming; Farm Expenses; Size, Tenure, and Value of Farm; Non-Farm Income; and Value of Products for Family's Own Use. The limited data used from the much larger Expenditure Schedule includes those from the sections on food, consumer products, home furnishings, and clothing expenses. Every household identified as Amish, Mennonite, or Plain was located. These designations appeared most often in the Recreation section of the Expenditure Schedule as interviewers found it necessary to explain why no entertainment outlays were listed. There were notes in other locations as well, such as personal care expenses and clothing expenses for women, noting costs of bonnets or material to make bonnets. The surveys, which were confidential, have no questions regarding name, religious affiliation, language spoken, or ethnicity, but they do designate township. Other than African American families in the South, New York City, and Columbus, Ohio, the ethno-religious groups in Lancaster County are the only ones identifiable in the entire survey collection. Many schedules have unofficial, handwritten marginal notations identifying the family as Amish or Mennonite to, as mentioned above, explain their unusual recreational, hair grooming, clothing, labor, and transportation expenses.

The surveys labeled "Amish" in the Recreation section were evaluated according to the presence or absence of automobile, telephone, electricity, and household appliances. Households having none of these items of technology were treated as Old Order Amish and those having an automobile as "Car/Church Amish." Surveys labeled "Mennonite" in the Recreation section received similar treatment: households without an automobile were labeled Old Order Mennonite and those with an automobile Mennonite. Households labeled "Plain" were considered to be Church of the Brethren (formerly Dunker) or Brethren in Christ. Employing this methodology identified 74 Old Order Amish households among the Lancaster County SCP respondents with a high degree of confidence. To include an element of random selection, all surveys with the fifth schedule were copied and results were also compared with a random sample constructed at the University of Michigan.[3]

Taking the survey plans into account, several precautions are necessary in using the data for historical and statistical study. First, the SCP is not a random sample of a population. Planners chose specific locations using specific criteria, and selected households in those locations based on a screening protocol. Statistical comparisons are useful and interesting, but not necessarily definitive.

Second, the surveys record income and expenses for the previous twelve months. They are not similar to postmortem probate inventories of all property. The two exceptions are automobile(s) owned and "equipment" (mostly household appliances) owned, such as radios and refrigerators. Of course, any money earned or spent in the middle of the Great Depression—a period just about halfway between the stock market crash in October 1929 and US entry into World War II in December 1941—is significant.

Third, household members are counted as an "economic unit"—that is, children and adults currently living in the house. Older children who had moved out and elderly parents or grandparents who might be living in an attached *Grossdawdyhaus* (grandfather's house) are excluded by definition. Old Order Amish households did contain significantly more children no matter how the surveys are categorized (table A2.2), even when the age of parents, number of acres, and other covariates are added to the statistical analysis of variance (ANOVA) (table A2.3).

Fourth, there can be a degree of uncertainty in pinpointing the ethno-religious identity of some households. The survey takers often wrote "Amish" or "Mennonite" or some other notation in the margins, which although helpful to later scholars, might have been stretching the rules at the time. The tables in this appendix illustrate the different ethno-religious categorizations as the research progressed on the data over the years: one grouping is based on initial analysis of the data (Grouping 1; used in our 1993 article in *Agricultural History,* for which see note 3 for this appendix), another developed after further study and adoption of stricter criteria (Grouping 2), and yet another according to mode of transportation, that is, horse and buggy or automobile for Plain households and "Mennonite" written somewhere on the survey (Grouping 3). In each grouping, including a disaggregation of horse-and-buggy households, Old Order Amish households contain more children.

These caveats do not reduce the importance of this gigantic accumulation of economic data. Rather, they indicate certain elements of caution to be used in interpreting the information gathered by WPA workers.

Plain Anabaptist Groups in Lancaster County, ca. 1938

	Congregations or meetinghouses[1]	Members (baptized adults)	Alternate names
Lancaster Mennonite Conference[2]	59	11,270	
Church of the Brethren, Eastern Pennsylvania District	16	4,728	Dunkers
Old Order Mennonites	8	2,050	Horning Mennonites, the car-driving segment; Wenger Mennonites, the horse-driving segment
Old Order Amish	16	1,699	House Amish
Brethren in Christ[2]	13	1,101	River Brethren
Ohio Mennonite and Eastern Amish Mennonite Conference[3]	2	938	Church Amish
Reformed Mennonite Church[4]	6	441	
Weavertown Amish-Mennonites[5]	1	150	John Stoltzfus Church, later affiliated with the national Beachy Amish group
Old Order River Brethren	1	Unknown number	Yorkers
Total		22,377	

Sources: For Amish and Mennonite groups, 1938 figures, *Mennonite Year Book and Directory* (1939); for Church of the Brethren, 1938 figures, *District Conference Booklet of Seventy-Second District Meeting, Eastern District of Pennsylvania, Church of the Brethren, April 27–28, 1938*; for Brethren in Christ, archives, Messiah University, 1937 figures; for Reformed Mennonites, 1932 figures, private files.

Note: Lancaster County's total population in the late 1930s was approximately 200,000; the 1930 census had reported 196,882 people. Plain Anabaptist church members thus accounted for about 11 percent of the county's population. If unbaptized children are included, and assuming sizable families, the Plain people would easily have constituted a fifth of Lancaster County's population. The unbaptized children of many Brethren did not dress plainly.

Lancaster County was also home to three Mennonite churches whose members did not dress plainly or adhere to a distinctively plain lifestyle. These congregations were part of the General Conference Mennonite Church and together had about 165 members.

1. The designation is church districts in the case of Old Order Amish and Old Order River Brethren, neither of which had meetinghouses.

2. Before World War II, most Lancaster Mennonite Conference congregations had multiple meetinghouses that functioned as "circuits," with preaching in a rotation every second or third week in each place. The 59 meetinghouses represented many fewer congregations. Similarly, in the 1930s, Brethren in Christ had three circuit congregations that collectively had 13 meetinghouses.

3. At least half of these members probably lived in Chester County, Pennsylvania, and those who lived in Lancaster County resided near the Chester County border. Despite a keen continuing sense of historic Amish identity, these churches were by the 1930s increasingly tied to Mennonite institutions in the Midwest, such as the Mennonite Board of Missions in Elkhart, Indiana.

4. Unusual among the groups listed here, the Reformed Mennonites included a good number of mixed-status households, in which one spouse, usually the wife, was a church member and dressed plainly, but the other spouse and children were not church members and were not Plain.

5. In some circles, the Weavertown church might also have been called Church Amish, but the congregation was quite different from the main Church Amish group—the Ohio Mennonite and Eastern Amish Mennonite Conference.

Ethno-Religious Categories in Reschly/Jellison Sample of the Study of Consumer Purchases,
Lancaster County, Pennsylvania, 1935/36 (total sample: 394 of 1,266, or 31.1%)

		Number	Percentage
A.	**Grouping 1 (Some attributed)**		
0	None (no religious group specified, no notes)	86	21.8
1	Old Order Amish	103	26.1
2	Car Amish	23	5.8
3	Old Order Mennonite	17	4.3
4	Mennonite	91	23.1
5	Plain, unspecified	74	18.8
B.	**Grouping 2 (Precise, as noted somewhere on survey)**		
0	None (no religious group specified, no note at all)	86	21.8
1	Old Order Amish (Amish noted on survey)	74	18.8
2	Old Order Mennonite (Mennonite noted, no auto)	14	3.6
3	Horse and buggy Plain (unspecified)	42	10.7
4	Car Amish (Amish noted, with auto)	23	5.8
5	Car Plain (unspecified)	64	16.2
6	Mennonite (Mennonite noted, probably Lancaster Conference)	91	23.1
C.	**Grouping 3 (Aggregate groupings)**		
0	None (no religious group specified, no note at all)	86	21.8
1	All horse and buggy groups (1, 2, 3 in table A2.2A)	130	33.0
2	All Plain car groups (4, 5 in table A2.2A)	87	22.1
3	All Mennonite (Mennonite noted, probable Lancaster Conference)	91	23.1
D.	**ICPSR Random Sample of Farm Households, Study of Consumer Purchases Surveys in Lancaster County, Pennsylvania, 1935/36**		
	All	108/1,266	8.5
0	None (no religious group specified, no note at all)	83	76.9
1	Old Order Amish	9	8.3
2	Car Amish	4	3.7
3	Old Order Mennonite	0	0
4	Mennonite	6	5.5
5	Plain (unspecified)	6	5.5

Note: ICPSR = Inter-university Consortium for Political and Social Research

Analysis of Variance: Children in Surveyed Households

A. Number of Children, Grouping 1

Variable	All	1 Old Order Amish	2 Car Amish	3 Old Order Mennonite	4 Mennonite	5 Plain	Other	Variance F-Ratio	Sig F
Reschly/Jellison sample	394/1266	103	23	17	91	74	86		
Percentage of sample	31.1%	26.1%	5.8%	4.3%	23.1%	18.8%	21.8%		
Mean	2.53	3.37	2.91	2.35	2.11	2.24	2.11	6.70	***
Standard deviation	1.89	1.96	1.78	1.97	1.76	1.75	1.75		

Significance: * = .1 level ** = .05 level *** = .01 level

B. Number of Children, Grouping 2

Variable	All	0 No Note	1 Old Order Amish	2 Old Order Mennonite	3 Horse and Buggy Plain (unspecified)	4 Car Amish (Amish noted)	5 Car Plain (unspecified)	6 Mennonite (noted)	Variance F-Ratio	Sig F
Reschly/Jellison sample	394	86	74	14	42	23	64	91		
Percentage of sample	31.1%	21.8%	18.8%	3.6%	10.7%	5.8%	16.2%	23.1%		
Mean	2.53	2.12	3.43	2.36	2.86	2.81	2.30	2.11	5.12	***
Standard deviation	1.89	1.75	1.94	2.05	2.05	2.05	1.72	1.76		

Significance: * = .1 level ** = .05 level *** = .01 level

TABLE A2.3 (*Continued*)

C. Number of Children, Grouping 3

Variable	All	0 No Note	1 Horse and Buggy	2 Car Plain	3 Mennonite	Variance F-Ratio	Sig F
Reschly/Jellison sample combined	394 31.1%	86 21.8%	74 18.8%	14 3.6%	42 10.7%		
Mean	2.53	2.12	3.13	2.46	2.11	7.69	***
Standard deviation	1.89	1.75	2.01	1.75	1.76		

Significance: * = .1 level ** = .05 level *** =.01 level

D. Number of Children, Horse and Buggy Plain Disaggregated from Grouping 3

Variable	All	1 Old Order Amish	2 Old Order Mennonite	3 Horse and Buggy Plain (unspecified)	Variance F-Ratio	Sig F
Reschly/Jellison sample combined	394	74 21.8%	14 18.8%	42 3.6%		
Mean	2.53	3.43	2.36	2.86	2.31	*
Standard deviation	1.89	1.94	2.02	2.05		

Significance: * = .1 level ** = .05 level *** =.01 level

A2.1 Map of Cities, Towns, and Farming Regions Surveyed in the Study of Consumer Purchases, 1935/36. Dotted lines represent farm counties and villages in those counties.

Study of Consumer Purchases: Geographical Categories and Locations

To improve legibility, not all of the locations listed have been located and labeled on the map.

TO BE SURVEYED BY THE BUREAU OF LABOR STATISTICS

METROPOLISES (2)

New York, NY
Chicago, IL

LARGE CITIES (6)

Providence, RI
Atlanta, GA
Columbus, OH
Omaha, NE–Council Bluffs, IA
Denver, CO
Portland, OR

MIDDLE-SIZE CITIES (14)

Haverhill, MA
New Britain, CT
New Castle, PA
Columbia, SC
Mobile, AL
Muncie, IN
Springfield, IL
Dubuque, IA
Springfield, MO
Pueblo, CO
Butte, MT
Aberdeen-Hoquiam, WA
Bellingham, WA
Everett, WA

SMALL CITIES (29)

Westbrook, ME
Greenfield, MA
Wallingford, CT
Willimantic, CT
Beaver Falls, PA
Connellsville, PA
Albany, GA
Griffin, GA
Gastonia, NC
Sumter, SC
Mt. Vernon, OH
New Philadelphia, OH
Logansport, IN
Peru, IN
Lincoln, IL

Mattoon, IL
Beaver Dam, WI
Boone, IA
Columbia, MO
Moberly, MO
Dodge City, KS
Billings, MT
Greeley, CO
Logan, UT
Provo, UT
Astoria, OR
Eugene, OR
Klamath Falls, OR
Olympia, WA

VILLAGES (140)

NEW ENGLAND (14)

MASSACHUSETTS: Avon, East Bridgewater, Hebronville, Kingston, North Dighton, North Easton, North Raynham, South Hanson–Bryantville

VERMONT: Bristol, Essex Junction, Northfield, Richford, Swanton, Waterbury

NORTH CENTRAL (46)

ILLINOIS: Atlanta, Bement, Cerro Gordo, Farmer City, Maroa, Monticello, Mount Pulaski, Tuscola

IOWA: Brooklyn, Bussey, Dallas, Earlham, Eddyville, Melcher, Montezuma, New Sharon, Pleasantville, State Center, Victor

MICHIGAN: Blissfield, Chelsea, Concord, Grass Lake, Hudson, Jonesville, Parma, Tecumseh

OHIO: Bellville, Cardington, Fredericktown, Mount Gilead, Perrysville, Plymouth

PENNSYLVANIA: Denver, Marietta, New Freedom, New Holland, Quarryville, Spring Grove, Wrightsville

WISCONSIN: Horicon, Lake Mills, Mayville, Mount Horeb, Sun Prairie, Waterloo

SOUTHEAST (34)

GEORGIA: Comer, Commerce, Greensboro, Jefferson, Madison, Social Circle, Washington, Winder

MISSISSIPPI: Drew, Hollandale, Indianola, Itta Bena, Leland, Moorhead, Mount Bayou, Rosedale, Ruleville, Shaw, Shelby

NORTH CAROLINA: Elm City, Franklinton, Louisburg, Nashville, Spring Hope, Wake Forest, Whitakers, Zebulon

SOUTH CAROLINA: Bishopville, Camden, Lake City, Lamar, Manning, Summerton, Timmonsville

ROCKY MOUNTAIN (22)

COLORADO: Glenwood Springs, Meeker, Red Cliff, Rifle

KANSAS: Bucklin, Cimarron, Fowler, Kinsley, Meade, Spearville

MONTANA: Forsyth

NORTH DAKOTA: Casselton, Cooperstown, Finley, Hatton, Hillsboro, Hope, Lidgerwood, Mayville, Portland

SOUTH DAKOTA: Belle Fourche, Sturgis

PACIFIC NORTHWEST (24)

CALIFORNIA: Beaumont, Brea, Ceres, Elsinore, Hemet, La Habra, Manteca, Newman, Oakdale, Placentia, San Jacinto, Tustin

OREGON: McMinnville, Newberg, Sheridan, Silverton, Woodburn

WASHINGTON: Arlington, Blaine, Burlington, Lynden, Marysville, Monroe, Snohomish

FARM COUNTIES (66) (*farm types studied in italics*)

NEW ENGLAND (4)

MASSACHUSETTS: Bristol, Plymouth—*dairy and poultry*

VERMONT: Chittenden, Franklin—*dairy*

NORTH CENTRAL (18)

ILLINOIS: De Witt, Logan, Macon, Platt—*corn or cash grain*

IOWA: Madison, Mahaska, Marion, Marshall, Poweshiek—*animal speciality*

MICHIGAN: Lenawee—*dairy and general*

NEW JERSEY: Camden, Gloucester, Salem—*truck*

OHIO: Crawford, Knox, Richland—*general*

PENNSYLVANIA: Lancaster—*general*

WISCONSIN: Dane—*dairy*

SOUTHEAST (22)

GEORGIA: Clarke, Elbert, Greene, Jackson, Madison, Morgan, Oconee, Wilkes—*cotton*

MISSISSIPPI: Bolivar, Leflore, Sunflower, Washington—*cotton*

NORTH CAROLINA: Jackson, Macon—*self-sufficing*

NORTH CAROLINA: Edgecombe, Nash—*cotton and tobacco*

SOUTH CAROLINA: Clarendon, Darlington, Florence, Lee, Marion, Sumter—*cotton and tobacco*

ROCKY MOUNTAIN (13)

COLORADO: Eagle, Garfield, Rio Blanco—*range livestock*

KANSAS: Edwards, Ford, Gray, Meade—*wheat or cash grain*

MONTANA: Custer—*range livestock and cash grain*

NORTH DAKOTA: Barnes, Cass, Griggs, Steele—*wheat or cash grain*

SOUTH DAKOTA: Pennington—*range livestock and cash grain*

PACIFIC NORTHWEST (9)

CALIFORNIA: Orange, Riverside—*fruit*

CALIFORNIA: San Joaquin—*fruit and dairy*

OREGON: Clackamas, Marion, Multnomah, Polk, Washington—*part-time*

OREGON: Marion, Polk—*general and fruit*

WASHINGTON: Whatcom—*poultry and dairy*

The original survey documents cited in this book are from the Study of Consumer Purchases (SCP), record group 176, National Archives II, College Park, Maryland.

Introduction

1. The American Institute for Economic Research cost-of-living calculator was used to convert mid-1930s currency values to 2022 dollars: www.aier.org/cost-living-calculator. The conversion requires a multiplier of approximately 20.6. In each chapter, the first one or two dollar amounts are converted to provide contemporary equivalence for context of earnings and costs in the Great Depression economy.

2. Survey 1903, Study of Consumer Purchases (SCP), record group 176, National Archives II, College Park, Maryland. The survey is reproduced here in appendix I as an example of the survey instrument because it clearly represents an Old Order Amish farm household and incorporates all five survey schedules.

3. Some of the statistics in this book differ from those found in our first publication based on the SCP surveys: Steven D. Reschly and Katherine Jellison, "Production Patterns, Consumption Strategies, and Gender Relations in Amish and Non-Amish Farm Households in Lancaster County, Pennsylvania, 1935–1936," *Agricultural History* 67 (Spring 1993): 134–162. After exhaustive study, some identifying classifications were adjusted for accuracy, often from "Old Order Amish" to "Horse-and-Buggy Plain (unspecified)," when no specific note by the survey taker identified the family as Amish or when the household was located in a township with a sparse Amish population in the 1930s. These "Plain" households could be Old Order Mennonite (probably Groffdale Conference), Old Order River Brethren, or simply a farm household with no automobile expenses for the prior year. For more detail on the SCP and the processes we used to select and classify farm surveys from Lancaster County, see appendix II.

4. David L. Weaver-Zercher, *The Amish in the American Imagination* (Baltimore: Johns Hopkins University Press, 2001), 11–12, 22, 49; Janet Galligani Casey, *A New Heartland: Women, Modernity, and the Agrarian Ideal in America* (New York: Oxford University Press, 2009), 28–29, 37.

5. *The Budget*, a weekly established in Sugarcreek, Ohio, in 1890, became a medium of contact and communication among far-flung Amish and other Plain communities.

Since 1946, *The Budget* has been published in local and national/international editions. For researching Plain communities in the 1930s, *The Budget* is a significant historical resource. For discussion of *The Budget* and its reliance on Old Order Amish and other Anabaptist women as reporters, or "scribes" as the Amish preferred, see Steven M. Nolt, "Inscribing Community: *The Budget* and *Die Botschaft* in Amish Life," in *The Amish and the Media,* ed. Diane Zimmerman Umble and David L. Weaver-Zercher (Baltimore: Johns Hopkins University Press, 2008), 181–198; and Elmer S. Yoder, *I Saw It in THE BUDGET* (Hartville, OH: Diakonia Ministries, 1990). For discussion of government photographers' portrayal of Lancaster County Amish and related religious groups in the 1930s and 1940s, see Steven D. Reschly and Katherine Jellison, "Research Note: Shifting Images of Lancaster County Amish in the 1930s and 1940s," *Mennonite Quarterly Review* 82 (July 2008): 469–483.

6. See Karen M. Johnson-Weiner, *The Lives of Amish Women* (Baltimore: Johns Hopkins University Press, 2020); Julia A. Ericksen et al., "Fertility Patterns and Trends among the Old Order Amish," *Population Studies* 33 (July 1979): 255–276; Eugene Ericksen, Julia A. Ericksen, and John A. Hostetler, "The Cultivation of the Soil as a Moral Directive: Population Growth, Family Ties, and the Maintenance of Community among the Old Order Amish," *Rural Sociology* 45 (Spring 1980): 49–68; Julia A. Ericksen and Gary Klein, "Women's Roles and Family Production among the Old Order Amish," *Rural Sociology* 46 (Summer 1981): 282–296; Marlene Epp, *Mennonite Women in Canada: A History* (Winnipeg: University of Manitoba Press, 2008); Royden Loewen, *Mennonite Farmers: A Global History of Place and Sustainability* (Baltimore: Johns Hopkins University Press, 2021). For a useful overview of scholarship on the Amish, see Cory Anderson, "Seventy-Five Years of Amish Studies, 1942–2017: A Critical Review of Scholarship Trends (with an Extensive Bibliography)," *Journal of Amish and Plain Anabaptist Studies* (hereafter *JAPAS*) 5 (Spring 2017): 1–16.

7. The exception to the neglect of Amish women's Depression-era experiences is our own previously published scholarship, which includes Reschly and Jellison, "Production Patterns"; Katherine Jellison, "An 'Enviable Tradition' of Patriarchy: New Deal Investigations of Women's Work in the Amish Farm Family," in *The Countryside in the Age of the Modern State: Political Histories of Rural America,* ed. Catherine McNicol Stock and Robert D. Johnston (Ithaca, NY: Cornell University Press, 2001), 240–257; Katherine Jellison, "The Chosen Women: The Amish and the New Deal," in *Strangers at Home: Amish and Mennonite Women in History,* ed. Kimberly D. Schmidt, Diane Zimmerman Umble, and Steven D. Reschly (Baltimore: Johns Hopkins University Press, 2002), 102–118; Katherine Jellison and Steven D. Reschly, "Working Together: Women and Men on the Amish Family Farm in 1930s Lancaster County, Pennsylvania," *JAPAS* 8 (Autumn 2020): 113–124; Katherine Jellison, "Relation hommes-femmes en milieu rural: une communaute amish dans les annees 1930," *Le Mouvement Social,* no. 277 (October–December 2021): 167–179.

8. Based on the research and theorizing of French sociologist Pierre Bourdieu, Steven D. Reschly has proposed three core elements of a shared Amish *habitus,* or repertoire of community, shaped by historical experience: estrangement from and suspicion of the world outside the church, developed in the context of persecution in early modern Central Europe; visible community rather than invisible individualistic faith; and portable community and successful migration, attracted by land ownership in North America and

driven by persecution and wars in Europe. Opportunities for changing agricultural practices resulted from the devastation and depopulation of the Thirty Years War, in the seventeenth century, creating a coherent agricultural system that was, in effect, a fourth element of a shared Amish habitus. See Steven D. Reschly, *The Amish on the Iowa Prairie, 1840 to 1910* (Baltimore: Johns Hopkins University Press, 2000), introduction and chaps. 1 and 2. The present book adds gender differentiation to this core, sometimes presenting as patriarchal authority, sometimes presenting as cooperative labor in house and barn, as described in chapter 1. The entire book can, in fact, be considered an extended development of the communal habitus of sustainable agriculture and cooperative household and farm management.

9. See Carolyn E. Sachs, *The Invisible Farmers: Women in Agricultural Production* (Totowa, NJ: Rowman and Allanheld, 1983); Deborah Fink, *Open Country, Iowa: Rural Women, Tradition and Change* (Albany: SUNY Press, 1986); Nancy Grey Osterud, *Bonds of Community: The Lives of Farm Women in Nineteenth-Century New York* (Ithaca, NY: Cornell University Press, 1991); Sonya Salamon, *Prairie Patrimony: Family, Farming, and Community in the Midwest* (Chapel Hill: University of North Carolina Press, 1992); Katherine Jellison, *Entitled to Power: Farm Women and Technology, 1913–1963* (Chapel Hill: University of North Carolina Press, 1993); Mary Neth, *Preserving the Family Farm: Women, Community, and the Foundations of Agribusiness in the Midwest, 1900–1940* (Baltimore: Johns Hopkins University Press, 1995); Grey Osterud, *Putting the Barn before the House: Women and Family Farming in Early Twentieth-Century New York* (Ithaca, NY: Cornell University Press, 2012); Jenny Barker Devine, *On Behalf of the Family Farm: Iowa Farm Women's Activism since 1945* (Iowa City: University of Iowa Press, 2013).

Chapter 1 · Working Together

1. Wolf Helmhard von Hohberg, *Georgica curiosa aucta, Das ist: Umständlicher Bericht und klarer Unterricht von dem Adelichen Land- und Feldleben . . .* (Nuremberg: Endters, 1682), quoted in Marion W. Gray, *Productive Men, Reproductive Women: The Agrarian Household and the Emergence of Separate Spheres during the German Enlightenment* (New York: Berghahn Books, 2000), 71, 73. According to Gray, who translated the title of Hohberg's book as *Careful Husbandry Improved: Guide to Noble Life in Land and Field,* "In the patriarchal culture, this harmony was a means of upholding the husband's authority over the household" (73).

2. Gray, *Productive Men, Reproductive Women,* 52, 55–56. The date of the first Amish arrivals in Pennsylvania is unclear, but some have suggested as early as 1727. Clearer, though incomplete, evidence points to 1734. For more on this, see the work of genealogists such as Robert L. Reeser, *The West Conestoga: Lancaster County's First Amish Settlement* (Strasburg, PA: R. L. Reeser, 2011), and Hugh F. Gingerich and Rachel W. Kreider, *Amish and Amish Mennonite Genealogies, Revised Edition with Additions and Corrections* (Gordonville, PA: Pequea Bruderschaft Library, 2007).

3. Steven D. Reschly, *The Amish on the Iowa Prairie, 1840 to 1910* (Baltimore: Johns Hopkins University Press, 2000), 8.

4. Gray, *Productive Men, Reproductive Women,* 34, 59.

5. Gray, *Productive Men, Reproductive Women,* 13, 63.

6. Quoted in Gertrude Enders Huntington, "The Amish Family," in *Ethnic Families*

in America: Patterns and Variations, ed. Charles H. Mindel, Robert W. Habenstein, and Roosevelt Wright, Jr., 3rd ed. (New York: Elsevier Science Publishing, 1988), 379.

7. Reschly, *The Amish on the Iowa Prairie*, 35–38.

8. Reschly, *The Amish on the Iowa Prairie*, 25, 43–44; James T. Lemon, *The Best Poor Man's Country: A Geographical Study of Early Southeastern Pennsylvania* (Baltimore: Johns Hopkins University Press, 1972), 3–5.

9. Mark Häberlein, *The Practice of Pluralism: Congregational Life and Religious Diversity in Lancaster, Pennsylvania, 1730–1820* (University Park: Pennsylvania State University Press, 2009), 144–146; Richard K. MacMaster, *Land, Piety, Peoplehood: The Establishment of Mennonite Communities in America, 1683–1790* (Scottdale, PA: Herald Press, 1985), 110; and Lemon, *Best Poor Man's Country*, 10.

10. Benjamin Rush, *An Account of the Manners of the German Inhabitants of Pennsylvania* (1789; repr., Lancaster, PA: Pennsylvania German Society, 1910), 68.

11. For a detailed narrative by one immigrant whose descendants later became a sizable share of the Lancaster Amish community, see S. Nicholas Stoltzfus, *German Lutheran to Pennsylvania Amish: The Stoltzfus Family Story* (Morgantown, PA: Masthof Press, 2019).

12. John M. Byler, comp. and ed., *Amish Homesteads of 1798* (Taberg, NY: J. M. Byler, 2016). There is evidence that Amish families, as relative latecomers to Lancaster County, ended up on more marginal lands than, say, the earlier-arriving Mennonites. See MacMaster, *Land, Piety, Peoplehood*, 70–72, 86–88, 125–127.

13. John S. Umble, trans. and ed., "Memoirs of an Amish Bishop," *Mennonite Quarterly Review* 22 (April 1948): 101–104.

14. The division between Old Order and change-minded Amish transpired at different times in Amish communities across North America from the 1850s to the 1880s. For specifics on the schism in Lancaster County within a broader national context, see Paton Yoder, *Tradition and Transition: Amish Mennonites and Old Order Amish, 1800–1900* (Scottdale, PA: Herald Press, 1991), 171, 208–210, 266–273. The Amish settlement in central and eastern Lancaster County largely became Old Order. Those on the eastern edge of the settlement constituted the Church Amish, and the meetinghouses they eventually built—one near Morgantown and another in Millwood—were near the border with Chester County. A third meetinghouse, built in 1909, was in Chester County itself, near the village of Atglen.

15. On subsequent developments among the Old Order Amish in Lancaster County, see Donald B. Kraybill, *The Riddle of Amish Culture*, rev. ed. (Baltimore: Johns Hopkins University Press, 2001); for subsequent developments among the Church Amish in the area, see Grant M. Stoltzfus, *Mennonites of the Ohio and Eastern Conference, from the Colonial Period in Pennsylvania to 1968* (Scottdale, PA: Herald Press, 1969), 146–149, 213–216. For broader agricultural history, see Sally McMurry, *Pennsylvania Farming: A History in Landscapes* (Pittsburgh: University of Pittsburgh Press, 2017), chap. 22.

16. Aaron Lapp, Jr., *Weavertown Church History: Memoirs of an Amish Mennonite Church* (Kinzers, PA: Aaron Lapp, Jr., 2003).

17. Gray, *Productive Men, Reproductive Women*, 13.

18. Grey Osterud quoting Mary Neth in Osterud, *Putting the Barn before the House: Women and Family Farming in Early Twentieth-Century New York* (Ithaca, NY: Cornell University Press, 2012), 6. See also material throughout Nancy Grey Osterud, *Bonds of Community: The Lives of Farm Women in Nineteenth-Century New York* (Ithaca, NY:

Cornell University Press, 1991); Mary Neth, *Preserving the Family Farm: Women, Community, and the Foundations of Agribusiness in the Midwest, 1900–1940* (Baltimore: Johns Hopkins University Press, 1995); and Katherine Jellison, *Entitled to Power: Farm Women and Technology, 1913–1963* (Chapel Hill: University of North Carolina Press, 1993).

19. The Old Order Amish were the most obvious, but not the only, twentieth-century farming community that continued to view farming primarily as a way of life rather than a business. Anthropologist Sonya Salamon characterizes these competing attitudes toward farming as the "yeoman" versus "entrepreneur" models of agriculture. In her study of late twentieth-century Illinois, she found that farm families of German descent embraced the yeoman model while those of "Yankee" stock were more likely to be entrepreneurs. See material throughout Sonya Salamon, *Prairie Patrimony: Family, Farming, and Community in the Midwest* (Chapel Hill: University of North Carolina Press, 1992).

20. Jane C. Getz, "The Economic Organization and Practices of the Old Order Amish of Lancaster County, Pennsylvania," *Mennonite Quarterly Review* 20 (January 1946): 59. Getz quotes here from field notes for Walter M. Kollmorgen, *Culture of a Contemporary Rural Community: The Old Order Amish of Lancaster County, Pennsylvania*, Rural Life Studies, vol. 4 (Washington, DC: Government Printing Office, 1942).

21. Katherine Jellison, "An 'Enviable Tradition' of Patriarchy: New Deal Investigations of Women's Work in the Amish Farm Family," in *The Countryside in the Age of the Modern State: Political Histories of Rural America,* ed. Catherine McNicol Stock and Robert D. Johnston (Ithaca, NY: Cornell University Press, 2001), 240–257.

22. For further discussion of SCP methodology as applied to Lancaster County Old Order Amish, see appendix II, and Steven D. Reschly and Katherine Jellison, "Production Patterns, Consumption Strategies, and Gender Relations in Amish and Non-Amish Farm Households in Lancaster County, Pennsylvania, 1935–1936," *Agricultural History* 67 (Spring 1993): 134–135, 140–143. The original survey documents cited in this book are from the Study of Consumer Purchases (SCP), record group 176, National Archives II, College Park, Maryland.

23. Profit and acreage statistics are from the second, reclassified grouping, for which see appendix II in this volume.

24. Sarah Elbert, "Women and Farming: Changing Structures, Changing Roles," in *Women and Farming: Changing Roles, Changing Structures,* ed. Wava G. Haney and Jane B. Knowles (Boulder, CO: Westview Press, 1988), 261.

25. SCP Surveys 1930 and 1017.

26. For discussion of mainstream farm families' use of mechanized equipment during this period, see Jellison, *Entitled to Power,* chaps. 3 and 4.

27. SCP Surveys 1583, 1903, 1937.

28. "One Day in the Life of an Amish Woman," *Independent* (New York), June 11, 1903, 1397. Scholars have long debated the authenticity of the *Independent* article and whether its author interviewed any actual Amish women for the piece. Among scholars who have recently included the article as a legitimate source in their bibliographies is Karen M. Johnson-Weiner, *The Lives of Amish Women* (Baltimore: Johns Hopkins University Press, 2020), 281.

29. For discussion of the use of this rhetorical strategy in non-Amish farming communities in other regions of the country, see Carolyn E. Sachs, *The Invisible Farmers: Women in Agricultural Production* (Totowa, NJ: Rowman and Allanheld, 1983), and Deborah

Fink, *Open Country, Iowa: Rural Women, Tradition and Change* (Albany: SUNY Press, 1986).

30. Cordelia Beattie, "Economy," in *A Cultural History of Childhood and Family in the Early Modern Age,* ed. Sandra Cavallo and Silvia Evangelisti (London: Bloomsbury, 2014), 54–56.

31. SCP Survey 1933.

32. Katie F. Lapp, "Gordonville, Pa.," *The Budget,* October 11, 1934; Mary Ann Byler, "Atlantic, Pa.," *The Budget,* November 8, 1934. The Lancaster Amish, both Old Order and change-minded, had a longstanding practice of assigning children their mother's maiden name as their middle names. For example, all the children of John and Anna Fisher, née Esh, would have Esh as their middle name. This practice underscored the significance of matrilineal lines for the Lancaster Amish conception of extended family.

33. SCP Survey 1357.

34. SCP Survey 1930. For discussion of the preference of Amish households for Amish laborers, see Kollmorgen, *Culture of a Contemporary Rural Community,* 52–53.

35. SCP Survey 1930.

36. SCP Survey 1930.

37. SCP Survey 1930; Kollmorgen, *Culture of a Contemporary Rural Community,* 46.

38. SCP Survey 1930. For discussion of Lancaster County potato and tobacco farming practices, see Gideon L. Fisher, *Farm Life and Its Changes* (Gordonville, PA: Pequea Publishers, 1978), chaps. 8 and 11.

39. Reschly and Jellison, "Production Patterns," 151.

40. B. H. Slicher Van Bath, *The Agrarian History of Western Europe, A.D. 500–1850,* trans. Olive Ordish (London: Edward Arnold Publishers, 1963), 27. The 1752 Steinselz Discipline and the 1779 Essingen Discipline, for example, both forbade "smoking tobacco and taking snuff." See the texts of European Amish church disciplines in Joe A. Springer, trans. and ed., *Montbéliard Mennonite Church Register, 1750–1958: A Sourcebook for Amish Mennonite History and Genealogy,* vol. 1, *Transcription and Translation* (Goshen, IN: Mennonite Historical Society, 2015), 559–571.

41. Franklin Ellis and Samuel Evans, *History of Lancaster County, Pennsylvania, with Biographical Sketches of Many of Its Pioneers and Prominent Men* (Philadelphia: Everts & Peck, 1883), 891; Daniel B. Good, "The Localization of Tobacco Production in Lancaster County, Pennsylvania," *Pennsylvania History* 49 (July 1982): 193–194.

42. Kollmorgen, *Culture of a Contemporary Rural Community,* 34.

43. "One Day in the Life of an Amish Woman," 1394. For further discussion of the Columbian exchange, see Alfred W. Crosby, Jr., *The Columbian Exchange: Biological and Cultural Consequences of 1492,* 30th anniversary ed. (Westport, CT: Praeger Publishers, 2003).

44. Fisher, *Farm Life and Its Changes,* 167–169.

45. SCP Survey 1930.

46. SCP Survey 1116. The household represented in this survey document is classified as "Car Plain (Unspecified)" in the Reschly/Jellison sample, on which see appendix II. It was located in West Lampeter Township and categorized as "Plain," with no recreation expenses, and with a bonnet expense on the wife's clothing survey, but the family also owned a 1929 Dodge automobile and had grid electricity. Given their geographic loca-

tion, the family was almost certainly either Lancaster Mennonite Conference or Reformed Mennonite.

47. SCP Survey 1116.

48. SCP Survey 1116.

49. Reschly and Jellison, "Production Patterns," 148, 151.

50. SCP Surveys 1116 (non-Amish) and 1930 (Amish).

51. SCP Surveys 1116 (non-Amish) and 1930 (Amish).

52. For discussion of farm women's activities in other northern US communities during this period, see Deborah Fink, *Agrarian Women: Wives and Mothers in Rural Nebraska, 1880–1940* (Chapel Hill: University of North Carolina Press, 1992), chaps. 5 and 7; Catherine McNicol Stock, *Main Street in Crisis: The Great Depression and the Old Middle Class on the Northern Plains* (Chapel Hill: University of North Carolina Press, 1992), chap. 6; Jellison, *Entitled to Power*, chaps. 3 and 4; Osterud, *Putting the Barn before the House*, conclusion; and Neth, *Preserving the Family Farm*, passim.

Chapter 2 · Quilts and Clothing

1. For discussion of the "making do" concept, see Mary Neth, *Preserving the Family Farm: Women, Community, and the Foundations of Agribusiness in the Midwest, 1900–1940* (Baltimore: Johns Hopkins University Press, 1995), 30–31.

2. For further comparison of treadle sewing machine ownership across Lancaster County ethno-religious groups, see Steven D. Reschly and Katherine Jellison, "Production Patterns, Consumption Strategies, and Gender Relations in Amish and Non-Amish Farm Households in Lancaster County, Pennsylvania, 1935–1936," *Agricultural History* 67 (Spring 1993): 155.

3. Lydia Stoltzfus, interview with Louise Stoltzfus, Lancaster County, Pennsylvania, April 17, 1995, and Naomi Fisher (pseudonym), interview with Louise Stoltzfus, Lancaster County, Pennsylvania, April 29, 1995.

4. Katie Y. Beiler, "Ronks, PA," *The Budget*, February 6, 1936; Patricia T. Herr, "Quilts within the Amish Culture," in *A Quiet Spirit: Amish Quilts from the Collection of Cindy Tietze and Stuart Hodosh,* ed. Donald B. Kraybill, Patricia T. Herr, and Jonathan Holstein (Los Angeles: UCLA Fowler Museum of Cultural History, 1996), 52–53; Fannie Esch (pseudonym), interview with Katherine Jellison and Steven D. Reschly, Lancaster County, Pennsylvania, January 10, 1997; Esch, interview with Louise Stoltzfus, Lancaster County, Pennsylvania, April 29, 1995.

5. For definitions of *Ordnung* and the variations among church districts and affiliations, see material throughout Donald B. Kraybill, Karen M. Johnson-Weiner, and Steven M. Nolt, *The Amish* (Baltimore: Johns Hopkins University Press, 2013), and particularly material throughout Steven M. Nolt and Thomas J. Meyers, *Plain Diversity: Amish Cultures & Identities* (Baltimore: Johns Hopkins University Press, 2007). For meanings of "affiliation," see especially Christopher Petrovich, "More Than Forty Amish Affiliations? Charting the Fault Lines," *Journal of Amish and Plain Anabaptist Studies* 5 (Spring 2017): 120–142.

6. Not all households completed all five survey schedules. Fifty-two of 74 (70%) Old Order Amish households filled out a clothing schedule for each family member, while 64 of 86 (74%) English households did so. For a general comparison of average clothing expenditures for men, women, and children across Lancaster County ethno-religious

groups, see Reschly and Jellison, "Production Patterns," 154. Specific averages are from the second, reclassified Reschly/Jellison sample, on which see appendix II in this volume.

7. SCP Survey 1016. All survey households provided general information about clothing costs per family member on page 5 of the Expenditure Schedule—Farm. Families like the one represented in Survey 1016, who chose to go on and complete the lengthy Clothing Purchases during Schedule Year survey, provided much more detailed information about their wardrobe expenses. Discussion of clothing costs in this chapter relies on data from this lengthier, more comprehensive portion of the survey instrument. For discussion of farm women's use of feed sacks in their sewing projects of the era, see Lu Ann Jones, *Mama Learned Us to Work: Farm Women in the New South* (Chapel Hill: University of North Carolina Press, 2002), 171–183.

8. SCP Survey 1016.

9. SCP Survey 1016.

10. SCP Survey 1016.

11. SCP Survey 1175.

12. SCP Survey 2089.

13. SCP Surveys 1854, 1016, 1762.

14. Elizabeth Benner, interview with Katherine Jellison, Lancaster County, Pennsylvania, July 25, 1997.

15. Benner, interview, July 25, 1997.

16. Louise Stoltzfus, *Amish Women: Lives and Stories* (Intercourse, PA: Good Books, 1994), 12–13.

17. Jerrold Smoker and Marie Smoker Breneman, Hannah Beiler Smoker's grandchildren, interview with Katherine Jellison and Steven D. Reschly, Lancaster, Pennsylvania, December 17, 2008.

18. Esch, interview, April 29, 1995.

Chapter 3 · Kitchen and Market

1. Steven D. Reschly and Katherine Jellison, "Production Patterns, Consumption Strategies, and Gender Relations in Amish and Non-Amish Farm Households in Lancaster County, Pennsylvania, 1935–1936," *Agricultural History* 67 (Spring 1993): 152–153.

2. SCP Surveys 1933 and 1453.

3. SCP Surveys 1116 (non-Amish) and 1930 (Amish).

4. SCP Survey 1930.

5. SCP Survey 1116.

6. SCP Surveys 1116 and 1930. For statistical data on average household food production in mid-1930s Lancaster County, see Reschly and Jellison, "Production Patterns," 152.

7. SCP Surveys 1116 and 1930. The remark about eating potatoes three times a day was made by Hazel Bergey, interview with Katherine Jellison, Lititz, Pennsylvania, August 12, 1997.

8. For data on the average Lancaster County household, see Reschly and Jellison, "Production Patterns," 150.

9. SCP Surveys 1762 and 1917.

10. Lydia Stoltzfus, a former Old Order Amish who converted to Church Amish, interview with Louise Stoltzfus, Lancaster County, Pennsylvania, April 14, 1995; Daniel,

Rebecca, and Amos Zook (pseudonyms), interview with Katherine Jellison, Lancaster County, Pennsylvania, July 22, 1997.

11. SCP Survey 1014.

12. SCP Surveys 1223 and 1903; Naomi Fisher (pseudonym), interview with Louise Stoltzfus, Lancaster County, Pennsylvania, April 29, 1995.

13. Fisher, interview, April 29, 1995; Mrs. John K. Lapp, "New Holland, Pa.," *The Budget*, October 29, 1936; SCP Survey 1488.

14. Elizabeth Benner, interview with Katherine Jellison, Lancaster County, Pennsylvania, July 25, 1997.

15. Stoltzfus, interview, April 14, 1995; Zook, interview, July 22, 1997; Bergey, interview, August 12, 1997; Grace Summy, interview with Katherine Jellison, Lititz, Pennsylvania, August 12, 1997.

16. Zook, interview, July 22, 1997; Stoltzfus, interview, April 14, 1995; Edith Thomas, interview with Katherine Jellison, New Danville, Pennsylvania, July 26, 1997; Paul Weaver, a Mennonite, interview with Katherine Jellison, Lititz, Pennsylvania, August 12, 1997; Anna Yoder (pseudonym), interview with Katherine Jellison and Steven D. Reschly, Lancaster County, Pennsylvania, January 10, 1997.

17. Fisher, interview, April 29, 1995.

18. Elmer C. Stauffer, "In the Pennsylvania Dutch Country," *National Geographic Magazine*, July 1941, 73–74.

19. Photograph 83-G-37609, Bureau of Agricultural Economics Collection, National Archives II, College Park, MD; photographs LC-USW3- 011286-E and LC-USW3-011295-E, FSA/OWI Collection, Library of Congress, Washington, DC. For further discussion of how Rusinow, Collins, and other photographers of the period portrayed Lancaster County's Plain people, see Steven D. Reschly and Katherine Jellison, "Research Note: Shifting Images of Lancaster County Amish in the 1930s and 1940s," *Mennonite Quarterly Review* 82 (July 2008): 469–483, and Katherine Jellison, "Peculiar Poster Girls: Images of Pacifist Women in American World War II Propaganda," in *Gender and the Second World War: Lessons of War*, ed. Corinna Peniston-Bird and Emma Vickers (New York: Palgrave Macmillan, 2017), 171–184.

Chapter 4 · Field and Barn

1. Lydia Stoltzfus, interview with Louise Stoltzfus, Lancaster County, Pennsylvania, April 14, 1995; Katie F. Lapp, "Gordonville, PA," *The Budget*, June 13, 1935.

2. Family size statistics are from the revised Reschly/Jellison sample, on which see appendix II in this volume.

3. Stoltzfus, interview, April 14, 1995.

4. Ada Lapp (pseudonym), interview with Katherine Jellison, Lancaster County, Pennsylvania, July 26, 1997.

5. Mahlon Hess, interview with Katherine Jellison, Lititz, Pennsylvania, August 12, 1997.

6. Elizabeth Benner, interview with Katherine Jellison, Lancaster County, Pennsylvania, July 25, 1997, and Edith Thomas, interview with Katherine Jellison, New Danville, Pennsylvania, July 26, 1997.

7. SCP Survey 1056; Daniel, Rebecca, and Amos Zook (pseudonyms), interview with

Katherine Jellison, Lancaster County, Pennsylvania, July 22, 1997; Paul Weaver, interview with Katherine Jellison, Lititz, Pennsylvania, August 12, 1997.

8. Fannie Esch (pseudonym), interview with Louise Stoltzfus, Lancaster County, Pennsylvania, April 29, 1995, and Esch interview with Katherine Jellison and Steven D. Reschly, Lancaster County, Pennsylvania, January 10, 1997.

9. Deborah Fink, *Open Country, Iowa: Rural Women, Tradition and Change* (Albany: SUNY Press, 1986), 34–35, 65, 107, 171. See also Mary Neth, *Preserving the Family Farm: Women, Community, and the Foundations of Agribusiness in the Midwest, 1900–1940* (Baltimore: Johns Hopkins University Press, 1995), and Grey Osterud, *Putting the Barn before the House: Women and Family Farming in Early Twentieth-Century New York* (Ithaca, NY: Cornell University Press, 2012).

10. SCP Survey 1903. The family had received their $192 payment from the Agricultural Adjustment Administration (AAA), an agency whose 1933 enabling act had been declared unconstitutional by the US Supreme Court 10 months prior to Hambright's visit. Amish man quoted in John M. McCullough, "Amish Curb Crops—But Not for AAA Pay," *Philadelphia Inquirer*, April 2, 1933.

11. All the first names, like the surname, are pseudonyms. Like all SCP participants, the family is anonymous in the study's records.

12. SCP Survey 1903. Although Agent Rigdon completed the majority of the survey for this family, Agent R. Groome completed a small portion of the survey's clothing section, and Hambright was responsible for the sample menu and daily activities sections.

13. SCP Survey 1903; "Leola, Pennsylvania," *The Budget*, September 24, 1936; Mrs. M. P. Stoltzfus, "Ronks, Pa.," *The Budget*, September 19, 1935. For a thorough first-person account of a Lancaster County Amish family who relied heavily on tomatoes as a cash crop in this period, see Aaron S. Glick, *The Fortunate Years: An Amish Life* (Intercourse, PA: Good Books, 1994), 77–89.

14. Fannie Beiler, "Lancaster, Pa.," *The Budget*, September 24, 1936; "Leola, Pennsylvania," *The Budget*, September 24, 1936; Mrs. John K. Lapp, "New Holland, Pa.," *The Budget*, October 8, 1936.

15. SCP Survey 1903.

16. SCP Survey 1903.

17. SCP Survey 1903.

18. SCP Survey 1903.

19. Reschly and Jellison, "Production Patterns," 151.

20. SCP Survey 1903.

21. SCP Survey 1903.

22. Quotation about Amish division of labor from "One Day in the Life of an Amish Woman," *Independent* (New York), June 11, 1903, 1397.

Chapter 5 · Friends and Frolics

1. References to recreational expenses are from section IX, page 4, of the Expenditure Schedule—Farm unless otherwise specified.

2. SCP Survey 1019. Meals furnished information appears on Schedule IV, page 3, of the survey form.

3. Katie F. Lapp, "Gordonville, PA," *The Budget*, June 14, 1934, and June 13, 1935.

4. Katie F. Lapp, "Gordonville, PA," *The Budget*, June 14, 1934, and August 23, 1934.

See John A. Hostetler, *Amish Society*, 4th ed. (Baltimore: Johns Hopkins University Press, 1993), 167.

5. See Carroll Smith-Rosenberg, "The Female World of Love and Ritual: Relations between Women in Nineteenth-Century America," *Signs: Journal of Women in Culture and Society* 1 (Autumn 1975): 1–30. For discussion of Amish wedding and childbirth practices, see chapters 6 and 7 in this volume.

6. Mary Neth, "Leisure and Generational Change: Farm Youths in the Midwest, 1910–1940," *Agricultural History* 67 (Spring 1993): 171; M. H. Yoder, "Hadley, PA," *The Budget*, October 11, 1934, and Mrs. Sam M. Miller, "Hadley, PA," *The Budget*, October 25, 1934.

7. Section X of the SCP survey focuses on family reading expenses and is located on the same page as, and immediately below, survey questions regarding recreation.

8. Fannie Esch (pseudonym), interview with Louise Stoltzfus, Lancaster County, Pennsylvania, April 29, 1995; Lydia Stoltzfus, interview with Louise Stoltzfus, Lancaster County, Pennsylvania, April 17, 1995; Paul H. Weaver, interview with Katherine Jellison, Lititz, Pennsylvania, August 12, 1997; Rebecca Zook (pseudonym), interview with Katherine Jellison, Lancaster County, Pennsylvania, July 22, 1997.

9. Entry for January 18, 1934, from the diary of B. E., private collection of Tom Conrad, Worthington, Ohio.

10. For further discussion of twentieth-century dating and its history, see Beth Bailey, *From Front Porch to Backseat: Courtship in Twentieth-Century America* (Baltimore: Johns Hopkins University Press, 1988).

11. SCP Survey 1260; "The Biggest Money Making Stars of 1934–1935," *Motion Picture Herald*, December 28, 1935. Statistics about movie attendance in the 1930s are from Katherine Jellison, *It's Our Day: America's Love Affair with the White Wedding, 1945–2005* (Lawrence: University Press of Kansas, 2008), 150. Data from Survey 1260 do not indicate that the woman had previously avoided motion picture attendance for religious reasons. Records for her family provide no evidence that they belonged to a Plain denomination. The family had highline electricity and an automobile they had purchased a decade earlier. They also purchased a radio for $125 during the survey year, and family members patronized the barber shop and beauty parlor.

12. Neth, "Leisure and Generational Change," 177–179.

13. SCP Surveys 1780, 1645, 1693.

14. Statistics from revised Reschly/Jellison sample, on which see appendix II, in this volume.

15. John Renno, "Belleville, PA," *The Budget*, January 31, 1935.

16. Robert Staughton Lynd and Helen Merrell Lynd, *Middletown: A Study in American Culture* (New York: Harcourt, Brace, 1929), and *Middletown in Transition: A Study in Cultural Conflicts* (New York: Harcourt, Brace, 1937).

17. Lynd and Lynd, *Middletown*, 251, 253 (carriage and auto statistics), and 253, n. 3 (quotation). The Lynds included their discussion of the automobile in chapter 18 of *Middletown*, "Inventions Re-making Leisure." The radio, of course, was another of those inventions, like automobiles, telephones, and so on, not found in Old Order Amish households.

18. Lynd and Lynd, *Middletown*, 258, and *Middletown in Transition*, 163, n. 33.

19. SCP Survey 1219.

Chapter 6 · Religion and Rituals

1. Entry for January 31, 1938, from the diary of A.S., private collection of Tom Conrad, Worthington, Ohio. Annie Smucker is a pseudonym.

2. John A. Hostetler, *Amish Society*, 4th ed. (Baltimore: Johns Hopkins University Press, 1993), 210–219; Donald B. Kraybill, Karen M. Johnson-Weiner, and Steven M. Nolt, *The Amish* (Baltimore: Johns Hopkins University Press, 2013), 77–90.

3. Mrs. M. P. Stoltzfus, "Leola, PA," *The Budget*, November 5, 1936; Fannie Beiler, "Lancaster, PA," *The Budget*, November 26, 1936; Mrs. M. P. Stoltzfus, "Leola, PA," *The Budget*, November 22, 1934.

4. Mrs. M. P. Stoltzfus, "Leola, PA," *The Budget*, November 22, 1934, and November 8, 1934.

5. Mrs. M. P. Stoltzfus, "Leola, PA," November 8, 1934.

6. Mrs. M. P. Stoltzfus, "Leola, PA," November 8, 1934; SCP Surveys 1601 and 1384. Funeral expenses appear on page 6 of the latter expenditure schedule, under section XVIII, Other Family Expense. SCP records for the family of the deceased man, who died halfway through the 1935/36 survey year, indicate that most family members were not affiliated with any Amish, Mennonite, or other Plain denomination. They used highline electricity, subscribed to numerous magazines, and had a car, radio, and telephone. No one in the household attended movies, but family members purchased tickets to attend plays and lectures. His parents only had an eighth-grade education, but his only surviving sibling, a 17-year-old sister, had 12 years of formal schooling. Further evidence that his was not a predominantly Plain household appears in the Toilet Articles and Preparations section of the survey, which includes purchases of cold cream, powder, nail polish, and perfume. The only clue that perhaps one member of the household was affiliated with a Plain church appears in the mother's clothing record, where the SCP agent recorded the purchase of a $5 "bonnett" [*sic*]. A possible interpretation is that the family's wife and mother was a member of the Reformed Mennonites. The denomination did not require youngsters to dress plainly until they joined the church, encouraged formal education, and included many women whose husbands were not members of the church. The SCP records provide no indication of the cause of the young man's death. For an overview of Old Order Amish funeral customs, see Hostetler, *Amish Society*, 200–208; and Kraybill, Johnson-Weiner, and Nolt, *The Amish*, 247–249, 344–345.

7. Hostetler, *Amish Society*, 202; Stoltzfus, "Leola, PA," November 22, 1934.

8. Fannie Esch (pseudonym), interview with Katherine Jellison and Steven D. Reschly, Lancaster County, Pennsylvania, January 10, 1997; SCP Survey 1161.

9. Esch, interview, January 10, 1997. The description of Amish dress material is from Agent Rigdon, SCP Survey 1016.

10. Esch, interview, January 10, 1997; Hostetler, *Amish Society*, 192–200; Kraybill, Johnson-Weiner, and Nolt, *The Amish*, 232–236; Louise Stoltzfus, *Amish Women: Lives and Stories* (Intercourse, PA: Good Books, 1997), 33.

11. Jane Marie Pederson, *Between Memory and Reality: Family and Community in Rural Wisconsin, 1870–1970* (Madison: University of Wisconsin Press, 1992), 205–210, 212–215; Carol K. Coburn, *Life at Four Corners: Religion, Gender, and Education in a German-Lutheran Community, 1868–1945* (Lawrence: University Press of Kansas, 1992), 106–108; Mary Neth, *Preserving the Family Farm: Women, Community, and the Founda-*

tions of Agribusiness in the Midwest, 1900–1940 (Baltimore: Johns Hopkins University Press, 1995), 67–68; Katherine Jellison, "From the Farmhouse Parlor to the Pink Barn: The Commercialization of Weddings in the Rural Midwest," *Iowa Heritage Illustrated* 77 (Summer 1996): 50–65; Gordon Marshall, "Shivaree: A Midwestern Welcome to Marriage," *Iowa Heritage Illustrated* 77 (Summer 1996): 66–69; Rebecca Sharpless, *Fertile Ground, Narrow Choices: Women on Texas Cotton Farms, 1900–1940* (Chapel Hill: University of North Carolina Press, 1999), 29–32; Martha Kohl, *I Do: A Cultural History of Montana Weddings* (Helena: Montana Historical Society Press, 2011), 50–57, 176–177.

12. SCP Survey 1240 contains information about the bride and her family for the period January 1-December 31, 1935. Survey agents' notations indicate that the young woman resided with her birth family for the first 50 weeks of that period before then marrying and leaving the household.

13. SCP Survey 1240.

14. SCP Survey 1240. The $100 wedding expense appears on page 6 of the second expenditure survey schedule, under the Other Family Expense section.

15. SCP Survey 1240.

16. SCP Surveys 1017 and 2013. For further discussion of bridal wear purchases in mainstream rural America during this time, see Jellison, "From the Farmhouse Parlor to the Pink Barn," 50–65.

17. SCP Survey 1240. Information about wedding gifts appears on page 5 of the second expenditure schedule, under section XIV, Gifts, Community Welfare, Taxes.

18. SCP Surveys 1785 and 1694. Information about family loans and repayment appears on page 6 of the second expenditure schedule, under section XXI, Changes in Family Assets and Liabilities during Schedule Year. For further discussion of Amish strategies for helping young couples establish a farm, see Hostetler, *Amish Society*, 129.

19. Esch, interview, January 10, 1997. For extended discussion of changes in mainstream wedding practices since the Depression, see Katherine Jellison, *It's Our Day: America's Love Affair with the White Wedding, 1945–2005* (Lawrence: University Press of Kansas, 2008).

20. Hostetler, *Amish Society*, 99, 148–149, 192–200; Kraybill, Johnson-Weiner, and Nolt, *The Amish*, 232–236. For young men, marriage as the passage to Amish adulthood takes one uniquely male form: only after marriage are Old Order Amish men allowed to grow beards.

21. Amos Zook (pseudonym), interview with Katherine Jellison, Lancaster County, Pennsylvania, July 22, 1997.

Chapter 7 · Accidents and Illness

1. Steven M. Nolt, "Inscribing Community: *The Budget* and *Die Botschaft* in Amish Life," in *The Amish and the Media*, ed. Diane Zimmerman Umble and David L. Weaver-Zercher (Baltimore: Johns Hopkins University Press, 2008), 182, 188–190, and 197, n. 24. As Nolt notes, in 1946 *The Budget*'s publishers began printing two separate editions—a Sugarcreek edition, which printed conventional local news and features, and a national version, which consisted exclusively of readers' correspondence.

2. Katie F. Lapp, "Gordonville, PA," *The Budget*, June 14 and June 28, 1934; Mrs. M. P. Stoltzfus, "Leola, PA," *The Budget*, November 8, 1934; B. F. King, "New Holland, PA," *The Budget*, November 1, 1934.

3. Katie F. Lapp, "Gordonville, PA," *The Budget*, February 15, 1934; John B. Smucker, "New Holland, PA," *The Budget*, December 20, 1934.

4. Katie F. Lapp, "Gordonville, PA," *The Budget*, June 28, 1934, August 15, 1935, and August 29, 1935; John B. Smucker, "New Holland, PA," *The Budget*, April 5, 1934, and November 15, 1934; Mrs. B. K. Stoltzfus, "Gap, PA," *The Budget*, October 10, 1935.

5. Katie F. Lapp, "Gordonville, PA," *The Budget*, June 27, 1935; Mary M. Beiler, "Ronks, PA," *The Budget*, September 19, 1935; Nettie M. Yoder, "Springs, PA," *The Budget*, February 21, 1935.

6. Katie F. Lapp, "Gordonville, PA," *The Budget*, June 28, 1934.

7. SCP Surveys 1202 and 2204.

8. References to medical expenses are from page 4 of Expenditure Schedule–Farm, Medical Care, unless otherwise specified.

9. SCP Surveys 2036, 1138, 1696, 1694.

10. SCP Survey 1903.

11. SCP Survey 1198.

12. SCP Survey 2036.

13. Elizabeth and David Benner, interview with Katherine Jellison, Lancaster County, PA, July 25, 1997.

14. Lydia Stoltzfus, interview with Louise Stoltzfus, Lancaster County, PA, April 17, 1995.

15. SCP Survey 1652. The family did hire household help for 20 weeks during the survey year, but the hired girl's period of employment did not seem to coincide specifically with the wife's appendectomy-related absence or convalescence. The length of the young woman's employment would indicate instead that she worked in the home during the usual busy period of fruit and vegetable canning, from late spring through mid-fall.

16. On the Reschly/Jellison sample, see appendix II in this volume.

17. SCP Survey 2086. The family represented in this survey was likely Church of the Brethren or Brethren in Christ.

18. SCP Surveys 2063, 1376, 1010.

19. Lily and Emma Sauder, interview with Louise Stoltzfus, Lancaster, PA, April 24, 1995; SCP Survey 2223.

20. SCP Survey 1396.

21. For further discussion of Amish living arrangements and practices regarding the senior years, see John A. Hostetler, *Amish Society*, 4th ed. (Baltimore: Johns Hopkins University Press, 1993), 167–170.

22. For comparison with Amish women's birthing experiences at this time, see the discussion of North Dakota farm women in Katherine Jellison, *Entitled to Power: Farm Women and Technology, 1913–1963* (Chapel Hill: University of North Carolina Press, 1993), 91–92, 94.

23. Katie F. Lapp, "Gordonville, PA," *The Budget*, May 17, 1934, and February 14, 1935; Katie Y. Beiler, "Ronks, PA," *The Budget*, February 6, 1936.

Chapter 8 · *Insiders and Outsiders*

1. Diaries of F.L., 1937 and 1939, private collection of Tom Conrad, Worthington, OH.

2. Carl C. Taylor to O. E. Baker, November 22, 1937, O. E. Baker Folder (1936–1940), General Correspondence (1923–1946), box 62, records of the Bureau of Agricultural Eco-

nomics, record group 83, National Archives II, College Park, Maryland (the collection hereafter cited as Baker Folder).

Taylor observed a sharp contrast between small-scale family farms, with farming seen as a way of life to be preserved, and large-scale business farms operated for profit. Given Taylor's training as a sociologist and his service as president of the Rural Sociological Society (1939) and the American Sociological Association (1946), he was doubtless familiar with the sharp dichotomy between the *Gemeinschaft* (community) and *Gesellschaft* (society) proposed by German sociologist Ferdinand Tönnies in 1887 and elaborated as "ideal types" by German sociologist Max Weber in the early 1920s. See Tönnies, *Gemeinschaft und Gesellschaft* (Leipzig: Fues's Verlag, 1887), of which there were several subsequent editions, and Max Weber, *Wirtschaft und Gesellschaft* (Tübingen: J. C. B. Mohr, 1922).

3. Carl C. Taylor, "My Memory of the Conceptual Development of the Community Stability-Instability Study," August 28, 1944, American Farm Community Study Project Files (1941–1946), general correspondence (1923–1946), box 538, records of the Bureau of Agricultural Economics, record group 83, National Archives II, College Park, Maryland (collection hereafter cited as AFCS Project Files). Walter M. Kollmorgen to O. E. Baker, June 6, 1938, Baker Folder; Walter M. Kollmorgen, interview with Katherine Jellison and Steven D. Reschly, Lawrence, Kansas, March 20, 1994.

4. Walter M. Kollmorgen to Carl C. Taylor and Conrad Taeuber, March 4, 1940, and Walter M. Kollmorgen to Carl C. Taylor, March 2, 1940, Baker Folder; Walter M. Kollmorgen to Carl C. Taylor, April 2, 1940, and Carl C. Taylor to Walter M. Kollmorgen, April 8, 1940, AFCS Project Files. Kollmorgen quotations from his March 2 letter to Taylor.

5. Kollmorgen to Taylor and Taeuber, March 4, 1940, and Walter M. Kollmorgen to O. E. Baker, March 1, 1938, Baker Folder; Kollmorgen, interview with Jellison and Reschly, March 20, 1994; Walter M. Kollmorgen, interview with Steven D. Reschly, Omaha, Nebraska, March 8, 1995; Elizabeth Louise Bennett, "Economies of Valuation and Desire: How New Deal Photography Made the Amish Modern" (Ph.D. diss., University of California, Berkeley, 2012), 28.

6. Charles P. Loomis to Carl C. Taylor, April 22, 1940, AFCS Project Files. Many years later, Loomis published his account of living and working with the Lancaster County Amish during this period. See Charles P. Loomis, "A Farm Hand's Diary," *Mennonite Quarterly Review* 53 (July 1979): 235–257.

7. Walter M. Kollmorgen to Carl C. Taylor, April 2, 1940, AFCS Project Files.

8. Walter M. Kollmorgen, *Culture of a Contemporary Rural Community: The Old Order Amish of Lancaster County, Pennsylvania*, Rural Life Studies, vol. 4 (Washington, DC: Government Printing Office, 1942), 105.

9. Kollmorgen, interview with Jellison and Reschly, March 20, 1994.

10. Kollmorgen, *Culture of a Contemporary Rural Community*, 90.

11. Kollmorgen, *Culture of a Contemporary Rural Community*, 47, 60, quoted language on 47.

12. Kollmorgen, *Culture of a Contemporary Rural Community*, 47–48.

13. Kollmorgen, *Culture of a Contemporary Rural Community*, 90; Lydia Stoltzfus, interview with Louise Stoltzfus, Lancaster County, Pennsylvania, April 17, 1995; Shoemaker comments from SCP Survey 1175. Further discussion of Stoltzfus's and Shoemaker's remarks appears in chapter 2 of this book.

14. Carl C. Taylor, foreword to Kollmorgen, *Culture of a Contemporary Rural Community*, n.p. Johanna Kollmorgen's part in her brother's research is unclear. Interviewed at age 87 in 1994, Kollmorgen did not recall that his sister played any role in his Lancaster County research. Taylor's introduction to the published study contradicts Kollmorgen's memory, and art historian Elizabeth L. Bennett's research indicates that Johanna Kollmorgen served as her brother's typist during his fieldwork among the Amish. In his 1994 interview with the authors, Kollmorgen indicated that the siblings had been almost inseparable since suffering polio together as toddlers. They attended college together and rearranged employment when possible so that they could reside in the same city. When Kollmorgen moved to Lawrence, Kansas, in 1946 to take a teaching position at the University of Kansas, his sister relocated there also. At the time of the 1994 interview, Walter and Johanna Kollmorgen were residing in the same Lawrence retirement complex, and they were ultimately even buried together in the same Lawrence cemetery plot. His sister's presence during Kollmorgen's 1940 fieldwork, therefore, would have conformed to a familiar pattern. For further information on Johanna Kollmorgen and her relationship with her brother, see her obituary and gravesite at *Find a Grave*, https://www.findagrave.com/memorial/23865620/johanna-julia-kollmorgen.

15. Conrad Taeuber to Ed Hulett, Charles P. Loomis, and John H. Provinse, July 5, 1940, and Carl C. Taylor to Charles P. Loomis, November 6, 1941, AFCS Project Files.

16. Charles Suter to Bureau of Agricultural Economics, April 2, 1943, and Peter H. DeVries to Charles Suter, April 27, 1943, AFCS Project Files. According to historian Steven M. Nolt, the Civilian Public Service camp at Howard, Pennsylvania, provided labor for the Soil Conservation Service and was in existence for only a short time, from June 1942 to June 1943. At its height, the camp was home to 44 conscientious objectors, including Assistant Director Suter, a General Conference Mennonite from Ohio who had previously had little experience with the Amish or other Plain Anabaptists. In total, only seven Old Order Amish men resided at the camp, six from Ohio and one from Mifflin County, Pennsylvania. The only Lancaster County resident at the camp was a Church Amish man. Most Lancaster County Old Order Amish had received farm deferments under the era's draft laws and thus did not end up in CPS camps. Steven M. Nolt, email communication with the authors, February 11, 2022. For further discussion of the era's draft laws, farm deferments, and their impact on Lancaster County, see Katherine Jellison, "Get Your Farm in the Fight: Farm Masculinity in World War II," *Agricultural History* 92 (Winter 2018): 5–20.

17. James MacGregor Burns, *Roosevelt: The Soldier of Freedom* (New York: Harcourt Brace Jovanovich, 1970), 423. Taylor to Loomis, November 6, 1941, Conrad Taeuber to Ray E. Wakeley, June 22, 1942, Carl C. Taylor to E. W. Burgess, August 2, 1942, Ralph R. Nichols to Wayne C. Neely, September 26, 1944, AFCS Project Files.

18. Walter M. Kollmorgen, "Kollmorgen as a Bureaucrat," *Annals of the Association of American Geographers* 69 (March 1979): 84.

19. Bennett, "Economies of Valuation and Desire," 22, 27; Kollmorgen, *Culture of a Contemporary Rural Community*, 61, 65, 80.

20. Grant M. Stoltzfus to Peter H. DeVries, September 14, 1943, AFCS Project Files. Stoltzfus was later a professor of sociology and church history at Eastern Mennonite College and Seminary and author of the important Anabaptist studies text, *Mennonites of the Ohio and Eastern Conference: From the Colonial Period in Pennsylvania to 1968* (Scottdale,

PA: Herald Press, 1969). See his profile at *Genie*, https://www.geni.com/people/Grant
-Stoltzfus/6000000010150970157, and John A. Lapp, "Stoltzfus, Grant Moses (1916–
1974)," *Global Anabaptist Mennonite Encyclopedia Online* (GAMEO, 1989), https://gameo
.org/index.php?title=Stoltzfus,_Grant_Moses_(1916–1974)&oldid=118750.

21. Bennett, "Economies of Valuation and Desire," 22.

22. Bennett, "Economies of Valuation and Desire," 1–2, 10–11, 25; Jerrold Smoker
and Marie Smoker Breneman, interview with Katherine Jellison and Steven D. Reschly,
Lancaster, Pennsylvania, December 17, 2008. Smoker and Breneman, Hannah Beiler
Smoker's grandchildren, verified that she and her parlor were depicted in this set of
photos. The subsequent saga of the Smoker farm pictures highlights the ahistorical
uses to which many of the public domain BAE photos have been put. For example, the
"special features" section of the season 2, DVD box set of the television series *Mad Men*
features the wartime picture of Smoker baking bread in her farm home as an illustration
of the post–World War II suburban domestic ideal. A picture of one of Hannah Smoker's
sons sorting tobacco leaves appears in a history of tobacco advertising "special feature" in
the *Mad Men* season 3 box set. Seasons 2 and 3, *Mad Men*, produced by Matthew Weiner
(Santa Monica, CA: Lionsgate Home Entertainment, 2009 and 2010), DVDs.

23. Bennett, "Economies of Valuation and Desire," 25. MacLeish was the son of the
nation's Librarian of Congress at the time, poet Archibald MacLeish, who himself had
written the text for a book-length FSA photographic essay, *Land of the Free* (New York:
Harcourt, Brace and Company, 1938). Kenneth MacLeish was co-author, with Kimball
Young, of the Landaff, New Hampshire, community study.

24. Kollmorgen, *Culture of a Contemporary Rural Community*, 8, 47. Caption for photograph 83-G-37556, Bureau of Agricultural Economics (BAE) Photograph Collection,
National Archives II, College Park, Maryland (hereafter BAE Photograph Collection).

25. Kollmorgen, *Culture of a Contemporary Rural Community*, 43; caption for photograph 83-G-37585, BAE Photograph Collection.

26. Caption for photograph 83-G-37548, BAE Photograph Collection.

27. Caption for photograph 83-G-37532, BAE Photograph Collection.

28. SCP Survey 1010; Naomi Fisher (pseudonym), interview with Louise Stoltzfus,
Lancaster County, Pennsylvania, April 29, 1995.

29. Kollmorgen, *Culture of a Contemporary Rural Community*, 65.

30. See material throughout Earl H. Bell, *Culture of a Contemporary Rural Community:
Sublette, Kansas*, Rural Life Studies, vol. 2 (Washington, DC: Government Printing Office, 1942). For further comparison of women's activities in the Lancaster County Amish
and Sublette communities, see Katherine Jellison, "An 'Enviable Tradition' of Patriarchy:
New Deal Investigations of Women's Work in the Amish Farm Family," in *The Countryside in the Age of the Modern State: Political Histories of Rural America*, ed. Catherine
McNicol Stock and Robert D. Johnston (Ithaca, NY: Cornell University Press, 2001),
240–257.

Conclusion

1. Entries for 1937 and 1939 from the diary of F. L., private collection of Tom Conrad, Worthington, Ohio; Tom Conrad, conversation with Katherine Jellison, Columbus,
Ohio, December 18, 1996.

2. Earl H. Bell to Carl C. Taylor, October 16, 1944, American Farm Community

Study Project Files (1941–1946), general correspondence (1923–1946), box 538, records of
the Bureau of Agricultural Economics, record group 83, National Archives II, College
Park, Maryland. See also Katherine Jellison, *Entitled to Power: Farm Women and Technology, 1913–1963* (Chapel Hill: University of North Carolina Press, 1993), chap. 4.

    3. Karen M. Johnson-Weiner, *The Lives of Amish Women* (Baltimore: Johns Hopkins
University Press, 2020), 167–179; Lydia Stoltzfus, interview with Louise Stoltzfus, Lancaster County, Pennsylvania, April 17, 1995.

Appendix II · The Study of Consumer Purchases:
Background, Findings, and Use

    1. "General Instructions for Field Agents" (March 18, 1936), Consumer Purchase
Study Records (1935–1936), box 2, folder 2, record group 176, National Archives II,
College Park, Maryland (hereafter SCP). The authors first conducted research using
these records when they were temporarily on loan to the Gerald R. Ford Presidential
Library, Ann Arbor, Michigan, for use in a random sample data entry project by the
Inter-university Consortium for Political and Social Research (ICPSR) at the Institute
for Social Research (ISR), University of Michigan, Ann Arbor.

    2. "Interim Report of Plans for a Study of Consumer Purchases, to Be Conducted as
a Federal Works Project, January 13, 1936," quoted in ICPSR 8908 codebook as "Introduction: Data Collection Description, Original ICPSR Codebook," part I, 9–10, Inter-
university Consortium for Political and Social Research, Ann Arbor; "Summary of
Scope and Method" (April 18, 1938), box 6, folder 1, SCP; "Instructions for Collection
of Schedules: Farm" (March 31, 1936), box 2, folder 2, SCP.

    3. The ICPSR constructed a first, random sample dataset consisting of 5,000 records
from the 300,000 families, and 6,000 records from the 61,000 families who completed at
least the first and second schedules. The second dataset is a large sampling and thus can
be analyzed with a high degree of confidence, although it must be remembered that these
are, to some extent, self-selected families who were willing to give all this information.
ICPSR organized the sample into four datasets: (1) urban income; (2) village and farm
income; (3) urban expenditure schedule; (4) village and farm expenditure schedule. With
6,000 of the 61,000 schedules included in the sample, statistical analysis can be performed
with a 1.6% margin of error at a 99% confidence level. By way of contrast, a typical Gallup
poll surveys about 1,000 adults of the 332 million people in the United States, producing
a margin of error of about ± 4% at a 95% confidence level. These files are massive. The
small town / farm dataset has 2,869 variables and 3,034 cases, producing 8,704,546 individual cells. The farm and small town codebook from ICPSR is 6,849 pages in length.
See "Study of Consumer Purchases in the United States, 1935–1936 (ICPSR 8908)," version 3, http://dx.doi.org/10.3886/ICPSR08908.v3. For further discussion of these records
as they pertain to Lancaster County, see Steven D. Reschly and Katherine Jellison, "Production Patterns, Consumption Strategies, and Gender Relations in Amish and Non-
Amish Farm Households in Lancaster County, Pennsylvania, 1935–1936," *Agricultural
History* 67 (Spring 1993): 134–162.

Page numbers in italics refer to illustrations; the letter *t* following a page number denotes a table.